PEOPLE'S
PARTICIPATION

CHALLENGES AHEAD

COMPILED AND ANALYZED BY
ORLANDO FALS BORDA

The Apex Press
New York

Intermediate Technology Publications
London

Copyright 1998 by Orlando Fals Borda and Faiep, Bogotá
All Rights Reserved

Published in the United States by The Apex Press, an imprint of the
Council on International and Public Affairs, 777 United Nations
Plaza, New York, New York 10017, Tel. Fax (800) 316-2739
e-mail: cipany @ igc.apc.org

Published in the United Kingdom by Intermediate
Technology Publications, 103-105 Southampton Row,
London WC1B4HH, Tel. 0171 436 9761; Fax 0171 436 2013;
e-mail: itdpubs @ gn.apc.org

This book is published simultaneously in Spanish by:
Instituto Colombiano para el Fomento de la Educación Superior
ICFES
Instituto de Estudios Políticos y Relaciones Internacionales Universi-
dad Nacional IEPRI
Instituto Colombiano para el Desarrollo de la Ciencia y la Tecnología
COLCIENCIAS

A CIP record for this book is available from the British Library
and from the Library of Congress.

ISBN 0-945257-98-8 (US)
ISBN 1-85339-445-9 (UK)

Typeset, Printed and boundy by Tercer Mundo Editores, S.A.
Bogotá, Colombia

CONTENTS

Part I
THE FORMAL OPENING

Part II
Underpinnings

Part III
Theoretical and Practical Experiences

*Orlando Fals Borda, with contributions by speakers,
rapporteurs and work group coordinators*

Part IV
THE FUTURE OF PARTICIPATORY CONVERGENCE

APPENDICES

Authors cited, Rapporteurs and Coordinators of Work Groups

Alemán, Máximo
Arocha, Jaime
Babüroglu, Oguz
Bonilla, Elssy
Borrero, Camilo
Barraclough, Solon
Brenes, Carlos
Chambers, Robert
Checkland, P. B.
De Roux, Gustavo
Escobar, Arturo
Galeano, Eduardo
Gaventa, John
Giraldo, Luz Mery
Goulet, Denis
Greenwood, Davydd
Gustavsen, Bjørn
Hall, Budd
Hoyos, Guillermo
Jackson, Ted
Josefson, Ingels
Kemmis, Stephen
Lammerink, Marc
Leal Buitrago, Francisco
Levin, Morten
Lleras, Ernesto
Martín Barbero, Jesús
McGuire, Patricia

McTaggart, Robin
Molano, Alfredo
Osorio, Jorge
Osorio, Miguel Angel
Palshaugen, Øyvind
Park, Peter
Parra, Ernesto
Parra, Rodrigo
Pyrch, Timothy
Quijano, Aníbal
Rahman, Md. Anisur
Ramírez, Socorro
Reason, Peter
Rojas, Fernando
Rojas, Humberto
Roy, Bunker
Rudqvist, Anders
Salas, Maruja
Sanz de Santamaría, Alejandro
Schratz, Michael
Sevilla Casas, Elías
Stavenhagen, Rodolfo
Swantz, Marja Liisa
Tandon, Rajesh
Tillmann, Timmi
Tokatlián, Juan
Toulmin, Stephen
Villasante, Tomás R.
Wignaraja, Ponna

INTRODUCTION

The present book tries to collect and synthesize the most outstanding expressions of the World Congress of Participatory Convergence in Knowledge, Space and Time held at the Convention Center and the Convent of St. Francis at Cartagena de Indias, Colombia, from May 31 to June 5, 1997. It also wants to stimulate a wider consideration of the subjects there discussed. The Congress was attended by 1,850 persons from 61 countries, most of them young people, professionals and university students. The event was multidisciplinary with many scholars from sciences considered "hard" such as engineering, and from disciplines considered "soft" including social sciences, literature and arts. There were 165 papers presented in Spanish and English (Appendix A). The Congress was a motive for national pride and satisfaction to show to the world the forgotten scientific and cultural face of Colombia. According to published statements, Cartagena had seldom seen an event of such an intellectual scope and ambition.

It was a Participatory Convergence because two series of sister trends came together: one, Participatory Action Research (PAR), whose First World Symposium was held at Cartagena in 1977, organized by the Foundation for the Analysis of the Colombian Reality (FUNDARCO); and the other series of Action Research, Action Learning and Process Management whose first World Congress was held at Queensland University in Brisbane (Australia) in 1990, organized by the Australian ALARPM Association. For the first series, the 1997 Congress was the 8th, and previous rites had been held in Ljubljana (1979), Calgary (1989) and Managua (1989), besides the ALARPM ones. For the second series, meetings were held twice in Brisbane (1990, 1992), with the coordination of Ortrun Zuber-Skerritt, and another one at the University of Bath, England

(1994), with Jack Whitehead, Moira Laidlaw, Pamela Lomax, and Terry Hewitt as organizers.

The decision to come to Cartagena in 1997 was taken at Bath. One justification was to pay tribute to the First World Symposium. But there were other weighty reasons. During this period the idea of participation associated with social, economic and political research, had spread through the five continents. Many related schools emerged, at least 32 according to a preliminary count.

Therefore, the need was felt to consider in what ways these schools differed or converged in theory as well as in practice, and to examine what they had been doing. This important objective to determine the vitality of the movement was amply achieved during the Congress. This was a solemn act of reaffirmation, with the advantage of serving also as a generational bridge between those of us who were present in 1977 and today's audience that, as explained above, was mostly of young people. Continuity was assured with the formation of a dozen international networks (universities, educators, diverse activists) during the Congress. And solidarity and exchange between Southern countries were reinforced.

Our 1997 meeting at Cartagena became reality thanks to the sponsorship of four Colombian universities: Nacional, Andes, Valle and Cartagena, whose authorities released five professors to conform the Executive Committee: Gustavo De Roux (agronomist), Alejandro Sanz de Santamaría (economist), Ernesto Lleras (engineer), Socorro Ramírez (political scientist) and Orlando Fals Borda (sociologist, Coordinator of the Committee). Important financial and intellectual contributions were received from COL-CIENCIAS (Colombian Institute for Scientific Research) and Director Fernando Chaparro, Juan Plata, Carl Langebaek, Hernán Jaramillo, Penélope Rodríguez and Julia Aguirre. Further support was given by Colombia´s Bank of the Republic and its Library Luis Ángel Arango with General Director Miguel Urrutia and Director Jorge Orlando Melo; the Presidency of the Republic of Colombia with the Advisor for Social Policies, Carlos Castillo Cardona and his staff; the Ministry of Foreign Affairs with Ministers Rodrigo Pardo and María Emma Mejía; ICFES and ICETEX, with Jaime Niño Díez (present Minister of National Education) and directors Luis

Carlos Muñoz and Carlos J. Buriticá; CINEP with Gabriel Izquierdo; UNESCO with Subdirector General, Francine Fournier, and the PNUD in Bogotá; the Dutch Ministry of Development Cooperation with Minister Jan Pronk and Hans Slot; The Presidency of the Federative Republic of Brazil with President Fernando Henrique Cardoso and the Ambassador in Colombia, Synesio Sampaio Góes; the FES Foundation, with Director Mauricio Cabrera; and the devoted friends from Australia´s ALARPM (Ron Passfield, Patricia Weeks, Joanne Semple, Anne-Marie Carroll).

Other supports were given by the Cultural Funds of the Colombian Departments of Bolívar (David Ernesto Peñas) and Córdoba (Carolina Patiño and Víctor Negrete); the Social Foundation and Workers Circle (Raúl Paniagua) and COREDUCAR (Rosa Díaz de Paniagua) at Cartagena, enthusiastic colleagues who organized concerts and visits to local communities, and who facilitated the Convent.

Our Congress really started one year ahead with preparatory workshops. Seven of them were held in Colombia, with the presence of the noted Brazilian educator and sociologist João Francisco de Souza, former coordinator of the PAR network of CEAAL (Latin American Council for Adult Education). Such meetings took place at Cartagena (organized by Raúl Paniagua and Rosita de Paniagua, Carmen Cabrales and Javier Hernández), Medellín (Alfredo Ghiso at CLEBA), Bogotá (Marco Raúl Mejía, Marco F. Vargas at CINEP), Cali (Elías Sevilla Casas, Gustavo De Roux and José María Rojas at Universidad del Valle), Bucaramanga, Villavicencio, Pamplona, Neiva and other cities. In these workshops regional papers were presented which later enriched Congress discussions.

We were informed about similar preparatory workshops in England, Singapur, Australia, New Zealand, Venezuela, Bolivia, Costa Rica, Cuba, United States, Canada, India, Mexico, Spain and Holland. A special exchange was made with Vietnam, China and South Africa. An E-mail roundtable about methods and schools was organized in Canada with the participation of eleven distinguished scholars from Europe and North America.

We would like to acknowledge the special support since 1994 from the Institute of Political Studies and Foreign Affairs of the National University of Colombia (IEPRI), with Directors Gonzalo

Sánchez and Álvaro Camacho; and from the Foundation of IEPRI
Friends (FAIEP) with Directors Socorro Ramírez, Flor Alba Romero
and Rosita Roa de Rojas, and Martha Correa as secretary.

Once on the march, the Congress was efficiently managed by
Rosita de Rojas, Ruby Pardo, Víctor Jiménez and Olga Maldonado,
with the assistance of Miguel Borja and Carla Shafer (Cornell
University) for the INTERNET connection, and Eurípides Silva Torres
and Magdalena Velásquez at the Bogotá office. Technical support
from the Cartagena Convention Center came from the team led
by Gustavo Devoz, Henry Martelo and Virginia Peña. Simultaneous
interpreters were coordinated by Carol Keeney.

Other efficient collaborators at Cartagena were Adolfo Meissel,
Director of the Bank of the Republic and Silvia Marín, Director of
the Library; Rector Manuel Sierra Navarro and colleagues at the
University of Cartagena; Piedad Zuccardi de García and Isabel
Marrugo Navarro of Cinco Estrellas (T-CI) Tourist Agency.
Translations from Spanish into English for the present book were
done by Fereshte Ebrahimzadeh, Anthony Letts, Rosa María Salazar
and Julia Salazar. The Spanish edition was supervised by Carmen
Inés Bernal at ICFES; the English one by María Teresa Barajas at
Tercer Mundo Editores.

We have had to summarize papers, hopefully with respect for
the spirit or intention of the authors. Those who want to read or to
consider carefully the whole manuscripts may ask our office for
copies and videotapes, following instructions (see Appendices).

Part III of this book is an attempt to combine Congress workgroup
discussions with personal reflections and writings by the
undersigned. This is a response not only to our contract with
COLCIENCIAS, but also to meet the need for information widely felt
as soon as the event was over. I recognize the risks of simplification
that this speedy effort represents, and I assume the responsibility
for the present synthesis. This is because it seems to me preferable
to have on hand this sort of preliminary reference work to feed
necessary discussions, than to be inexplicably silent in the face of
the historic commitment renovated at Cartagena.

It is important that exchange and diffusion of Congress ideas
and materials take place. In this respect it is well to remember that
the 165 authors, workgroup convenors, and rapporteurs are

authorized to edit and publish whatever they consider proper and by the means at their disposal, in all languages. Only the reference to our Congress is required. There are also 15 videotapes available which show diverse aspects of the event. (See Appendix B).

* * *

For reasons explained in Part III of this book, in the following chapters we have used the terms Participatory Research (PR) interchangeably with Participatory Action Research (PAR) that have been in use since the 1970s.

Orlando Fals Borda
Congress Coordinator

POSTHUMOUS MESSAGE FROM PAULO FREIRE
(Recife, September 19, 1921 - São Paulo, May 2, 1997)

São Paulo, February 28, 1997

Dear Friends of the Convergence:

For different reasons —one of them being my health which though not seriously threatened needs to be taken care of— I could not answer before concerning the invitation to your interesting meeting. I kept on postponing the answer in the hope that eventually my condition would become better. But this has not been the case, thus I feel that I cannot wait any longer to let you know my impossibility to be with you at the Cartagena Congress.

I hope we can meet in another opportunity to reminisce and to think about how to continue with our struggles. Above all we must fight against the power of the dominant neoliberal ideology that keeps on offending and attacking the human nature while reproducing itself socially and historically, threatening dreams, utopias, and hopes.

With cordial affection to all of you,

Paulo Freire

PART I

THE FORMAL OPENING

The World Congress for Participatory Convergence in Knowledge, Space and Time was considered a State project by the Colombian Government. It offered a good opportunity to correct the image of the country abroad, so that more representative situations of local social realities could be shown; and it was meant to foster direct contacts of Colombian scientists and intellectuals with foreign colleagues. Enough resources and political supports were therefore given to the Congress organization, thanks to the good offices of President Ernesto Samper Pizano, the Ministers of Foreign Affairs, Rodrigo Pardo and María Emma Mejía, and the Minister of National Education, Jaime Niño Díez. The Congress was also sponsored by President Fernando Henrique Cardoso of Brazil, and by the Brazilian Ambassador at Bogotá Synesio Sampaio Góes for reasons of colleagueship and Latin American solidarity. UNESCO was represented by Sub-Director General Francine Fournier, for present and historical reasons as it had also sponsored the First Action Research Symposium of 1977.

These official supports plus obvious facts of protocol unavoidable in Colombian circumstances led to an opening session characterized by hierarchy (abundant presence of high public officials), patriarchy (a majority of men on the stage) and an absence of the Indian, Black, and Oriental colleagues at the head table.

This initial formality was criticized by alert delegates because it diminished general participation. Participatory levels had in fact been higher in the previous, smaller Congresses held in Australia and England. The problem was compounded by the unexpectedly high number of registrants, which kept increasing up to the last day of the event. They were of course welcome, but the cumbersome initial situation underlined a deeper fact: that the organizers had not succeeded in modifying the cultural format of academic meetings to give way to other spaces set up in accordance with the democratic orientations of Participatory Research. We were expected to be more consistent in relating our ideals to our practices.

It was fortunate that such tensions were soon eased by the participants themselves through happily spontaneous means derived from programmed cultural and artistic activities, and also from positive interventions made by group rapporteurs like Peter Reason, Gustavo De Roux, Budd Hall, Marja Liisa Swantz, Pat McGuire, and others who acted promptly and constructively. In a similar way, women delegates who felt an early discrimination organized themselves and took over the final sessions, presiding with eloquence and distinction. With such inputs, the Congress gained its internal participative equillibrium and held it until the final days.

According to further reports, general satisfaction came from the variety and flexibility of the intellectual and artistic menu offered by the event. Each person was able to "make her/his own Congress", to enjoy a "happening" or vivencia according to anyone's interests. The most intense recollections appear to be those related more to that informal programming than to the scheduled items. For these reasons, according to Davydd Greenwood of Cornell University (USA), "the Congress became a social event which showed progress in three ways: 1. The universal encounter of diverse schools and trends within our field, something unthinkable before. This taught us so many things that the event must be seen as a milestone in the history of our disciplines; 2. The more intense North South dialogue and the contact between the Souths; and 3. The discovery of the Latin American dynamic activism and of the importance of Spanish as an international language".

Part I recalls important moments at the formal inaugural session, including comments on the First World Symposium of 1977, an exhortation for peace, a tribute to our pioneers, pertinent declarations of official policies, plus an extraordinary personal and political reflection by President Cardoso of Brazil.

1. CARTAGENA REVISITED: TWENTY YEARS ON

Alfredo Molano (Colombia)
Sociologist and Journalist

Alfredo Molano wrote a brilliant critical foreword for the publication of the Proceedings of the First World Symposium (Crítica y Política en Ciencias Sociales, Vol. I, Bogotá: Punta de Lanza, 1978 pp. IX-LXI). This led him to reflect from the Colombian standpoint on what has happened since then.

The momentous changes which we are suffering from in Colombia today were first formulated in the 1970s. In April 1977 we met and talked —with great perspicacity, of course— about research, action, and revolution while behind our political backs-far reaching changes were already quietly under way. In particular, there were the drug-traffickers and the guerrillas, who have affected the lives of all of us ever since. They are two phenomena which have their roots in our history, each taking its own course. Drugs are the natural result of the farming crisis and the concentration of ownership of land. The guerrillas are a new chapter of the history of our civil wars, and are the result of a narrow-minded, corrupt democracy.

The fight for land which peasant-farmers had started in the 1930s came to a crisis at the end of Carlos Lleras Restrepo´s administration. First, because the dominant Conservative and Liberal parties signed an agreement in Chicoral to destroy the little that had been achieved in agrarian reform up to that time; second, because the movements of the farmers and indigenous communities were scattered by machine-gun fire; third, because coffee ceased to be the great force for settling the land and became simply another big business, doing away with the small grower and his economy which had for half a century been a solution to the concentration of ownership, had helped to create a domestic market and was the secret of the economic stability of the political regime. These changes left thousands of peasant-farmers out of work, and industry —which was also in crisis— could not absorb them. The only way out was to settle new lands, since there was no further advantage to be gained from land already exploited. This process had been going on since the years of the *violencia*, but in the 1970s it spread along the hillsides, down the valleys, up the mountains and on the massifs of the Andes; and nowhere did the settlers find welfare, prosperity or peace. The expropriation of the best land by the great landowners led to the formation of the haciendas, and "colonization" was at best simply a means of driving the peasant farmer off them.

The pioneers, who had arrived before this new wave, were men who understood guns, fighting and resistance against authority. They had had armed cadres for many years, some more tightly organised than others. The centres of resistance were Tolima, Cauca, the middle Magdalena and the *piedemonte* of the eastern plains. The brutal repression of the 1970s, under the protection of the Public Safety Law, intensified armed conflict and forced these bands to reorganize themselves, to formulate national strategies based on experience and to find their own sources of supply although many accused them of being armed puppets of Moscow or Cuba.

In the mid-1970s, when we first met in Cartagena, the ELN (National Liberation Army) had just been shattered, almost destroyed, at Anorí; the FARC (Revolutioonary Colombian Armed Forces) had not recovered from the ambush at La Sonora in Tolima, where Manuel Marulanda was on the point of doing what his adversaries wanted; and the EPL (People's Liberation Army) was teetering after the death of its founder, Pedro Vásquez. And towards the end of the decade General Camacho, the Defense Minister of the devious Turbay administration, was able to claim that in Colombia there were only 1,800 guerrillas left, with a mere 1,000 guns between them.

While we sat in Cartagena, ton after ton of marihuana left that same Caribbean coast. Soon, when the United States began to produce marihuana, the Colombia producers switched to cocaine, coming from the land onto which the exiled peasant-farmers had been driven "manna from heaven"—as they themselves said. There was a boom and the settlers lived not from taking their maize to the marketplace but from selling the landowners the "improvements" they extracted from the jungles. Coca allowed them, for the first time, to earn a fair return on their work, and therefore convert the "improvements" into a farm of their own. These were the great changes which coca brought, and which only coffee had made possible before. Historically, the colonization caused by coca can be explained by the depletion of the colonization achieved by coffee, and the rise of the guerrillas by the systematic removal of political guarantees for opposition.

In April 1977, as we sat there by the Caribbean, the Social Sciences were trying to break away from a Positivism without principle and at the same time become a critical, and thus all embracing, discipline. In Colombia, we had studied sociology or anthropology or economics (instruments of analysis which we had picked up more or less successfully at university) but none of them were of the slightest use in our attempts to understand what was actually happening before our eyes. If we looked at events in terms of the functionalism, which we had learned something of, with little enthusiasm, we would conclude that very little was happening, although everybody knew what was in fact happening; the violencia, denounced by Germán Guzmán, Orlando Fals Borda and Eduardo Umaña in their classic book, was still alive. Camilo Torres was in his mountains, the peasant farmers were seizing land, the workers were calling strikes; and we, the students, were throwing stones, burning cars and trying to build a road to heaven. Nothing out of the ordinary.

Luckily for most, the university eventually pushed us out onto the street to earn a living. To do that, or to change our lives, we had to take refuge in some modest day-to-day realities: a world of give and take, a world of decisions. Some were consumed, destroyed, or driven off course. Others were drawn into the fight, but nothing that we had learned in the lecture rooms and no law that had passed through our congress was of any use at all. In the fight —an indeed, in the fight for survival— we started to take a new look, and a more critical and realistic one, at what was happening. This new way of looking at things or rather, perhaps, of listening was what came to be called Participative Action Research. As with all great things, it had no single inventor. Nobody discovered it. It was the result of an atmosphere rarefied by the clash between clear-cut scientific explanations and a rough reality which hardly gave us time to experience it. If the conventional sociological interpretation had been blown away, our dreams persisted; in our dreams of Utopia, we could still be radicals in the name of Participative Action Research, casting down the dogmatism which dominated our thoughts about Marxism, and above all else, about the commonplaces which functionalism offered us under the cloak of science.

If we go back to the work of Cartagena in 1977, and recall the spirit which dominated that meeting, we will remember that we were trying "to show that personal commitment and political militancy for social change could in themselves be serious scientific tasks".

And we were right. We who adopted Action Research inherited two forms of radicalism: fundamentalism, tied to the Cross and the sword; and political radicalism, a road opened up by Mariategui, Gaitán and Che Guevara. Our radicalism was tempered by the militant tolerance of an Ulf Himmelrstrand, an Andrew Pearse, a Paulo Freire or a Rodolfo Stavenhagen. In most of our papers, there were direct references to the class struggle and frequent quotations from classical Marxists or the famous intellectuals of the left. But it must also be said that as a matter of principle, Action Research distanced itself from revolutionary parties and the schematic discourse of the Communists. Not one speaker at that meeting invited us to try to seize power. Action Research was more an invitation to scepticism, opening the door to criticism with greater freedom, and to commitment with greater sincerity. It is true that initially Action Research was stigmatized by many "organic intellectuals", but today, after some years of work, those who professed their faith in action are in general still on the side of the popular movements. The same cannot be said of some of the high priests of the Social Sciences of those days.

The dogma of class struggle crumbled to the ground with the Berlin Wall. Those who condemned real socialism and applauded the capitalist society, thought that the downfall of communism means the end of opposition in society and in ideology, and that from that day forward there would only be rivers of milk and honey. Their illusions, like ours, did not last long. Today, the cracks in the walls built from the ruins of a socialist Utopia have begun to become visible, and through them we can see the misery which those walls have failed to hide from us.

In Colombia, however, despite our incorrigible complacency towards any intellectual fashion which comes along, like any other imported goods, radicalism was not brought down by its intellectual or academic enemies. It was rounded up by the purveyors of tendentious opinion in the media, and shot to death. Today, the man in the street feels no better for it. The unemployment figures, unsatisfied needs and violence walk hand in hand with profit figures, return on capital, and margins. But now, armed conflict, violence and death are not only not on the way to extinction: they are reaching appalling levels of prevalence. The violation of human rights has pushed this country to the brink of attracting international intervention.

Social conflict has become deeper, more widespread and more intense in the last ten years, as has the crisis in finding an explanation for it. All that is left of Marxism, which for years had made its limitations obvious, is a handful of its most critical concepts. Positivism and Functionalism, retooled and called Post Modernism have become steadily more feeble as the battle against the dinosaurs abates. Their hegemony, as we know, helped to bring them down. But when ideologies fall into crisis, there is a correspondingly greater need for critical interpretation, and the ethical dimension of knowledge becomes the star of hope. In Cartagena we had predicted that behind any revolution in theory (to put it in the terms of those days) there was a political position. And we liked to add, but not quite so firmly, that behind political positions there was an ethical view which is, as it should be, always unsatisfied.

Today, when we in Colombia are beset by violence, and in the rest of the world the illusions of post modernism have lost their shine, ethics brings criticism down to earth. Participative Action Research has survived the wreck of the grand theories because it has stayed on the alert to unsatisfied needs, always searching and researching its ground. It has always shunned the comfortable life. Research has dropped all that has been drying on its golden boughs from its theoretical structure. It has stopped studying Marxism and its rigid application and passed on to the reconstruction of the lives which ordinary people actually live, in the search for a new reason to fight. In 1977 we thought that we knew where we were going. Today, by good fortune, we have no idea where we are going and we make progress because we are lost and we are forced to use the compass of Action Research. In those days, we thought that history was the bus to the New Jerusalem. Today our eyes are sharper, and we can see that history is a bus without a destination board.

Looking at the papers to be delivered at this meeting, twenty years on, I would like to try and make a timid and hesitant attempt to describe the profile of Action Research today. The great step forward has undoubtedly been to put ethics back on its rightful throne, after so many years of suffering as servant of politics. The first victim of this has been the idea that political parties and their satraps are needed for any form of action, and therefore for any intellectual work. Researchers today are interested in walking side by side with the ordinary man rather than one step ahead. The confession that we do not know where we are going but that we are there, shoulder to shoulder in the battle line, is, I think, an irreversible step.

In Colombia we have passed from the dictatorship of the bourgeoisie to the struggle for full respect for human rights, or in other words, we have stopped fighting against the State, and are now fighting for it. Before, we were concerned with militancy; now, our eyes are on participation. It is as if Action Research had made us more modest. Today we are prepared to accept equality; we are undergoing a far-reaching redefinition of our own relevance. The idea that the people need to be led has fortunately been replaced by the excitement of being among the people and the wonder of its creative ability. Subjectivity has gained ground, and allowed the heart to win some points against the head.

For us Colombians, the twenty years since Cartagena 77 have in no sense been short of important events. But at the end of the day, the story is one which illustrates the bankruptcy of the political system. Its illegitimate children have brought it to the brink of ruin: drugs, in an economic sense, and the guerrillas in the political sense. As I noted at the beginning, these two phenomena are tied to the inability of the system to press for political reform and to satisfy the collective interest. The system has preferred to sacrifice itself as a State of law rather than curtail the interests which it holds so dear.

The general climate of violence shows that the State is incapable of keeping order or a monopoly of arms. It is besieged by emerging forces which have built up their own legitimacy and their own jurisdictions. In Colombia today, there are several different systems of justice, and different sources of power which impose them. The State has been losing legitimacy, and its real power has been passing to the army, thus making social and economic conflict more intense. But the forces of law and order have in turn given up exercising their authority within the framework of the law, and have endorsed the actions of the paramilitaries as agents of their mission. It is an appalling paradox that as conflict grows more intense, and the struggle against the violation of human rights increases, the chosen solution, the paramilitaries, has brought us to the edge of total civil war. Every day we come closer under the gaze of the international community, which cannot understand how the State can remain sanguine and impotent in the face of the crimes which are committed every day around this country, the most recent of them being the horrific murder of Mario Calderón, Elsa and Carlos. For them, I ask not for a minute's silence, but for a roar of applause: they made us renew our faith in life.

The situation of the opposition and criticism is growing worse. In 1980, the chances were that one would be tortured in the stables of the cavalry regiments. In 1985, after the seizure of the Palace of Justice, it was more likely that one would disappear. And now, ten years later, the threat is not torture or disappearance but being shot to death in one's own living room. And all the time, incredibly, everything is kept hidden away, under cover. It would seem as if the political system, in its efforts to strengthen its position, had given a licence to kill to gangs of hired killers; but the effect has been that it has only speeded up its own decay and made it weaker. So today, Participative Action Research must inescapably turn its attention to the struggle for human rights.

In the last twenty years the guerrillas have multiplied tenfold. The 2,000 or so under-equipped men reported by General Camacho have now swelled to 20,000 under public safety laws, suspensions of Constitutional guarantees, the taking and retaking of La Uribe, the War Tax , the rural civil defense groups, and the offer of rewards for turning in wanted men. The guerrillas have created so many battlefronts that the army has admitted that it cannot control them. And this is why the paramilitaries have mushroomed in the way that they have. Today, nobody doubts that the tolerance of the army, the complacency of the media and the money of the business conglomerates and the drug traffickers are responsible for the birth of this new element in the war. And the war is the clearest of evidence that the State is incapable of restoring order, and worse, incapable of finding a political solution since it left the waging of this disastrous and bloody war in the hands of the army. It has been forced to do so, not only because it is afraid of guns, but also because the system of political patronage and narcotics have rotted the foundations of its legitimacy and brought its authority to its knees.

There is increasingly less room for social research and civil political action. The war, the drugs, the destruction of the State and the bankruptcy of the political system condemn us to being observers from afar, because any attempt to come closer to events would be to put our lives in danger. In Colombia, Action Research is not a scientific challenge or even, as in the 1980s, a political challenge. Today, Participative Action Research is practically suicide.

But this does not mean that we should think again because, amongst other things, there is no other way forward.

2. KNOWLEDGE AND POLITICAL PRACTICE

Fernando Henrique Cardoso
President, Federative Republic of Brazil.

Videotaped Message, Palace of Alborada, Brasilia, May 1997.

It is with great pleasure that I am sending this message to the participants in the World Congresses, Fourth on Action Research, Action Learning and Process Management and Eighth on Participatory Action, being held in Cartagena, a beautiful city which shows visible signs of our common Latin American history as well as the kindness and hospitality of the Colombian people.

First of all, I would like to congratulate the people responsible for this event, in particular Doctor Immanuel Wallerstein who is presiding over the meeting, and Doctor Orlando Fals Borda who has invited me to participate by way of sending this message from Brasilia. Immanuel and Orlando, besides being very good friends, are distinguished intellectuals whose participation in this Congress augurs well for the development of the work to be carried out there and is a guarantee that the event will be succesful.

I am especially pleased to notice that this Congress is paying tribute to my friend and fellow citizen Paulo Freire who has totally reformed the concepts on education both in Brazil and all over the world, and who has called our attention to the relation between education and the promotion of the human being as a citizen, as a social actor capable of changing his or her own destiny by means of participating in the political life. Paulo Freire's passing away was a significant loss for his friends as well as for the Brazilian and the Latin American social thought. For all those who think about society and about action towards social changes, Paulo Freire will continue to be a symbol of the struggle towards a more egalitarian society and the efforts to give education the credits it deserves amongst the most important rights of citizens. I take this opportunity to sincerely acknowledge the remarkable work done by this great Brazilian.

My dear friends and colleagues:
The debates to be held during this Congress shall refer to some key issues for the understanding of the current historic moment and for a better evaluation of the position and the role played by the researcher in our society, as well as to discuss the challenges faced by the researcher in our society, as well as to discuss the challenges faced by the researcher and the importance of his democratic participation, instrumental for the economic and social development of our countries.

The title of this event itself in putting together the ideas of research and participation emphasizes a permanent issue for the social scientist, i.e., the relation between political and academic activity.

I wish to share with you some personal thoughts and questions arising from my double experience both as a politician and as a sociologist, as a Government person and as an academic.

I would like to do that as an intellectual taking some distance from my political background. But this is not an easy task to accomplish. In the political sphere when someone who is in a public position speaks, the important aspect to be considered is not the content of the speech itself but the way it is delivered. Speech and speaker are inseparable. I reaffirm once more my intention to stick to an academic approach.

Perhaps the most traditional framework we should use in order to discuss the relationship between academy and politics is the distinction Weber made between the two activities. Accordingly, we should consider two distinct and separate logics corresponding to facts and values respectively. The scientific studies about society would be guided by the ethics of freedom as a *sine qua non* for the search of the truth. On the other hand, political action would be oriented by the logic of necessity and would be linked to the world of values, being necessarily influenced by ideologies, interests, and would constantly take consequences into consideration.

The distinction is actually very strong and is undoubtedly a very important tool that helps us in the study of the differences between the two activities.

We have noticed in the evolution itself of the social thought in Brazil (and I am sure that the same applies to all other countries) that sometimes there has been opposition between a pure academic approach guided by the scientific method of research and another approach leaning more towards the transformation of the social structures, for which the political goal of social change is a priority. Scientific method has been left, so to speak, to a secondary position. That was what happened, for instance, in the beginning of the sixties with the relation between the school of thought of the Sao Paulo University, more concerned with scientific purity , and the group of intellectuals gathered together in the Higher Institute for Brazilian Studies, ISEB, who were committed to the elaboration of guidelines for a national project.

Today, taking advantage of retrospective wisdom, it looks clear to me that, to a certain extent, both sides of this controversy were right since both deal with real problems. On one hand it was and it is still necessary to give more consistency to the knowledge of reality so that we achieve higher levels of precision and increase the scientific quality of research. On the other hand, from a different and equally legitimate point of view, it was and it still is impossible for an intellectual to ignore an unfair reality in which inequality was the rule and authoritarian practices prevailed.

Referring to another example, the history of the evolution of the Latin American social thought within CEPAL is another very interesting alegory of the relation between knowledge and political project. There is no doubt that research carried out within the framework of CEPAL, in particular Raul Prebisch's conclusions, bear in mind the establishment of strict parameters of analysis of Latin American economic reality. However this research was simultaneously influenced by a necessary project due to the deterioration of the terms of exchange. It was considered to be necessary to substitute imports. In that case knowledge had the precedence over political action.

It has not always been this way though. The question of trying to find out what comes first —knowledge or political project— hides a complex reality in which the two terms are dialectically linked within the structure of human action.

Now, if we combine the two opposite traditions —the one of the intellectual in his ivory tower and the one of theory as a necessary and ideal spring-board for political action— we will have to examine some interesting issues:

Is it possible to conciliate scientific method and political project? What is the role of knowledge in the political project?

Is it possible to know with some objectivity the better project for each given historical circumstance? Does knowledge prevail over project?

Those are two questions that I invite the Congress to consider.

The study of the subject indicates that there is a complex relation between knowledge and social reality. And that complexity is particularly evident when we study more carefully the question of social change, of the transformation of societies which is a main subject for those who work as sociologists or politicians in Latin America. This is a subject that dialectically combines reflection and project, thought and action. Whenever we tackle the question of transformation, we necessarily refer to values, goals and directions of transformation. Values are the instruments that can politically mobilize and articulate the social basis for the change.

Within the framework of the relation between academy and political action we can ask ourselves: Who takes the lead of the change? And how are the parameters that guide the efforts towards transformation defined?

When we examine those two questions in the light of our practical experience we realize that very often approaches taken by academics and politicians lead to a paradoxical inversion of the initial perspective relating to the separation between facts and values. We actually find in many cases that academics defend pure values, morally superior to the traps and contingencies of political life. According to this vision politicians would be condemned to live in a world in which harsh truth would leave no space for an authentic ethical reference. Academy would thus be in the Weber sense the representative of an ethics of conviction, while politics would belong to the world of responsibility as an abstract form separate and opposite to pure conviction.

But if we examine these issues more carefully this interpretation also becomes insufficient. In a democratic society there should not and there cannot be monopolists of values, truth or the ideals of change. If we assume that those who have a political activity have the monopoly over the definition of values, academic political thought would then be reduced to technical knowledge that could be used indifferently for any project with regards to social change. If we assume, on the contrary, that intellectuals and academics have the monopoly of ethics, then the purity of academy is the only space for the affirmation of authentic values. Political activity would then be reduced to technical action aiming at the maximization of vested interests without any reference to an ethical perspective.

In any of those cases the results would be unsatisfactory: they would mean a disqualification both of academic work and political action.

The distinct perspectives —the one of the intellectual, the one of the politician as well as the one of the leaders of social movements within NGOs— should all contribute to the public debate so that we reach a balance between the ideal and the possible.

It is exactly because dialogue is an indispensable tool for the construction of legitimate democracy (according to Habermas) that the positions of those who participate in public affairs cannot only be to defend unrealistic values, or simply obtaining mobilization gains and short-term advantages. The risk of a mere intellectual approach is to transform goals into tactics. And to convert goals into tactics means to create a gap between values and real political action.

On the other hand, the risk politicians incur is to forget values and to treat political activity as a goal in itself. This is something restricted to the power politics considerations and to guaranteeing personal or group advantages. In this sense, politics becomes a technique, the world of practical "consequences" prevails over the goals of common well-being.

In my personal experience in politics I consider that the benefits of intellectual reference rely exactly on the fact that it allows one to be conscious of the risks of political activity and to avoid them. I assume that to keep a constant dialogue with values is exactly what allows, or better said, encourages the politician to look further than the power game itself, to search for an ethical orientation, to bear in mind in every decision the question: Could it be better done in a manner that could benefit more people?

Furthermore I find that the intellectual can learn from the political activity that human and historical limits also constitute values that are important to moderate the easy forms of voluntarism.

That does not mean, under any circumstance, that one should reduce his ethical impulse or that the will to fight for a better world be disregarded. On the contrary, it means one should seek to build the conditions that will enable this will to find concrete ways of expression in reality. It means to realize that that will, emanating from an individual or from a specific social group, is only part of reality.

Conviction and responsibility are not necessarily opposed. In the light of the uncertainty that marks political decision, conviction (whenever it does not become a dogma distant from reality) can be instrumental in showing a way to society.

By way of a conclusion, I would like to make some remarks about the most recent trends which are evident both in our societies and on an international scale. To me those trends reinforce the importance of a permanent dialogue and of close interaction between academy and political world, between the intellectual and the politician.

First, the consolidation of democracy in Latin America has stressed even more the ethical dimension of our political life and at the same time it has made it more difficult and more complex, to cope with day-to-day facts of politics. Democracy entails an enlargement of the space in which social demands multiply and require urgent measures as social movements participate playing a more protagonic role. Societies acknowledge their intrinsic injustices in a much clearer way and demand urgency in solving their old social problems. At the same time, the instruments to be used in the solution of those issues must be negotiated.

Due to the conciliation effort of distinct sectorial interests expressed through ever-growing ways of participation that democracy should incorporate, the task of building a political dialogue capable of producing the universal from the individual has become more urgent. The thought, the reference to the universal, puts a new emphasis on the search for the common well-being.

In this sense Montesquieu's reflection on citizens' virtue as a leitmotiv of political action in a republican environment requires a new interpretation. In a democratic regime the exercise of citizenship means more than just periodically voting. It implies the debate, the thought and a certain kind of political wisdom without which political action would not be different from the behavior based upon individual or group interests.

It does not mean we should disqualify or ignore the existence of interests. After all it is part of legitimate democratic life that competition between groups, within a legal framework, to improve their positions economically or socially should exist. However, just as free market is a fact of economic reality but cannot answer all economic questions —since it does not include the element of ethical values— political competition, power politics, is not everything, it does not solve all the problems of democracy.

It indicates, first of all, that good political practice necessarily entails reflection, knowledge, and not only a reflection of a technical character, but of an ethical fashion; a reflection oriented to the universality of the *res publica*. Otherwise there would be no other way to avoid the risks of corporate interests and public space would then be in the hands of private group's interests.

At the same time that we experienced those changes typical of the consolidation of democracy, we have witnessed very quick transformations in social interaction within and amongst nations as a consequence of technological innovations that have drastically altered the standards of production, communication and transportation. There has been an acceleration in the process of change at such a pace that our capacity to react to this trend is often insufficient.

What is the importance of this tendency for the reflection on politics? A fundamental importance. Perhaps more than ever Government decisions have to be enlightened by thought. They have to be benefited from the long-term vision which constitutes the comparative advantage of academy.

Not to react to changes, and I would even add, not to anticipate those changes is a luxury we cannot afford. In wartime when knowing the terrain might mean the difference between life and death cartography would convert from an academical art to a prioritary security issue for the State. We are experiencing a period which is not wartime but it is full of very important changes in which the required cartography, the strict analysis of the opportunities and risks brought about by the new situations, may become the difference between development and marginalization, between success and failure of societies.

Accordingly more and more knowledge has to "illuminate" political action. Today we cannot adopt a vision of the relation between theory and practice, and unfortunately this sort of vision can still be often found both in our Universities and amongst those who dedicate themselves to political activity.

In the analysis of this subject Weber cannot continue to be taken as a paradigm. The challenges of the present situation require a certain kind of merging, without confounding them, between the two logics that I have mentioned in my initial comments: the logic of knowledge and the logic of action. Within the framework of our democracies, republican tradition in trying to merge thought and action in the fundamental concept of republican virtue results more productive, more updated than an abstract distinction between facts and values, or between conviction and responsibility.

It is in this spirit that I extend to the participants in the World Congresses my best compliments trustful that your work will bring an important contribution to solving the problems of our time in our societies. At the moment we are getting closer to a new century, full of new opportunities and hopes for those who, like me and yourselves, believe in knowledge and political action as tools for the construction of a more just society.

3. EDUCATION AND PARTICIPATORY RESEARCH

Jaime Niño Díez (Colombia)
Sociologist and Minister of Education

On behalf of the Government of Colombia and President Ernesto Samper Pizano, I extend to all of you attending this important international event, my warmest greetings to Colombia and to this beautiful city of Cartagena. Your presence does us great honour.

Both as Minister of Education and in personal terms, it gives me great pleasure and excitement to be able to take part in the inauguration of the Fourth World Congress of Action and Learning Research and the Eighth World Congress of Participative Action Research, held to mark the twentieth anniversary of the First World Symposium of Participative Action Research, which also took place here in Cartagena on April 18-24, 1977.

Twenty years of political and social ups and downs, twenty years of social protests and movements of great importance to the lives of all, have been the context or framework for the rise and progress of Participatory Action Research, the idea which Orlando Fals Borda has nourished among us throughout his fertile academic life, and which is so deeply dynamic as it generates processes by its own structure. In this case, the generation of a process does not depend on the decision or wish of the researcher: Participatory Action Research entails processes, since they are part of its nature.

Participatory Action Research becomes a process in the daily lives of individuals and entire peoples. It is the meeting point of personal space and time for those who promote it and for those who take part in reconstructing the meaning of the history which formed its roots, or in reconstructing the situation which shapes its present form. And it is that meeting-point in one's own space and time which makes our commitment inescapable. Different specifics and different times are interwoven in our present, in a commitment to construct the future.

With his proposal for Participatory Action Research, Orlando Fals Borda succeeded in tying down, in conceptual and technical terms, the dreams of a whole generation of social scientists, in such a way that they are never going to leave us. Action Research is now a way of practicing Social Sciences by transforming the world with all those who wish to build their own history. It is to be found in social affairs, in the academic world, in the progress of our peoples. This is why it will endure, to remind social scientists of the power which commitment has to bring about change and of the obstacles which block scientific objectivity at certain moments.

Action Research is also here as a bond of knowledge between people born on opposite shores, a meeting-point for us to work together, a guarantee of civic participation, a talisman against the curse of indifference and indolence.

And it is precisely all these processes of Action Research as a method of knowledge and transformation of social reality that have extended its influence rapidly and indeed have led to its adoption by large numbers of researchers all over the world: many highly reputable social scientists from over sixty countries give it their valuable and constant support.

This Congress of Action Research brings in all the mystery and excitement of a meeting of ways. It marks the end of a period of consolidation, and the beginning of a stage of diversification. Action Research can be many things: for example, it can be a basic instrument of participation, the recovery of identity, education in solidarity, or socialization of the commitment in every school in the country. Perhaps it is the instrument which the Institutional Projections required by the Colombian Education Law has been needing to integrate the education process into civil society and the educational community; to turn the school into a center of social development and participation; and to ensure that education would be adopted as a civic purpose. Action Research is perhaps what the Institutional Projections have been needing to anchor the schools into the hearts of communities. And perhaps it is what the schools were needing in order to learn how to conjugate the verb to do research .

Our campaign From the School, Peace in One Thousand Days launched by the government, finds in Action Research an instrument of singular importance for building up peaceful coexistence, stimulating many moments in daily life for creative acts of peace. Every primary school, every high school, every university and every education center must become a node in one great national network to bring Colombians together.

"May our schools and education be the bearers of the transition from the old culture of war to a new culture of peace, coexistence and human solidarity. "

As Minister of Education and as the sociologist that I am, I would like to express my very real pleasure at being here at the inauguration of these events, and my most sincere wishes go for the success of our discussions. Your theme is an expression of the development and importance of the participatory viewpoint as a form of research, as an approach for the transformation of realities through the social sciences. Your conclusions and contributions will be of the greatest value to Colombia and other countries.

Dr. Fals Borda, you and your team deserve our deepest gratitude for this legacy which gives to your former lectureship in sociology at the National University a place in Colombian history. Our whole country, and especially its Caribbean coast which is so close to your heart, know what this means.

4. UNESCO AND PARTICIPATORY RESEARCH

Francine Fournier
Sub-Director General for Social and Human Sciences, UNESCO, Paris.

On behalf of Dr. Federico Mayor, let me first thank you for inviting UNESCO to take part in this important scientific event, a very welcome initiative in this moment when different international organizations and national research centers pay careful attention to the interplay between social science research production and its use and application by political and societal agents.

Intellectuals have always sought to influence their societies, and modern times brought to this arena a new type of rapport between intellectual and the decision-maker. Intellectuals, and in particular social scientists, claim to have the definite credential por analysing and promoting social transformations: the new knowledge, based on scientific rigour.

Social sciences have acquired the status and the capacity to forecast and to intervene in everyday's life. Moreover, social sciences are currently expected to contribute to public policy processes. They play the special role of explicating the ideas and paradigms implicit in social movements, in the economic decision and in political change. Social sciences have a key role to play in the process of forecasting and preventing social disarrays.

In policy practice, there are stubborn controversies that tend to be enduring, relatively immune to resolution by reference to evidence, and seldom finally resolved. In fact, our times are marked by policy controversies (for instance, disputes over nuclear weapons, welfare, ecological degradation, the status of minorities, or the interplay between local and global processes) which pose the following epistemological predicament: What can possibly be the basis for resolving conflicts of frames when the frames or the paradigms themselves determine what counts as evidence and how evidence is to be interpreted? In other words, different views of the world create multiple social realities.

Realizing this preliminary difficulty is of the great relevance for the development of the relations between knowledge-producers and knowledge-users. Because the role of social science is not limited to the understanding of social relations or the mastering of nature; they are expected to contribute to problem-solving in society. I would consider that their aim is to produce, in close collaboration with decision-makers, citizen organizations and local communities, blueprints for the organization of society.

What can UNESCO offer in this connection?

In 1994, UNESCO launched the Management of Social Transformation (MOST) Programme. MOST is an international cooperative framework designed to bring together the decision making process with policy relevant knowledge production in the areas of multiculturalism and multiethnicity, cities and global-local linkages. The Programme promotes the use of social science research in policy formulation; the assessment of the social impacts of existing economic development policies; the development of methodological tools for evaluating the impact of social and economic development policies designed in follow up to the major UN conferences. The principal strength of the MOST Programme is its capacity to mobilize networks, coordinate projects from headquarters and field offices, provide high level expertise for upstream project preparation and evaluation at the national and regional levels, in cooperation with the UNESCO Field Offices and National MOST Liaison Committees responsible for the local development of the Programme and its projects. This support system reflects the viability of the cooperation between research producers and users recognized by Member States as critical improved development policies.

The MOST Programme seeks to conceptualize the policy process in innovative ways in order to clarify the relationship with policy oriented social science. Currently, 20 comparative long term policy research projects have started in the framework of MOST. One feature of these projects is their original dimension and conception, that is, regional networking and approaches to problem solving, regional scientific cooperation and sharing of expertise, dissemination of information, regional agreement towards achieving common and equitable development goals and making compatible regional strategies with national policy-formulation.

These long term MOST research and action projects are not designed only for scientific knowledge production. The user led principle (i.e. knowledge production responsive to needs of users, as expressed by users) is inherent in each project and constitutes a condition *sine qua non* for acceptance of a project by MOST. For instance, in each MOST project, policy-makers or other users participate in the formulation, design, implementation and evaluation of the project, alongside with professional researchers. This therefore differentiates MOST research projects from typical and traditional university-based research projects. Different Latin American research teams are participating in MOST projects. Among other themes, they are dealing with interaction and integration within MERCOSUR, the institutional modernization of social policies, social and economic transformations connected with drug trafficking, poverty reduction strategies in urban settings.

In sum, technical and scientific activities can ensure the betterment of the quality of life or cause self-destruction: they can produce new relationships between the world and life, a new cosmos. This can be considered as the real problematic of thinking and action. In the philosophy of science, Kuhn has distinguished (1962) periods of normal science, when scientists operate within a shared paradigm and agree on rules of the game for settling disagreements, from periods of scientific revolution in which scientific disagreement cuts across paradigms and there is no agreed upon framework for settling disputes. It seems that we are living this latter moment, since new paradigms in social science are being forged in replacement of categories coined mostly in the 19th century. The Social and Human Sciences Sector of UNESCO particularly through its MOST Programme, participates in this effort to reflect upon these changing paradigms.

In UNESCO´s Social Science programmes in general, and in the MOST Programme in particular, we share the same goals as the action research and action learning approaches, scientifically, practically, as well as ethically.

5. Pioneers gallery

With the presence of Mrs. Jean Pearse and daughters Gabriella and Joanna, from Trinidad / Tobago, the Congress plenary paid tribute to world pioneers of the participatory approach. The portraits of these pioneers and a biography of Paulo Freire written and sent by his widow Ana María Arújo Freire, were displayed at the Congress museum.

A. Letter to Paulo Freire, upon his death

Carlos Núñez Hurtado (México)
Federal Deputy,
President, LatinAmerican Council for Adult Education
(CEAAL)

Dear Paulo:

I am addressing this letter to you from Cartagena where I had hoped to meet you again, as we had done before at Havanna, to tell you what I am writing about. I will not ask you how you are as I am sure you are better than ever, enjoying peace and harmony, love and fulfillment, and reaping well what you have sown in life.

Many people who got to know you through your books probably discovered how human you were, as much as those of us who knew you personally and appreciated your lucid and dynamic thought. I have stated this several times, since the day when we first met in Costa Rica in the mid 70´s. You will remember that we went to visit the Atlantic Coast to get acquainted with a "Total

Language Pedagogy". There, in the forest as you said, walking on the dust of those paths, we learned about your "Letters to Guinea Bissau", still unpublished, which you read to us with passion. We heard about your experiences and achievements in Africa, a continent recently liberated from colonial bonds which was giving its first steps toward nationhood.

Certainly those who read your "Education as a Practice for Freedom" and "Pedagogy of the Oppressed" had to rethink their lives and reframe their work as educators, intellectuals or politicians. And many others had to alter their impositive attitudes and practices after hearing you talk about dialogue and reading the "Pedagogy of the Question".

Paulo, I feel that, for your natural humility, you never were fully conscious of the impact of your work. It is of course hard to measure, but I can assure that a great number of current educational, cultural, social and political practices in our continent (and elsewhere) have had inspiration or have adapted themselves through your rich thought and firm ethical commitment. You have always been coherent, giving much "political substance" to your conceptions and actions. Your profound philosophical, epistemological and pedagogical reflections were always on the side of the poor and oppressed, betting on hopes and dreams. This is perhaps the most subversive of your political ideas.

You gave us a "Pedagogy of Hope" to balance our pragmatic, mercantile and neoliberal world, and as another way to rediscover the "Pedagogy of the Oppressed". You wrote then: "This book is written with wrath but with love, something without which there is no hope. It is a defense of tolerance (that should not be confused with conviviality) as well as of radicalism".

You never forgot the presence of hard realities. But neither did you deny the need to struggle in order to change them. For this reason you also said that "hopelessness is concrete, but that it can be explained for historical, economic and social reasons. And also that we cannot conceive human existence and necessary efforts for improving it without recourse to hopes and dreams".

Dear Paulo, I read this letter in the presence of many friends and colleagues who are getting ready to discuss and to take a stance, as scientists, intellectuals and educators, on the present historical situation, which seems so difficult and hopeless. You should be here to give us your lucid opinions inspired by love and concern. You would be calling upon us to revive our capacities for indignation and amazement for the daily scenes which we observe see of hungry children on the streets, of the unemployed clowning for a few coins, of prostituted girls and boys, and of so many other faces of injustice and exclusion which are the gifts of the new goddess of the market. This certainly would be the subject of your talks.

As you have made such deep impression upon our thoughts and lives, for these very reasons, I am sure that you are here with us, impelling us to carry on with our struggle for that action which still is unachieved: the ethical revolution. This is characterized by love, tolerance, coherence and scientific knowledge combined with people's knowledge, culture, values and efforts, and everything guided by hope.

José Martí, the great Cuban apostle, once wrote: "Death is not true when one has done life's work well". You, dear Paulo, have done well and abundantly so. Thus I can now assert with much emotion that you are still alive and that you are here present together with all of us.

B. G.V. S. DE SILVA
(Colombo, Sri Lanka, June 3, 1928 - November 25, 1980)

Orlando Fals Borda
With notes supplied by Ponna Wignaraja and Md. Anisur Rahman.

G.V., as he was called by his friends, was a distinguished economist who studied at the University of Ceylon (1948) and the London School of Economics (1951). A government official and international expert on agriculture, fishing, and industry for many years, De Silva founded, in conjuction with Ponna Wignaraja, S. Tilakaratna and others, the influential and well known Participatory Institute for Development Alternatives (PIDA). From this institute, still active, participatory ideas, policies, and critiques have spread throughout Southeast Asia and the world. It received an Alternative Nobel Prize in 1985.

De Silva will be remembered above all for his active involvement in the mobilization of "adivasis", poor peasants of Maharashtra (India) during the 1960's. They formed a "Land Army" or "Bhoomi Sena". This great social, economic and political movement for people's self-reliance and justice in India's countryside produced a massive rural recomposition in Maharashtra and other states. It also fostered the creation of autonomous social and political forces. Millions of *adivasis* were motivated into action and progress thanks to the discovery of their own intellectual, political and economic possibilities.

This tremendous work took inspiration from G.V.'s thesis that "the economic problem is not due to instability of growth but to a lack of a self-reliant response to overcome endemic backwardness". He discovered that the economic sciences did not help him understand the real situation of his people. He then proposed alternative ways of explanation and action that differed from the "bankrupt orthodox economic theory", a solution which led him to articulate "constructive heresies", as he called them. This idea was a leading light for his further work.

Bhoomi Sena's impact was felt soon beyond India's borders, especially for the publication of a detailed report on its origins and developments written by De Silva, Wignaraja, Md. Anisur Rahman, and Niranjan Mehta. This report was translated into English and published by the Dag Hammerskjold Foundation at Uppala (Sweden) in its influential journal *Development Dialogue*, N° 2 (1979).

The rest of the Third World learned about Bhoomi Sena and its important pioneering accomplishments through that publication. It was a motive for inspiration and emulation in many parts of the world, where there were similar situations of injustice and exploitation especially in land tenure systems and political practices. Such was the case, for example, of the Colombian National Peasant Association (ANUC), one of the most significant popular movements of the present century in this country. Many of ANUC leaders got to know about De Silva's work in Maharashtra and to admire it.

For this reason and for many others of a personal nature —his selflessness and generosity, his intelligence and vision— G.V.S. De Silva will be forever remembered as a pioneer for people's participation throughout the world. Hence the present just recognition by our World Convergence Congress.

C. TRIBUTE TO ANDREW PEARSE
(Crewkerne, England, 1916 - Oxford, England, 1980)

Solon Barraclough
Consultant,
United Nations Research Institute for Social Development (UNRISD)

Andrew was born in Crewkerne, England, in 1916 during World War I. He held a Master of Arts in literature from Trinity College at Cambridge. During World War II he was a conscientious objector, and after the war he took part in "democratizing" the German school curriculum during the Allied occupation. He later was decorated by the French Republic for this educational work. He undertook adult educational programmes in Scotland for the Workers' Educational Association before moving on to Trinidad and Tobago where he worked with the University of the West Indies on social, cultural and ethnographic questions. Subsequently, Andrew worked as a UNESCO expert on the sociology of education in Brazil and Colombia as well as being a sociology professor and head of the Social Research section at the University of Bogotá. It was during this period that I first met Andrew and persuaded him to become an advisor to the Inter-American Committee for Agricultural Development's research project on land tenure and agricultural development that I was co ordinating.

Andrew came to the Chilean Agrarian Reform Research and Training Institute (ICIRA) in 1964 as a FAO expert to direct its rural sociology programme, where he remained until 1968, when he had to return to England for medical treatment. He then became a Senior Fellow of St. Antony's College at Oxford. In 1970 he moved to the United Nations Research Institute for Social Development (UNRISD) to direct its research on the social implications of the green revolution where he remained until 1975. After a brief stint as a project manager of a FAO/UNDP rural development project in the West Indies, he returned to England as a fellow at Queen Elizabeth House, Oxford. When I became UNRISD's director in 1977, I asked Andrew to help plan the Institute's programme and also to rewrite the draft overview report of the green revolution research as a book. He came frequently to Geneva from 1977 until his untimely death in December 1980, to help with UNRISD's research programme and to launch its project on Popular Participation. He was the intellectual leader of this research that continued into the 1980s much along the lines he had envisioned.

Andrew was one of the few social scientists during the 1960s and 1970s dealing with development issues whose principal concern was how the historical changes called "development" affected ordinary people in diverse real world situations. He always insisted on understanding what was happening in " development" from the standpoint of those who were most affected, often negatively. He did not tolerate fools or pretentiousness easily. Instead of expounding grand theories, he wanted to know what was really going on, who was affected and how and what the motivations of the different actors were. He insisted that we always look beyond the footlights: "It is not only the programme but the ongoing societal process with its diverse and often conflicting social forces that must be the object of research", he wrote.

He concluded that in poor countries the dominant process was the incorporation of peasants into the institutions of urbanizing nation states which, in turn, were increasingly incorporated into the world system. It was practically impossible to posit credible alternatives to a continuation of these processes, other than catastrophic ones.

Andrew believed that social researchers shared an obligation to use their position to try to influence social outcomes to the advantage of those who were being excluded. He was too realistic to expect that convincing the powerful of the need for popular participation would be enough to bring it about. Peasant organization, in his view, was a necessary but not a sufficient condition for greater popular participation. He warned that defending a popularly based strategy from internal abuse and from state and private exploitation was as difficult as bringing it about in the first place.

Andrew wrote two major books on development: *The Latin American Peasant* and *Seeds of Plenty, Seeds of Want*. His greatest influence, however, was not through his books but through his personal contacts and his numerous highly perceptive short papers and articles. He insisted on analyzing social processes at local levels from the perspective of the different social actors involved, taking fully into account the context of institutions, policies and values in which they were operating.

He found the cross country statistical correlations of abstract indicators so beloved by many development economists, sociologists and political scientists to be laughable at best. He suggested that to understand social change it is usually much more fruitful to read perceptive novelists as Tolstoy or Arguedas than to study social science texts and journals. He had read and digested an amazing number of novelists, historians and social scientists. Moreover, he spent a major part of his time in the field talking, drinking and eating with peasants, farm labourers, teachers, traders, landlords and political authorities.

Andrew was an outstanding social scientist whose pioneering work has not been adequately recognized by many of his peers. He was also a stimulating friend and teacher. The same is true of two of Andrew´s and my close colleagues at ICIRA in the 1960s who have now passed on. One was the well known Colombian economist and statesman, Antonio García, who headed the Institute´s programme on Cooperatives. Another was Paulo Freire, who headed its literacy programme and whom I had hoped to see again at this Congress. To them our tribute is also due.

D. Myles Horton
(Savannah, Tennessee, July 9, 1905 - New Market, Tennessee, January 19, 1990)

Helen M. Lewis,
Highlander Research and Education Center (USA)

Myles Horton was founder of the Highlander Folk School, later renamed Highlander Research and Education Center in the mountains of Tennessee (USA) in 1932. The school has educated three generations of activists and popular educators who have worked in the labor and civil rights movements in the South and Appalachia. It has also been a major catalyst for social change in the United States for over sixty years.

Seeking to develop a form of education to change society rather than maintain the status quo, Myles Horton created a pedagogy which leads people to challenge the system, to take risks. Myles called it the "two-eye" theory of teaching. You keep one eye on where people are, and one eye on where they can be, forever pushing, making them uncomfortable, stretching their minds, helping them grow in their understanding and critical consciousness.

Myles grew up in the rural South of the United States in the first quarter of the century. His philosophy, educational theory and values had deep roots in his Southern rural experiences. His family was from the hills of Tennessee. They were members of the Cumberland Presbyterian Church, a strongly egalitarian, frontier, anti-elitist denomination. From his family he inherited a down-to-earth theology, an old-time "primitive Christianity", which was simple, straight, hard-nosed, with clear ideas of right and wrong. His grandfather gave him a strong biblical sense of differences between rich and poor, and his mother instilled the importance of love and service. He was smart and proud, encouraged to read, learn and question. He had no sense of inferiority, and he approached life with a country arrogance, questioning and confronting ideas and issues in church, school and work.

He was influenced by his experiences on the farm, in factories and sawmills, working with the Student YMCA in college, and teaching Bible in rural schools. Through these experiences he became committed to fighting injustices and working to make the South more democratic. Later at Union Theological Seminary, at the University of Chicago, and at Danish folk schools, he developed his educational ideas and plans for an adult education center.

One of the most important elements of Highlander pedagogy is the recognition that the best teachers of poor and working people are the people themselves. Rather than bringing in "experts" as resource people, Highlander brings people together, developing a circle of learners who share the same problems. Together people share their experiences, analyze their problems and learn how to work toward basic changes in society. The goal is not reform or adjustment to an unjust society but the transformation of society.

It is an education for action. It is dangerous education, and although much emphasis is on forming strategies to confront the system without being destroyed, people are encouraged to push the boundaries, to be creative in solving problems. Often this means pushing to the place where they get into trouble. Myles insists that until people take some risks and gain some independence from the system they are not free to learn or to act. As people try to be part of the decision making process, they discover that learning about democracy involves working to replace, transform and rebuild society to allow for equal participation.

Although Myles developed this method of education from his own life and work with poor and working people in the rural South of the United States, it is not unique to Highlander and to Myles. Paulo Freire in Brazil and others working in similar situations in Chile, Colombia, India, Nicaragua, Kenya, Tanzania, and Europe have developed a similar pedagogy by observing how people learn and tying this to the need for basic changes in society.

Myles worked to build networks with people in popular education movements all over the world. Other Highlander staff members, John Gaventa, Sue Thrasher, Susan Williams, have been active in international adult education and participatory research groups working to link these movements. As people all over the earth use education for social transformation they are generating

an international social movement for political participation and
change. We at Highlander are honored to have Myles Horton and
Highlander recognized as pioneers and included among the vital
headwaters of this mighty human stream.

E. MENTIONS TO ANTON DE SCHUTTER (HOLLAND / MÉXICO) AND JOÃO BOSCO PINTO (BRAZIL / COLOMBIA)

The World Congress for Participatory Convergence went on to
remember and recognize the merits of two other pioneers. One is
the Dutch educator and social scientist Anton de Schutter, who
worked at CREFAL in Pátzcuaro (México). He was the first to combine
participatory research with pedagogical approaches in adult
education. He wrote in 1980 a classic book on this subject, which
had ample repercussion in Latin America where it is still used as a
text. Anton died in an unfortunate automobile accident in 1985.

The other pioneer is the Brazilian anthropologist and educator
João Bosco Pinto, a brilliant activist and theoretician of action
research. His techniques were tried successfully in the field,
especially in Colombia (at ICIRA, Interamerican Institute for Studies
in Agrarian Reform) and Central America. His seminars and
workshops had regional fame. Bosco Pinto trained a whole generation
of public officials and others who adopted the participatory
philosophy in their lives. He was author of several articles and
books on the subject, and died near Recife (Pernambuco, Brazil)
in 1996.

6. AN INVITATION FOR PEACE

Gustavo I. De Roux (Colombia)
Sociologist

The critical situation in Colombia should have been explained and described to the world without the intercession of the press in reference to the recent assassinations of Mario Calderón and Elsa Alvarado, fellow members of CINEP *(People's Education and Research Center), whose director, Gabriel Izquierdo, spoke out against the assassinations. The full Congress approved a strong motion of protest against the authorities that Alvaro Camacho Guizado, director of the Institute of Political Studies and International Relations at the National University of Colombia put forward. The next day, a large March for Life was organized which traversed the streets bordering the Convention Center with candles and finished in the San Francisco Cloister with a musical homage (see Videos 1 & 4).*

The Executive Committee of this Congress has wanted, since the inauguration of the same, to invite all of the participants to make known their reflections at this moment and place with regard to the unavoidable topic of peace. First of all, because this deals with an event that happened in Colombia, a country which competes for the painful distinction of the most violent country on the planet; a nation where about 30,000 homicides are committed annually which makes up one-third of those committed in the Region of the Americas. Also, because this Congress meets in a country that has shown in the last ten years a net destruction of human life.

Day by day, the Colombian citizen runs the highest risk of dying from a homicide. While 1.0% of the deaths in the world and 3.0% of the deaths in Latin America are due to homicides, in Colombia homicides account for one of every four deaths. The violence in Colombia has produced around 50,000 orphans. It causes an annual loss of 1,200,000 years of potential life, forces around 150,000 people a year from their homes and regrettably afflicts the citizen s security and ability to live together. Moreover, it produces incalculable economic costs as a result of the armed struggles, extortions, payments to kidnappers and for crimes against the patrimony. And there are the environmental costs which come as a result of guerrilla actions against petroleum installations and from the establishment and control of illicit crops.

There are many actors responsible for the diverse repertoire of violations against the right to life, to live in peace and to human rights. For example, those who make war a form of life, an obligation, a pathway to peace or to change society are responsible; others who are responsible are those few and anonymous who come out from among those who have received the constitutional mandate to guarantee the life and integrity of each citizen; those who act delinquently, be that common, organized or disperse are responsible also; finally, all of those who permit and use violence as a mechanism to resolve conflicts and daily disagreements.

Disappearances, assassinations, massacres and actions called "social cleaning" practiced by groups inspired in a lawfulness outside the realm of judicial law all make up the menu of violence. Also on the menu are groups that justify their enormous intolerance in supposed historical, natural, cultural or social laws to eliminate opposition politicians, Protestant pastors, beggars, homosexuals, prostitutes, drug addicts, street kids and young delinquents or those suspected of being young delinquents. What is more, the Heroic Cartagena, home of this Congress, was saddened by recent anonymous actions of social cleaning.

The Executive Committee has also wanted to invite everyone to remember that in the time which has passed since the World Symposium of Participatory Action Research which was held in Cartagena twenty years ago and today's conference, the lives of many intellectuals, and popular urban and rural leaders —especially in Asia, Africa and Latin America— have been sacrificed. These people held Participatory Action Research as a paradigm to construct enlightened ways of transformation and change. These were researchers for whom it was important that the people took a role in the search for progress in dignity reconciled with nature, and which opened spaces for participation in the defining of the future. These were researchers who tried through participation to find horizons without marginalizing or exclusion, where the forgotten of the earth would have capacity to come near to their little utopias of adequate housing, deserving wages, and health and education opportunities. Among these researchers are Mario Calderón and his companion, Elsa, who should be here with us today, but who were brutally assassinated two weeks ago near Bogotá for stubbornly keeping to their commitment with peasants hoping for a better life.

Paradoxically, Colombia is also a country full of good people who refuse to give up their dreams of peace. Millions of friendly and hospitable women and men who love life and who reject war and violence build on a daily basis counterweights to the intolerance and disrespect for civil and human rights through their honorable work and untiring solidarity. This is a country full of social, academic, political, syndicalist and religious groups and organizations which mobilize unceasingly for peace, struggling for initiatives that stir up the urban conscience to uphold mutual respect and the right to die a natural death.

The Committee has also wanted to remind the participants of the historic role of Participatory Action Research in the building of peace in a world which, at the end of the twentieth century, is facing two great tragedies: aggression between human beings and aggression by human beings against nature as their home and sustenance. This is a world in which there coexist unimaginable advances along with indescribable suffering, increases in prosperity and abundance along with a depressing growth in poverty. Remember that peace will not be a free gift but rather the result of the human capacity to construct social justice and combine it with solidarity. Participatory Action Research has maintained a serious commitment to the development of this capacity. A capacity which the Committee wants to be highlighted and affirmed.

Violence is an adulteration of social relations which doesn't result from the manifestation of instinctive human conduct but from the behavior of alienate peoples. Because it is socially produced, it can be socially prevented. The convergence of knowledge in this place and time (marked by the profound social crisis of incubated violence whose overwhelming dimensions have converted it into a norm) should alert us to keep up our capacity for astonishment and to impede our becoming apathetic toward violence. We should create beams of light to show the way to peace.

The Executive Committee also wants to make an invitation to this Congress, if the participants find it pertinent, to reaffirm before the world the general obligation to respect human rights and the importance of appealing to a peaceful and dialoged solution to conflicts. A call is also made to energetically defend the right to life and the right to live in peace as indispensable conditions to make this planet a kinder and friendlier place. We should demand that power be used for constructing just and decent societies. But, more than anything else, we urge you to exalt peace because it surely deserves a serious chance.

PART II

UNDERPINNINGS

This part includes the lectures on topics of general concern to participatory audiences which were presented at afternoon plenaries during the Congress. They are Immanuel Wallerstein's theory of SpaceTime; Manfred Max Neef's critique to classic economics and neoliberalism; Agnes Heller's conceptualization of modernity, ethics, and democracy; Rajesh Tandon's personal reflections on construction of knowledge, which have ample implications; Robert Chambers' methodological descriptions of rural change practice and diagnosis; and Robert L. Flood's discussion of systems theory and participatory research.

Not all of these thinkers and activists belong to PR schools, but they converged with congress purposes. They express here ideas and concepts which are highly pertinent and useful for the aims of social, political, economic and cultural movements at the heart of PR.

7. SPACETIME AS THE BASIS OF KNOWLEDGE

Immanuel Wallerstein
President of International Sociological Association.
Binghamton University (New York, USA)

Time and space are the most obvious parameters of our existence. They are among the first concepts a child learns. However uneducated people are, they will be able to identify the times and spaces in which they live and usually those in which others live. One would think these concepts would be at the center of any and all attempts at social knowledge. And in a sence they are. We discuss the sequence of events, and we say that processes have histories. We also regularly notice and seek to explain the fact that social conditions and social relations seem different in different places. So we appear to be taking into account not only time but space as well.

But in fact, in a more important sense, we ignore time and space completely, because we seldom, if ever, take into account the social construction of time and space, and almost never the social construction of their combinaton which I shall call TimeSpace. In a sense this is not surprising at all. Historical systems derive such stability as they have from the fact that most people located within them consider the social system natural and enduring, if not eternal. To do this, it is easiest to consider time and space as invariants, as Kant theorized.

"The moving finger writes," said the poet Omar Khayyam. "And having writ, moves on." Time rides forward imperturbably in a universe which surrounds us. No one is capable of changing time or space. Of course, for all practical purposes, this is true. But it is equally true that the meaning of time and space, the interpretations we make of time and space, the use we make of time and space concepts, the notice we take of time and space are not at all invariant. Just the opposite! And this has been nowhere as true as in the modern world-system in which we live, one of whose salient features is the room that it has given for multiple social constructions of TimeSpace, a feature that has given it great pliability and resilience, but at the same time an extraordinary ability to hide from its participants the reality of what they are experiencing.

Modern structures of knowledge have insisted that time and space are invariant exogenous factors of social reality within which everything we do and say somehow fits. We are subjects acting within objective reality. We are humans, and time and space are external to us, part of our natural environment. We exist immanently, but time and space persist despite us. Given this belief in a radical disjunture of humans and nature, which reflects the same binary, antinomic conceptualization of reality as the purposed disjunctures between the particular and the universal, the idiographic and the nomothetic, philosophy and science all part of the intellectual scaffolding of the modern world-system, we are logically forced into perceiving only two kinds of TimeSpace. On the one hand, there is that of the infinitesimally small events, which I call "episodic geopolitical Time Space, "and on the other hand, there is that of the infinitely large continuing realities, which I call "eternal TimeSpace."[1] The world of knowledge, for 200 years now, has required the analyst to choose among only these two possible TimeSapces to describe social reality.

Episodic geopolitical TimeSpace is the explanation of the immediate in time and space by the immediately prior in time and space, each vector being summarized as narrowly as possible. It is the analysis of events, which of course occur in an instant at a particular point, hence episodic in a series of episodes, an event in an endless series of events; and geopolitical in terms of the nominal definition of the space in which it occurs. Every episodic moment is equivalent to every other; hence no patterns which are trans-event can be discerned, because they cannot exist. The space is superparticular, and in its exceptionality equivalent to every other; hence no patterns which are trans-locality can be discerned because again they cannot exist. Eternal TimeSpace pretends to be the polar opposite. In eternal TimeSpace there exists nothing but generalizations, since the laws of human behavior hold, as it is said, across time and space, that is, without reference to the variations in time and in space. But since every time and space is in reality different, or it would not be specific, to assert eternal TimeSpace is entirely compatible with the assertion of episodic geopolitical TimeSpace. One asserts eternal TimeSpace by ignoring the differences between particular TimeSpaces despite the fact that one knows that they are there. The two TimeSpaces constitute the remote other ends of a logical continuum.

The problem is that the actors in this social reality (as opposed to their analysts) have not at all limited themselves to have not done so, because accepting this antinomy places an enormous constraint upon social action and thereby upon its correct analysis. But how is it possible that the analysts of social reality, those who are presumed to be the specialists, in fact use a framework of analysis that is less perceptive than the rest of the world, the so-called actors in the real world? It can only be so if the specialists have created for themselves a trained incapacity to perceive, and if so, then this training itself must itself be in turn explained.

To seek some insight into this complex situation, where the keys to rational explanation are themselves the major obstacles to rational explanation, we must trace the evolution of our modern structures of knowledge, and the role that they have played in the modern world-system. The story starts, as we know, in the European Middle Ages, when the Church was still able to assert its decisive control over the definition of truth. Truth existed as God revealed it, and as the Church interpreted this revelation.

The process of creating the modern world system, a capitalist world-economy, involved (necessarily involved) an effort to break out of the constraints imposed by this clerical monopoly. Enter the philosophers, or rather re-enter! The two great movements of ideas we associate with this period in which our world-system was born are the Renaissance and the Reformation. Both involved the assertion that truth can be ascertained directly by human beings, in one case by insight into the natural laws of the universe, in the other by insignt into the mysterious ways of God. But in both cases, truth was ascertained on the de facto authority of the one who had the insight, and in theory everyone might have such insight, or at least it was not an option that was linked to holding some office.

The capitalist world-economy centered its activity around creation, creation of capital, creation of goods and technology in order to create capital, creation of both states and an interstates systems as the necessary institutional framework for the accumulation of capital, creation of social categories in order to create the appropriate work force with both the capacity and willingness to assume roles in the creation of goods and technology, and the creation of structures of knowlwdge that would sustain all the other activities. There was no order of priority among these creative activities. They were all essential elements in the erection, maintenance, and flourishing of a historical systems based on the endless accumulation of capital.

The revolt of the philosophers against the theologians was therefore only the beginning phase of the intellectual restructuring that was in process. In time, a specialized group of more practical thinkers began to designate themselves as scientists, a term that came to denote an emphasis on an inductive road to truth, via empirical research and experimentation, a method that could furnish evidence that might validate hypotheses or generalizations, as the members of this group achieved more collective self-confidence in the seventeenth and eighteenth centuries in Europe, they began to speak out not only against the heavy hand of the theologians but against what they saw as the equally heavy hand of the philosophers. They charged the philosophers with being disguised theologians, and asserted that the former had no greater claim to access to truth than the latter.

Thus was consummated in the late eighteenth century in what has been termed the divorce between philosophy and science, a divorce that was institutionalized in the reviving university system by the establishment of separate faculties for the humanities (or letters or philosophy) and for the (natural) sciences, a segregation that remains to this day the form of most university structures throughout the world. This was the split between what we call today the two cultures, and the divorce was not at all amicable. The scientists were disdainful of the philosophers, arguing that their ratiocinations were intellectually irrelevant and that they could be, indeed should be, ignored. The scientists thereupon distanced themselves from "culture," which was defined as somehow subjective, and therefore neutral, investigators of external reality. The philosophers, in response, asserted that the scientists were ignorant of the fundamental values upon which social life (and indeed the very work of the scientists themselves) was based, that they neglected human (and therefore humane) concerns, and that they were incapable of promoting the good or appreciating the beautiful.

It must be said that, in this passionate war of words, neither side gave much ground to the other. Both were equally sure that they were right. The non-scholarly world however tended to find the arguments of the scientists more persuasive than those of the philosophers, since science was seen as more practical, that is, as having more useful applications in the material world. Thus, science rose steadily in public esteem throughout the last two centuries and philosophy moved into a defensive backwater. The world of knowledge was thereupon not merely deeply divided but arrayed by the larger society in a hierarchical order. In the nineteenth century, and the twentieth, those who sought to prevail in public argument and acquire public prestige usually felt it necessary to clothe themselves in the mantle of science. Ever since then, the world of knowledge has been engaged in one long epistemological debate between those who have a basically positivist view, between those who had a largely hermeneutic view, and between those who said it was knowable only by empathetic insight.

In the nineteenth century, as a result of the fundamental social change brought about in the wave of the French Revolution and the new widespread feeling that social change was both normal and inevitable, it suddenly seemed of urgent importance to understand the rules by which the social world operated, in order to be better able to control where it was going, and at what pace. This ideological need led to the creation of what we today call social science. Social science did not seem to fall obviously either into the domain of natural science or into that of the humanities. As a mode of knowledge, it came to be located, somewhat uneasily, in between the two. In fact, in many universities, a third, quite

separate faculty was established to house its practitioners. However, there was no third separate epistemology for this third faculty.
Rather, practitioners adopted one of the two competing epistemologies, and as a consequence, the social sciences were torn
apart by this struggle between the two cultures for the soul of the
social sciences.[2]

The battle raged as intensely within the social sciences as
between the humanities and the natural sciences. Indeed, it was if
anything more intense, since the two sides were in closer ongoing
social and intellectual contact within the social sciences than were
the original antagonists, the philosophers and the physical
scientists. The results for the social sciences were in the long run
largely negative. The two tendencies within the social sciences,
what Windelbrand called the nomothetic and idiographic positions,
each sought to demonstrate that it could fulfill, and fulfill better,
the now culturally dominant scientific ethos: objetivity and value-
neutrality. They chose however widely divergent paths to achieve
this objetive.

The so-called nomothetic, or universalizing, disciplines
(primarily economics, political science, and sociology) insisted that
objectivity was best guaranteed by the use of replicable, quantitative
data. They also insisted that the closer the social scientist was (in
time and space) to the source of the data, the les likely it would be
for the researcher that was concentrated on a few variables was
likely to contain fewer unanalyzed intervening phenomena (or
middle terms) that were difficult to control and to measure. If
one followed the logic of these methodological preferences, the best
data were absolutely contemporaneous data, as "hard" as possible,
collected in social situations where existed excellent infrastructure
for quantitative recording (which meant only in certain countries,
those that were wealthier and more bureaucratized), such data
permitting the researcher to measure accurately the correlation
between two variables over a relatively brief period of time.

From the point of view of TimeSpace, such data were inevitably
data couched in episodic geopolitical TimeSpace, with however a
very strange twist. Because the nomothetic social scientists insisted
that truth was universal, that is, that truth statements were valid
across all of time and space, they inferred that their findings, which

were actually based only on episodic geopolitical TimeSpace, were to be considered findings about eternal TimeSpace. The inference was a logical leap of considerable fragility, but it is nonetheless the one which a very large part of modern social science is based.

The so-called idiographic, or particularizing, social scientists (primarily historians, anthropologists, and Orientalists) turned this process upside down. They asserted a socio-psychological premise: the closer the scholar is to his/her data, the more likely he/she is to be motivated to distort the recording of the data, in order to serve immediate political and social ends. Value-neutrality is easiest, they said, if one studies what is far off, in time and space. On the other hand, idiographic social scientists were simultaneously arguing that interpretation was the heart of the scholarly exercise and that intelligent interpretation required a deep knowledge of the total context (the history, the culture, the language). Of course, one knows the context best of one's own times and one's own culture/ nation/group. And this seemed to push the researcher in the opposite direction, that of closeness. How then could the two demands be reconciled? The researchers solved the dilemma by combining two injunctions. They would study only the past, the chronological past in the case of the historians; the hypothetical, unchanging pre-present in the case of the anthropologists and the Orientalists. In this sense, they were standing remote from their data. But they would study them only after deep immersion in the context: by long acquaintance with both the archives and secondary sources, as well as linguistic knowledge in the case of the historians, by erudite scholarship and careful philological reading of the texts for the Orientalists, by participant observation for the anthropologists. Again there was a twist: close acquaintance with the context, but not with the people, who were dead for the historian; unvisited for the Orientalist; and left behind by the anthropologist (who was enjoined under no circumstance to "go native"). Thus, they stood intellectually close to, but presumably emotionally aloof from, their objects of enquiry. Finally, the emphasis on the context implied a lifelong commitment to a narrowly-defined segment of social reality, since it would be extremely difficult to devote the necessary time to the detailed study of more than one such segment, and without such investment of time the scholarship would inevitably be superficial (that is, would result in an inadequate interpretation).

In terms of TimeSpace what happened was that, in a manner parallel to the nomothetic social scientist was pushed in the direction of narrowing ever more the scope of his enquiry, towards in fact the use of episodic geopolitical TimeSpace, while at the same time arguing that in this microcosm, he was discovering something universal in human nature, a hint of eternal TimeSpace.

This historical evolution of social science —the lack of an autonomous epistemology, its consequent subjugation by the centrifugal pulls of the two cultures, its retreat to ever more narrowly-defined objects of investigation— reached its culmination in the period following the end of the Second World War, the period between 1945 and 1970. Social science was at that time and for the first time accorded considerable public recognition, not perhaps anything like that accorded the natural science, but nonetheless a great deal more than previously. The increased social recognition was rewarded with increased social and financial support, once again at a level far beneath the natural sciences, but at a far higher level than previously. And yet, social science was using this prestige and the financing to pursue primarily the microcosmic, deeply committed as it was to only two kinds of TimeSpace, each of which found the microcosmic methodologically more satisfactory.

It was precisely this entrenchment of the microcosmic, and the consequent inability to interpret the real world that was so obviously and rapidly changing at a macrocosmic level, that provoked a reaction and led to the long simmering critical self-assessment through which social science has been going for the last twenty years and which shall no doubt be continuing for another twenty. It is reflected on the one hand in widely-expressed complaints that the social sciences are falling apart (what the French call *émiettement*) and on the other hand in the widespread, almost desperate, search for new paradigms which it is hoped will somehow rescue social science. But rescue it from whom or from what? Perhaps from itself.

What had social science gained by concentrating on only two TimeSpaces, the immediate and ephemeral one of episodic geopolitical TimeSpace, and the unchanging one of eternal TimeSpace? For the primary consequence of this concentration on the microcosmic was political irrelevance, a sort of self-emasculation that was at once the price and the guarantee of public recognition and support. And what had those who supported this kind of social science gained by this emasculation? It seems quite obvious: both the avoidance of embarrassing insightful analyses into the dark corners of reality and the ideological masking of existing patterns of hierarchical privilege. The language of value neutrality was itself the major culprit of the intrusion of value distortion.

What kinds of TimeSpace were not noticed in this epistemological cul-de-sac of the social science? There were three, and each was evacuated from discussion in different ways. I have given names to each, and I shall discuss sucessively what they imply and why they were evacuated. I call them cyclico-ideological TimeSpace, structural TimeSpace, and transformational TimeSpace.

Cyclico-ideological TimeSpace should not be confused with cyclical theories of history, which are nothing but variations of eternal TimeSpace. The great cyclical theories all describe presumed eternal patterns, which however take the form of a wave instead of a straight line. But in these theories nothing ever really changes, because the laws of human behavior are eternal. I am not talking of such eternal cycles. Rather I am talking of the cycles that occur within the functioning of particular historical systems and which are in effect the regulatory mechanisms of these systems. All systems have regulatory mechanisms, or they would not be systems. Mammals breathe, for example. This has the function of both taking some external elements into the body and discharging other elements out of the body: this maintains a physiological balance of sorts, without which the body cannot function. When a mammal ceases to breathe, it ceases to live. We can measure these cycles. When the physician tests a human being's blood pressure, he records it in terms of systolic and diastolic lengths, because the heart contracts and relaxes, contracts and relaxes. When we have understood this cyclical pattern, we have understood something very important about the physiology of the body.

Analogous rhythms occur in historical social systems. If we wish to analyze the modern world-system, for example, it is crucial to discern the regulatory structures, which take the form of such cyclical patterns. A study of these patterns reveals what is happening which takes the form of such cyclical patterns. A study of these patterns reveals what is happening within the system, why, and when. Has it ever occurred to you how strange it is that most economists are perfectly willing to accept the reality of very short-term wave-like movements, generally called business cycles, that last 2-3 years at most, and which are usually over almost as soon as they have begun, but these same economists are extraordinarily reticent to accept the reality of longer cycles, those called Kondratieff cycles, which tend to have a 50-60 year life?

Why this curious inconsistency? Perhaps the answer lies in the inferences one can draw from the study of cycles of different lengths. If one notices very rapid, short-run cycles, we may infer that they are beyond their control (and hence for which no one needs be held responsible) but which also do not endanger their survival, since they reverse themselves very fast. If however we talk of 50-60 year cycles, of which the B-phase (or the negative phase) is 25-30 years, we can no longer be quite so indifferent. If a Kondratieff b phase is seen to be associated with increased worldwide reduction of wage employment, this is a serious matter with serios political implications. We will want to know at least what is responsible, if not who is responsible, for this negative period.

The analysis of medium-term cyclical patterns in the functioning of an historical social system lays bare the anatomy of the system, allows us to inspect its workings, and makes possible not only a scientific account of its mechanisms but ultimately a moral appreciation of its rationality as a system. The analysis of medium-term cyclical patterns puts us on the road to meaningful judgments about what can be done, but also about what cannot be done, to alter the operations of an ongoing system. It is extremely empowering. Why has social science historically tended to neglect this kind of study? Why has it often heaped obloquy on those who have attempted it, scorning such analyses on the grounds either that patterns do not exist (since only episodic geopolitical Time-Space exists) or that the data do not permit asserting them as eternal patterns within the framework of a specific historical social system, as they are indeed not eternal and do not pretend to be. They pretend to explain the functioning of a particular system, but one that extends over large space and long time, the *longue durée* of Braudel.

I have called this kind of SpaceTime cyclico-ideological, because the spatial parameters of such conceptions tend to have ideological markers, reflecting defined divisions within the geocultural norms of the historical system in question. We talk for example of mercantile, industrial, and post-industrial eras of modern capitalist history. We spoke until very recently of there being two blocs, two worlds, a free world and a Communist world, but this ideological space was in fact linked to a very specfic time period, 1945-1990. It exists no more, and it could not be considered to have existed in the period before 1945. What do such characterizations do when they single out and give names to particular cycles in a series of repetitive cycles? They tend to reify certain differences and simultaneously efface a considerable number of similarities. They tend to take phenomena that are cyclical, that is repetitive, and suggest that the cycles are less important than the qualitative shifts, which it is suggested are more fundamental than they are in reality. They divert attention, that is, from the structural, the realm of the fundamental qualitative characteristics. Thus, while perceiving cyclico-ideological TimeSpace does enable us to understand far better the functioning of a system, it has nonetheless its dangers. Through its ideological parameters, it can lead us into perceiving constant medium term novelty, which can encourage us into perceiving constant medium-term novelty, which can encourage us to slide back into the short-term, into episodic, geopolitical TimeSpace, and not so paradoxically at the same time into the arena of the total absence of novelty, eternal TimeSpace. Cyclico-ideological TimeSpace thus often undermines itself. Its function is for us to perceive the repetitive patterns of a system to be sure, but this is only useful if we remember that such repetitive patterns occur within the framework of a historical system limited in both time and space albeit long time and large space.

If we are to keep in mind the outer limits in time and space of any historical system, we need then to have a clear idea of structural TimeSpace. Historical system, like all systems, are organic in the sense that they have a genesis, a historical life, and an end (a collapse, a transformation) all of this locatable in both time and space. Structural TimeSpace is in fact the key concept in social science. When we locate it, we have the meaningful unit of analysis of social continuity and of social change. We have the basic parameters within which social interaction and social conflict occur. We know whereof we are speaking. Yet social science in the modern world has treated structural TimeSpace as though it were a high-voltage transmitter. We approach it with fascination, and we retreat when we get too close, afraid of being burned.

There is a sense in which social science in the modern world has been nothing but one long exercise in establishing what it is that is modern about the modern world, a sort of quest in self-discovery. Are we afraid of what we shall discover? Take the long hesitation of calling this capitalist world capitalist. Why are we searching for euphemisms? What is the fear of the term, when, as Braudel remarked, though we chase it out the front door, it always returns through the window? The answer is no doubt simple. There is nothing that so clearly shows up the limitations of both eternal TimeSpace and episodic geopolitical TimeSpace as the concept of structural TimeSpace. Nothing gets us as close to the story of human choice and human evolution as understanding what kinds of historical systems we have constructed, what their parameters and boundaries are, and why their existence is necesarily limited. Structural TimeSpace speaks to what we cannot change (the system in the short run) and what will surely change (the system in the long run), and why the system doesn't really change in the short run (the cyclical rhythms) and why it in fact does change in the long run (the secular trends, leading far from equilibrium).

Insofar as social science has failed to perceive structural TimeSpace, it has not merely failed in its mission but has manifestly misled us in our quest for self-knowledge. Social science has thereby disabled us in our ability to construct the world we wish to construct, the good society we prefer and covet, merely by denying the very possibility of doing this. This brings us to the last kind of TimeSpace we have neglected, what I call transformational TimeSpace. This is the brief, very rare, moment of fundamental change. It is the moment of transition from one kind of historical system to another, from one mode of organizing social life to another. These moments do not come often. They come only when an historical system has exhausted its mechanisms of reequilibrating itself, has used up the efficacity of the cyclical rhythms, has gone sufficiently far from equilibrium that the oscillations have become relatively wild and unpredictable. We enter then into the moment of which Prigogine speaks, the moment of bifurcation in which a new, but nonpredictable, order will emerge from the chaos into which the structure has acceded. Even then, we do not know if we are undergoing truly fundamental change. For it is always possible to recreate an analogous historical system, or one that is indeed morally worse. But it is also possible in these moments to create something better, more hopeful, more imaginative, more creative.

This moment of transformational change, or rather of the possibility of transformational change, has two vectors that are decisive. One is the political struggle between those who hold different, opposing-value systems. But the second is the struggle within the historical alternatives that we face, make more lucid our choices, both criticize and empower those who are engaged in the political struggle (from which of course the world of knowledge is unable to dissociate itself).

I have tried to present the case that the concept of TimeSpace, of the multiple social constructs of TimeSpace, is at the center of the intellectual task of the ongoing reconstruction of the world of knowledge which is necessary to enable the world of knowledge to fulfil adequately its role in this time of transformation. The extension and sequence of time and space may be beyond human control. But time and space affect social reality primarily in the ways in which they are assimilated within us as categories that provide the premises of our thought. Inside and outside, before and after, the same and the different are all defined in terms of boundary lines that we construct, and whose only possible justification is their social usefulness. But even then, the very term "social use-fulness" presumes time and space boundaries which are themselves socially constructed, and socialily disputed.

The emergence of complexity studies within the natural sciences is very illuminating in this regard, and offers great support and assistance for the reconstruction of social science. Just as the social construction of time and space was always true but was only recently (re)discovered as a key issue, so the concept of complexity within the natural sciences was always true but only recently (re)discovered as a key issue. Classical mechanics, which had been at the heart of the scientific enterprise since at least the seventeenth century, was based on the opposite premise, that of simplicity. There were said to be eternal rules that governed physical phenomena, rules that could be stated optimally in simple formulas. These equations were linear and deterministic. Once one knew these equations and any set of so-called initial conditions, one could predict perfectly the future and the past. Time was reversible, in the jargon of the enterprise. Whatever fluctuations occurred in the real world, largely the result of measurement errors, were swiftly tamed by a return to equilibrium. These Newtonian-Cartesian premises were the basis of the concept of eternal TimeSpace and of nomothetic social science.

Already in the last third of the nineteenth century, Henri Poincaré had demonstrated that the so-called three-body problem was insoluble, that the impact of a third body on the relations of two bodies moving under no influence other than gravitation could never be specified with total accuracy. And of course if it could not be specified for the virtually infinite number of bodies that exist in the real universe. But nonetheless it was not until the 1970's that concepts like asymmetry, non-linear and non-equilibrium thermodynamics, fractals, and strange attractors came to be taken seriously by a significant segment of the natural science community. The heart of the challenge to classical mechanics lies in the phrase, "the arrow of time." What is being asserted is that time is not and is never reversible, that everything that was affects everything that is and will be, that the past constrains the future but never determines it. In this conception of the physical world, equilibria are temporary, and all systems tend over time to move away from equilibria. When they move far enough away, the oscillations (the cycles) become dramatic and sharp and at a certain moment there is a bifurcation (technically the situation in which there are two or more solutions to an equation). The bifurcation is inevitable and therefore predictable, but it cannot be determined in advance which path the process will take. What we can say is that the world is complex, and getting ever more complex, and that the task of science is not to reduce this complexity to an impossible simplicity but to explain/interpret this complexity.

For social science, the rise of complexity studies represents an epistemological revolution. On the one hand, it undermines totally the basis of the concept of eternal TimeSpace, while at the same time rejecting that of episodic, geopolitical TimeSpace, substituting for it the rules of social processes for as long as these rules are relevant. For the "orders" that are represented by these rules constantly yield place to periods and loci of "chaos" out of which new "orders" are constantly regenerated. This is precisely the concept of structural TimeSpace with cyclico-ideological TimeSpace located within it, coming to moments of transformational TimeSpace. Since this model is coming to us from the natural scientists, the heartland from which social scientists had draw their views of TimeSpace, this critique of the impossibility of eternal TimeSpace cannot be considered the mere romanticism of those who reject science for irrational and reactionary reasons.

There is however a second element that is revolutionary in the impact of complexity studies on social science. Insofar as the study of social reality was distinct in the nineteenth century and early twentieth century from the study of physical reality, those who wished to bring the two into line with each other urged the social scientists to adopt more closely the model of classical physics. Today, however, although the drive for bringing the social sciences and the physical sciences closer is still there, the terms of their relationship are quite different. Now the proponents of complexity studies are urging upon physical scientists "the arrow of time," which is fundamentally a social science concept. The physical scientists are recognizing historical social systems as simply the most complex system in a world of systems to be analyzed in their complexity. There is thus occurring a "social scientization" of physical science, but it is social science as it might be and not as it has been.

At the same time, in the same period since the 1970's, we have seen the growth in the humanities of what is called cultural studies. Cultural studies has presented itself to us a radical critique of prevailing epistemologies in a way parallel to the critique that complexity studies has made of classical mechanics. Cultural studies has attacked "scientism," but in this regard, it has said little that has not long been argued by those of a so-called humanist bent. What is more significant in my view is its attack on the traditional humanities, on the concept of a self-evident aesthetics which can be summarized in so-called canons. Canons represent eternal TimeSpace within the humanities, whose protagonists were proclaiming it even as they were insisting that all aesthetic creation is irremediably particular, that is, located in episodic, geopolitical TimeSpace. In the humanities just as in the natural sciences, the supposedly contrasting epistemologies of eternal and episodic TimeSpace were in reality totally compatible one with the other.

What the proponents of cultural studies have been saying is that all is context, that texts are within specific contexts. There is hence no definitive meaning of any text, and a text is certainly not the unalterable property of an author. But what is the implication of this kind of assertion? Surely that there is a social meaning to a text, a meaning that evolves with the changing social situation. There are only two roads to go from this observation. One can go down the path of solipsism, in which the world exists insofar as the analyst conceives of it. But solipsism is a self-defeating perspective, since it renders communication not only impossible but irrelevant, and therefore all scholarship pointless. In any case, the solipsist may be in force some rude schocks, when the supposedly nonexistent outer reality suddenly impinges on his survival.

The other route from the observation of the contextuality of all texts is into the assertion of the social construction of reality, but therefore the existence of contingent, albeit not fleeting, rules that explain how we socially construct reality. The social construction of reality is a social, not an individual, process, constructed over structural TimeSpace and varying over cyclico ideological TimeSpace, which brings us to a central premise of social science. The only enduring outcome of cultural studies lies thus in the "social scientization" of the humanities.

So there we are. In the classic divorce between philosophy and science, the social sciences were caught in a tug-of-war between the two, and torn apart in the process. But in the bifurcation in the world of knowledge through which we are living, the synchronous rise of complexity studies in the natural sciences and of cultural studies in the humanities may be creating a new convergence around social science, in which a new epistemology may arise that will overcome the culture dichotomy and recreate a unified epistemology for the world of knowledge.

Why now, you may be thinking? Not so long ago, the concept of the two cultures seemed unassailable. In his famous essay, written in 1959, C.P. Snow was reduced to calling for greater comprehension between the practitioners of the two cultures. It apparently never occurred to him that the two cultures might become one again. Obviously, there have been developments internal to the world of knowledge which have led in this direction. There were problems in the physical sciences that seemed difficult to treat within the framework of classical mechanics, especially those dealing with the supermacroscopic and the supermicroscopic realms. But this had been true for a century already and it was only in the 1970's that these issues as a substantial alternative culture emerged within this community. Similary the canons had seemed dubious to many for quite a long time. However, like beeches in the wind, previously they had bent and modified their contours as required. Suddenly, the wind had become much stronger.

It seems clear to me that the dramatic shifts in the world of knowledge reflect dramatic shifts in the real world, in the workings of our modern world-system. Our modern world-system has been a remarkably stable system for one that is so dynamic and so seemingly ever-changing. The secret has been its ability to permit simultaneously the endless accumulation of capital (and a considerable accumulation at that), the ever-widening polarization of the world-system, and the willingness of the vast majority of the world's populations to tolerate the anomaly. There was a point in time, in the early nineteenth century, when it did not seem very possible to reconcile the accumulation and the polarization, and the specter of the "dangerous classes" (what Marx called the "specter of Communism") posed itself as an imminent threat to the stability of the system.

This specter seemed quite threatening in 1848, and then it seemed to recede, and despite much hullabaloo, was kept very much in check until 1968. How was this done? The basic mechanism was the achievement of a central place for liberal ideology in the geoculture of the world-system. Liberalism situated itself in the political center with a commitment to reformism through the use of the state machinery, but a reformism that was both gradual and "rational," that is, administered by experts. Initially put forward within Europe in the nineteenth century, liberalism combined three reforms: the suffrage, the welfare state, and political integration of the working classes via nationalism and racism (vis-à-vis the non European world). With this program, liberal ideology tamed both of its competitor ideologies, the conservative and the radical/ socialist, turning them into its avatars.

In the twentieth century, the dangerous classes were no longer to be found in the European world but had become the popular strata of the non-European world. Liberals attempted to replicate their formula for taming the dangerous classes: national independence and the development of underdeveloped nations substituting for suffrage and the welfare state. At first, this seemed remarkably successful. In the period 1945-1968, three noteworthy events ocurred. The United States was able to impose via its undisputed hegemony order and peace among the great powers. The world-economy knew its greatest expansion in the history of the modern world-system, with its benefits trickilng down to all parts of the world. And the great antisystematic movements (heirs of the radical/socialist ideology of the nineteenth century) came to power virtually everywhere: the Communists in Eurasia from the Elbe to the Yalu, the national liberation movements in Asia and Africa, populist movements in Latin America, and social democratic movements in Europe and North America.

The combination of these three events seemed to validate the enormous optimism that all the ideologies (liberal, conservative, and radical/socialist) professed about the future. It suggested that reformism was in fact working, and that we were on the verge of a worldwide social convergence, overcoming the pattern of polarization in the world-system. But it was hybris, and the world fell hard. The world revolution of 1968 marked the first great expression of disillusionment by the popular strata. They expressed this disillusion less with the liberal center than with the antisystemic left, which they saw as having been unable to deliver what they had historically promised.

This cultural earthquake was followed by the world economic stagnation of production and profit during the 25 succeeding years which led to considerably increased polarization within and between countries, a process that is continuing apace. One after the other, the governments of the old left fell in the various zones of the world-system, as the popular strata withdrew their legitimation both of these movements and of the state as a reformist institution. The collapse of the Communisms in 1989 was simply the last major event in this sequence of delegitimation. The impact on the old antisystemic left was devastating. But it was no less devastating to the liberal center, who had counted for over a hundred years on the tatical support for their program that came from the old left, behind whose fiery rhetoric lay essentially the same program of governmental action.

If then a crisis or an earthquake began to be felt in the world of knowledge as of the 1970's, it was clearly not without connection to this crisis or earthquake in the world of political economy. The loss of optimism and certainty in one sphere was quite congruent with its reconsideration in the other. If order out of chaos became a slogan in complexity studies and multiculturalism a theme in cultural studies, it was surely not within evident analogy with what serves as a new set of guidelines in the sociopolitical world.

Where then are we today? We are in the midst of the most difficult kind of period, socially and intellectually, a period of confusion, of violence, of uncertainty, and of transformation. It is a period which makes all its participants uncomfortable, and indeed fearful, for the immediate risks are enormous. But so are the long-run risks, since it will be during the next 25-50 years that we shall determine the main lines along which the world shall probably move for the next 500 years at least. The responsibility is thus quite awesome, while our vision seems least clear. But this is realistic. When we thought we had clear vision, we were in fact quite blind. Now that we acknowledge that our vision is blurred, we may perhaps be able to perceive dimly the directions in which to move.

What is needed is to recognize the TimeSpace in which we are living as, a transformational TimeSpace. We must be clear on what will be the outcome, a new structural TimeSpace. We must be aware that our historical choice is between alternative, indeed conflicting, visions of the good society, and that the battle will be ferocious, if often surreptitious. We must finally be aware that we cannot engage intelligently in the socio-political battle without reconstructing the world of knowledge as an essential element in the battle. It is not just any convergence that we want, but a good one, a just one, an intelligent one, a substantively rational one.

NOTES

1. I have defined what I conceive to be the five possible TimeSpaces in "The Inventions of TimeSpace Realities. Towards an Understanding of our Historical Systems", in *Unthinking Social Science*, Cambridge: Polity Press, 1991, 135-148.
2. For a brief history of these developments, see I. Wallerstein *et al.*, *Open the Social Sciences*, Berkeley: Standford University Press, 1996. (Gulbenkian Commision Report).

8. Economy, Humanism and Neoliberalism

Manfred Max-Neef
Rector, Universidad Austral, Valdivia, Chile
(Videotaped in Spanish)

My intention at this conference is to tell you about some deep concerns I have, which I am sure you will all share with me, and to describe some positive options and visions. I shall start with the area I am concerned about, for I firmly believe that in order to design any kind of a solution to a problem of the magnitude affecting us in the world today we need to know fairly clearly what it is we want to change. Strategically speaking, to win a battle it is essential to find out all you can about the enemy and the terrain he moves in.

Civilization and Culture

I should like to begin with an all-embracing premise to put things into context. Our world is characterized by a great diversity of cultures and a few civilizations. The difference between civilization and culture is, in my view, a relatively simple one. I see a civilization arising when there emerges among a multiplicity of different cultures an agglutinating element towards which they all converge while maintaining their diversity. That is to say, an element that agglutinates a considerable diversity. This agglutinating element may be long-lasting or short-lived, depending on the twists and turns of history. If we define civilization in this way (which is not, of course, the only way of defining it) and search history for agglutinating elements that have thus given rise to civilizations, we find that they are few and far between. I would say that the first major agglutinating factor was perhaps monotheism.

Belief in one deity had always existed, from times of great antiquity such as the era of Akhenaton in Egypt. But it had not become a factor capable of agglutinating diverse cultures around itself, a common occurrence this. Eventually, however, what we know today as Western civilization took shape around the concept of monotheism. It is interesting to recall that belief in one God remained an agglutinating concept until 500 years ago, maintaining an interesting diversity.

It was almost exactly 500 years ago, in 1492, that an event occurred which was to have equally important consequences, if not more so: the discovery of America, and the expulsion of the Arabs and Jews from Spain. I think what happened in that year (the expulsion of the Arabs and Jews) was perhaps the most tremendous mistake made in Western history. For that wound has remained unhealed from that day to this.

If we analyze most of the conflicts in the West, we still find an undercurrent in them of the three groups that originally united around the belief in one God: Judaism, Islam and Christianity. It was the Christian version of this monotheism that eventually became predominant.

What other agglutinating element has there been? Another element that also existed very long before becoming a point of convergence for diverse cultures —regardless of how well or ill or in how many ways it is defined— was the concept of democracy. Although the agglutination produced by the concept of democracy does not have the same limits or boundaries as in the previous case, democracy is indisputably an agglutinating element. It is something increasingly claimed to be in place, so much so that many of the most repressive regimes we have known have pronounced themselves to be highly democratic. Hence, democracy at least as a mask has been important because of its agglutinating force as a concept.

We are presently going through a new process of civilization. Before going on to describe it, I would point out that when I speak of a civilizing phenomenon I am not necessarily referring to something a priori good or bad. I simply mean an agglutinating element. Time will tell whether the historical outcome is good or bad. All the same, we can form an opinion of it beforehand, and I have one regarding what I am going to identify now as a new agglutinating element, which I consider to have negative consequences. This is the model of the new economic language that has begun to dominate the world, particularly in its form of neoliberalism.

It may seem surprising that I should place something as transcendental as monotheism and something as politically potent as democracy on the same level as neoliberalism, as agglutinators or as elements with agglutinating capacity. I do so not because I like to but because it is an inescapable fact, for if there is one thing to be credited to this pseudo-religion of neoliberalism it is that it has accomplished in a couple of decades what Christianity and Islam could not in 2000 years, that is, to conquer practically the whole world.

To use a strictly colloquial expression, that's not to be sneezed at. The question is, what has made this thing so powerful that it has managed to conquer so much in so little time? It is partly what I suggested a minute ago, that, like all acts of conquest, it has its own language, and this language actually only acquires any sense, content and logic if it is analyzed as a pseudo-religious language.

Because it is a dogmatic language. It has very definite dogmas: economic growth, free markets, globalization. These are dogmatic assertions not open to discussion. They are the Holy Trinity. We may later be allowed to discuss forms and frills, but the essence of these principles is not open to discussion. It is therefore a simplistic language containing all the usual promises: those who strictly follow the rules of the game will gain paradise, which, however, is sufficiently far removed for us ever to be able to claim our reward. But this too is part and parcel of the whole thing. There is, besides, a Vatican: the World Bank and the International Monetary Fund, which see themselves as infallible, for they have achieved something truly amazing in the history of humanity: they have managed to devise a single remedy for all ills: a structural adjustment to improve your health wherever you may be. This is a spectacular achievement that has so far eluded the real Vatican. The Roman Catholic Vatican may have more solutions than this other one for solving the world's problems, but there is no doubt that the latter has confronted us with something extremely powerful. What's to be done? As history has shown, when a group of people and organizations emerge that don't feel at one with the dominant religion, they form heretical movements.

HERESY VS. DOGMA

Heresy is the only response where there is deep nonconformity with a certain catechism. I should like to assume that I'm addressing a large number of heretics' this evening; I would find that very comforting. Let us see now from the heretics' side how we can convince those who still profess the dominant religion that they should come over to our side. The only way that occurs to me is to reveal, as any heretic or any Martin Luther would, the fallacies and errors of this catechism.

Let us begin with dogma number one: economic growth. Economic growth is said to be good by definition, hence the greater the economic growth, the better. Let us accept this as a working hypothesis: if it is good, it is because something has to occur that can show things to be better now than they were before such growth.

I am an economist who has remained somewhat anchored in classical economics perhaps through romanticism. So I still believe that economics is a discipline that has to reveal values, that it is the daughter of moral philosophy and has something to do with human beings. This is where I stand, and this is where I came to a stop. Actually I went beyond this point while I was studying, but decided to retrace my steps because other terrains seemed too dehumanized to me, from neoclassicism on. Today, of course, the question doesn't even arise, for man himself seems to be regarded as an impediment in economics: without him, the model would work so much better. Yet, if economics has anything to do with human beings, its goodness has to be revealed by improving the conditions of these human beings. This is the first thing I should like to discuss in the context of this dogma number one, the dogma of growth.

Today's world is like a wine glass, with the upper part representing the 20% richest people of the world, who appropriate 87% of the planet's wealth, while in the lower part the 20% poorest are left with 1.4% of the world's riches. This is our present-day world, a champagne-glass world, where there is phenomenal concentration of wealth. Things might be said to be going badly for that 20% in the upper part of this glass, but they were probably worse off before. In 1960 the difference between the poorest 20% and richest 20% was 1 to 30: that is, the upper part was 30 times as rich as the lower. In 1994 the difference between them was 1 to 61. In other words within the space of 30 years the inequity had doubled, even though the poorest 20% were now a little better off than they were 30 years back.

But the inequity gap has doubled. In a study by the World Research Institute, of Washington, published some three years ago, world economic growth in each one of the past four decades (I repeat, in each one) is estimated to have been equal to or greater than world's accumulated economic growth from the origins of civilization up to 1950. I repeat that in each one of these past four decades there has been as much growth as had accumulated over 2000 years.

Now, applying a minimal, elemental scientific approach to these two sets of information, one can say that there had never been so much economic growth in the history of humankind. But neither had the world seen before, as it did in these same four decades, so much destruction of the social fabric, so many ecological disasters, such crises from over-exploitation of natural resources, such global increase in poverty and wretchedness. There may be pockets here and there where things have improved, but overall there has never been such a great increase in poverty, in destruction of the social fabric, in environmental and ecological crises. These two sets of information tell me that never before has growth been so rapid or poverty so fast expanding. Even a minimal scientific approach should therefore make me willing to revise the hypotheses I am working with. Something hasn't worked out well for me with economic growth, something is missing. Economic growth by itself has only helped to produce greater concentration of wealth, sharper inequity, more widespread poverty and many other problems. This, it will be said, is a distortion produced by viewing the whole picture, for within the whole some factors perform well and others badly.

Statistically, it may be argued that the overall picture is being distorted by bad performance by factors that aren't behaving as they should. Very well, let us review the factors that are performing well, the ones we should supposedly emulate from the richer countries, from those countries that have established the guidelines and designed the models and performances to be followed.

When I was Director of the Alternative Development Center (CEPAUR), before taking over as Rector of the Universidad Austral, around 1985-1986, we conducted studies in 21 countries, based on the theory of development on a human scale, which grew out of the work of the Center in collaboration with various groups in Latin America. The methodology used was also designed around this theory. The studies were intended to discover to what degree people felt that the systems in place in their respective countries adequately met their basic human needs, as postulated by the theory of human-scale development.

Those of you who are familiar with the theory will recall that there are nine basic human needs: the need for sustenance, protection, love or affection, participation, understanding, creation, leisure, identity and freedom. We conducted studies using quite sophisticated methodology in 21 countries, including rich northern countries such as Scotland, England, Denmark, Germany, Sweden and Austria, southern countries, from Latin America, and a particular region respectively in Malaya and India. The findings were pretty surprising because we began to discover things we weren't looking for. We found rich countries exhibiting what could be called interesting levels of poverty, that is, strong dissatisfaction over some of these basic needs, which is how we define poverty. In contrast, we discovered riches in traditionally poorer countries. Thus some striking profiles began to emerge that formed the basis of a hypothesis known today as the "threshold hypothesis."

THE THRESHOLD HYPOTHESIS

The threshold hypothesis holds that in every society there would appear to be a period during which economic growth, conventionally defined and measured, improves the people's quality of life, but only until a certain point is reached, this being the threshold. If there is more economic growth beyond this point, the quality of life begins to deteriorate.

This was a bold hypothesis that provoked much debate and many reactions. However, as often occurs in the world of scientific research when a new idea emerges whose time may be said to have come, things converging in this same direction began to be detected independently in other places. Some six months after we put forward this hypothesis at a congress, a study was published in the United States whose authors had designed an indicator known as the sustainable economic well-being indicator. Like gross domestic product, this too is a compound indicator. It is made up of measurable and quantifiable items having an impact on the quality of life, for example on income distribution, production costs, cardiovascular disease, cost of accidents, road-accident growth, erosion, etc. This indicator was applied to the United States over the period 1950 1990 and provided the results. The upper curve represents per-capita income, which grew continuously. The lower curve shows the sustainable economic well being indicator. You will observe that more or less up until 1970 the two curves run parallel, they move in exactly the same way, but from then on, while growth continues, the economic well-being indicator begins to deteriorate, to decline.

If I had been giving this talk in 1970 and showing these two curves between 1950 and 1970, all the economists would have said, "Of course. What you're showing is obvious. We have always known this: economic growth improves people's standard of living." But I'm giving this talk in 1997. Twenty more years have gone by and today serious methodological criticism is being directed against that indicator, because it belies what we were accustomed to seeing, what seemed so self-evident to us. But that is the reality. For us it was a stupendous illustration of the threshold theory, using a completely different methodology from ours.

A single case is not enough, though: in science you need much more than a single case to begin to validate or reject a hypothesis. So we induced a study on the same lines for Great Britain, and the outcome was similar. Once again, the upper curve, representing per-capita income in Great Britain, and the lower one, the indicator relating to the quality of life, run perfectly parallel up until 1970. From then on the lower curve begins to plunge much more dramatically than in the case of the United States. The same for Germany: the last peak occurs more or less around 1980, then the curve begins to fall sharply. For Holland the curve starts to decline in 1980, and for Austria in 1983. The curves also start to separate significantly for Sweden and Denmark.

In short, we have studied nine cases of rich countries, that is to say, countries that have set what is supposedly the proper path to be taken, and in every case the same phenomenon has occurred.

Accordingly, with the phenomenon occurring in nine cases of rich countries, we can fairly say that our threshold hypothesis is a solid one. I should add that throughout these country studies, the indicator's composition methodology has consistently undergone improvements. The later measurements are much more rigorous than the initial one for the United States, because the indicator has been continuously fine-tuned.

IMPLICATIONS FOR DEVELOPMENT

Now, if the hypothesis is well-founded, we are faced with a situation involving a very serious, radical reformulation of economic theory, particularly development theory. For, if there really exists a threshold point in a society, then the economic policies I have designed for a society before reaching its threshold may well prove successful. But they will not serve after this point and will need to be considerably modified. Let us suppose, for example, that a country reaching its threshold point is still beset with great poverty, or a significant percentage of poor people. Before reaching this point, there is no doubt that more economic growth is essential for it to eradicate such poverty, but once it has crossed this threshold, more growth is not going to do away with poverty. The only thing that will do so is better income distribution. For a very simple reason: beyond the threshold, every marginal dollar of product growth will be spent on resolving problems created by this same growth, instead of being properly invested in development.

To understand what is happening in a large city like Bogotá, consider its economic growth. But spending in Bogotá exceeds revenues generated, and more of it is going on solving problems created by the city's growth than on fostering true development there.

And the same would be true for any society taken as a whole. This is what we are seeing today. But economic theory has not yet accepted this fact, so that we are in the absurd position of facing problems that are increasing and growing worse, while we try to deal with them by applying more of the same. We are thus, paradoxically, making the problems rapidly worse instead of resolving then. This is an extremely serious paradox we are trapped in across the world.

Unemployment is an alarming and growing problem in every country, presenting different aspects in countries of the north. In a country like Spain, unemployment among young people is as high as 45%. Imagine what their vision of the future is in these conditions, in that same Spain where something like 3600 townships and villages have been completely abandoned in recent decades. Imagine the human history behind this. And this is happening in the name of an economic model purported to be the most successful in human history.

This then is the balm being sold by this catechism, and this is the effect it is producing in the countries we try to emulate. It is not very difficult nor does it need much imagination to see what dogma number one will involve for countries like ours if we continue in this direction.

THE DOGMA OF FREE TRADE

Let us now turn to the dogma of free trade. I shall deal with this more quickly because I won't be showing any illustrations. First, let us assume there is in fact something called "free trade," which to start with is a colossal fabrication. The only genuine example of free trade I know of that corresponds exactly to the description of a free market in economics textbooks is Old Domingo's Indian market, where there is complete transparency, full information, and everyone knows one another: there the model really works. But Old Domingo's market model, the only one that actually works, is looked down on in economic theory, and we have invented this other fiction.

Let us assume once again as a hypothesis that this other model works as it is claimed to do by the catechism hawking it, that those who practice it, and do so properly, will obtain results to their benefit, in other words that it is a delightful game in which there are no losers. What a fascinating thing. Of course, I'll buy it immediately.

What is the free-trade theory based on? It is based on the principle of comparative advantage, which holds that if in a given country I specialize in something for which I have greater possibilities and somewhere else someone specializes in something else, and we trade together, we will both benefit thereby. This theory arose from a classical model designed in the last century by the great English economist David Ricardo. It is a beautiful model in which Ricardo showed that if Portugal were to specialize in producing wine and port, and England in producing textiles, both would have comparative advantage and would benefit mutually by exchanging their products.

But it was essential to the working of Ricardo's theory and model that capital should remain at home. That is, the model assumes national immobility of capital: capital will move within the national territory until it finds a niche where it will provide greater return. The same would occur in the other country, and this is how comparative advantage would operate. But this is just what is not happening today, because nowadays it is precisely capital that has full mobility. Financial capital moves at the speed of light, all computerized, while physical capital is transported at the velocity of planes or ships.

What does this signify? That where there is capital mobility comparative advantage disappears and absolute advantage accrues to the owner of capital. How do absolute advantages apply? If adverse changes occur in the conditions under which the capital was invested, it can move off immediately in search of some other country to be placedt. This is what we are constantly seeing today.

What advantage is there for capital in moving from place A to place B? That in place B, for example, wages, tax and environmental requirements are less onerous than in place A.

What does a treaty like the North-American Free Trade Agreement, between the United States, Canada and Mexico, signify to the United States? It signifies something extremely simple: that large transnational oligopolies of American origin, desiring to remain competitive, move to Mexico, where conditions are less strict than in the US. They generate apparent benefits for Mexico and general unemployment in the US. The situation begins to become regulated slowly.

If this continues and becomes widespread at global level, wages and prices will tend to become equalized; this is recognized by economic theory itself. And this is where the sixty-million dollar question arises: will they be adjusted upward or downward?

They will obviously be adjusted downward. In a country like ours such capital inflows will mean immediate acceptance of a ceiling that I cannot exceed, making me move downward not upward because otherwise this capital will go somewhere else where it is offered better conditions.

There must be many people in this hall wearing Nike sneakers, for example, which are American but made in Indonesia. Why are they made in Indonesia? Because the wages received by Indonesian women for making them is barely a dollar a day. That is highly competitive! These are the best selling sneakers in the world, pretending to be American. I have, of course, heard people refuting this by saying that if it weren't for Nike these women wouldn't even be getting that dollar. In other words, the situation is much to their benefit, which is a pretty stupid assertion, for it ignores a whole historical process in which a couple of decades ago these women were probably living in self-sustaining rural systems. When forced migrations were set on foot, the women ended up in city slums and from such slums rose to become Nike workers. A little historical perspective is needed to refute the benefits of this kind of situation.

The Dogma of Globalization

I want to describe another thing that is happening, and I think all economists, regardless of what school they belong to, will agree about this. Looking at a country we recognize that there is an economic power there manifesting itself through the market, and also a political power, manifesting itself through State institutions (all economists agree on this); we further recognize that every time this economic power causes distortions in the market, the State may legitimately intervene to rectify such market imperfections. In other words, it is legitimate at this point for the political role, the role of the State, to rectify market distortions. Any economist, even the most absurd neoliberal, agrees with this.

What is being explicitly recognized here? The need for economic power and political power to exist together and to balance each other at some point. But what is happening with globalization? What is being globalized? Here we come to the third dogma, the dogma of globalization, which we are told is a good thing. What has been globalized is economic power, without any corresponding globalization of political power that would make it possible to rectify any imperfections generated by this economic power in the global market. And the lack of such countervailing power has led to the great paradox that intelligent behavior by international oligopolies has turned into irresponsible behavior. For if they internationalize their costs within their prices (I mean their environmental costs and the social costs they generate) they will lose markets, and no-one can force them to do so. Certainly not the World Trade Organization.

The second paradox arising from this is that, in these conditions, it is not the large transnational oligopolies that are competing to make investments in Third-World countries, rather it is the governments of these countries competing against each other to attract such investments. How are they competing? By offering better conditions. What better conditions? As I said before, lower wages, low taxes, fewer requirements of all kinds. In many cases and tragically in many African countries, by undertaking large prior investments in infrastructure —involving extremely heavy indebtedness— in order to appear more attractive.

These then are the three dogmas: growth, free trade and globalization.

Lastly, with further regard to globalization, supposing, in strictly theoretico-mathematical terms, that there are N number of players, all of them playing this game optimally, then the final outcome will be a zero-sum game. It is foolish to play a zero sum-game. In actual fact, however, it is not going to be a zero-sum game but one in which there will be a few large winners and many losers.

Who are the large winners? The major transnational oligopolies.

We continue with the fiction of international trade, believing that our countries trade with other countries: Colombia trades with Germany and Japan, and Japan trades with all the others, etc. In our national accounts Colombian exports are reported in relation to German imports, and so we talk of trade between countries, which is increasingly a greater fabrication. Because today as much as 75% of all international trade is controlled by major transnational companies, and it is Nestlé of Colombia that imports from Nestlé of Switzerland, which in turn imports from Nestlé of the Philippines.

This is registered as trade by the three countries, though it is completely controlled by several oligopolies. At this juncture in history oligopolies no longer have any national loyalties and should rather be regarded as truly transnational entities. They are no longer national companies. General Motors today is not what it was forty years ago, when it was said, "If it's good for General Motors, it's good for the United States," because that is how it operated at the time. Then they were still companies with truly national or local loyalties. All that is over now.

Today we have countries and we have these new entities, which some identify with a new Middle Ages, the lords of the manor, with large castles. There is Mitsubishi, Shell, Nestlé and their kind, surrounded by large and ever growing numbers of serfs. It is they who are incontestably the largest beneficiaries, who hawk the model, who have the final say, who can sell this catechism very attractively packaged, very well marketed, full of promises. What's to be done in the face of this? Heretics of the world, unite!

Here is a piece of information I had forgotten to mention. Between 1987 and 1994, that is, precisely during the seven hardest years of application of the IMF's structural adjustments, something amazing occurred. In 1987 there were in the whole world 145 people, individuals identified by name, not families or companies but persons in their individual capacity who were billionaires, that is, having a personal fortune of more than a thousand million dollars. In 1994 their number had gone up to 358, an increase of 150% in seven years in the number of the world's billionaires. The personal income of these 358 individuals, who would barely occupy a small part of this hall, is equal to the income of 45% of the world's population.

MOSQUITOES VS. RHINOCEROS

This and other things are made possible by a model of this kind. If we analyze how financial speculation has been functioning, we find that it has reached absolutely astronomical levels and is completely out of control. To face up directly to anything so powerful, if you think about it, is quite disheartening. In this connection, I thought up an allegory when I was running for president of my country in 1993, because after every speech, in talks with people someone would inevitably say, "But what can we do? We are weak and powerless compared with these giants." Such a defeatist, depressive attitude is paralyzing and there is nothing to be done. So I devised this allegory, which I think opens a path to a solution. I would tell them, "If you were in an open field with an angry rhinoceros about to charge at you, the silliest thing you could do would be to imagine you were a rhinoceros too. The outcome would be obvious. What can you do, faced with a rhinoceros, to get the better of it eventually and come away unharmed? What is the only thing, in this case, that is more powerful than a rhinoceros? Why, a swarm of mosquitoes.

Whether you call them NGOs, or organizations of civil society, or what you will, women's, ecologists', pacifists' movements, and a thousand others have been going at it incessantly. They are growing and growing, buzzing and buzzing, and are beginning to achieve a few things. More than once they have managed to make some of the world's largest factual-economic powers give in. In several countries in South-East Asia, and in Malaysia, consumer organizations have obtained resounding victories over pharmaceutical companies.

Victories of this kind, however, are not sensational and get no media coverage. They cannot and never will, because the media are clearly a part of the oligopolistic scheme of things. Perhaps the largest transnational oligopolies being created in the world today are precisely in the communications industry. The merger between Times-World and Siemens provides on its own control over the world's news, over what is shown or not shown. So the efforts of the mosquitoes and heretics go unsung, but they are working, and working better all the time.

This can be seen by considering what has happened to the ecologists' movements. Twenty years ago, and even as recently as ten years ago, ecologists were regarded as friendly, ignorant, romantic airheads, divorced from reality and unable to understand what was what, but withal decent types, semi-poets, fond of little birds and flowers. We used to be ridiculed. Today we are the target of the most brutally hostile attacks. Why? Because the movements are now much more powerful, they even have money and can organize spectacular campaigns and put paid to many strategies that would otherwise be carried out with impunity. An event occurring today in any given place can attract a tremendous wave of international solidarity. Such a situation has arisen recently in Colombia; I learnt of it in Manizales just before coming here. At a conference I was directing there, a delegation of U'wa Indians, who are threatened by oil exploitation, handed me a tremendously moving letter with a set of documents, asking me whether I would join their cause and seek further international support for them. They have already obtained very extensive support from the international community. I cite this as an example.

Nowadays, in situations of this kind people do not feel quite so alone and international support has begun to prove effective. It is also beginning to generate fear, which explains the growing attacks against the movements and the increasingly intensive efforts to discredit them by every possible means. This is a sign of success, though. And instead of bitterly resenting such attacks, one should develop an appropriate degree of sadomasochism to enjoy them. For when I am attacked more sharply, that means that I have become more dangerous, that I'm producing a greater effect and a greater impact.

Evaluation of processes

I should like to end this talk by drawing your attention to one final point. It is disturbing to see the enthusiasm, bordering sometimes on fanaticism, that is shown in following the laws of a model such as this, which is beginning to dominate the world, despite such powerful evidence against its purported benignity and benefits. I am from Chile, which is the example that everyone in Latin America is supposed to follow these days. We are so successful that we have become the blue-eyed baby of the IMF and the World Bank. There is talk of the Chilean miracle, and it certainly is a miracle, but only to those blind to everything but the simplistic vision of macroeconomic indicators.

In terms of growth Chile is a leader, but it is at the same time one of the countries in the world with the worst income distribution.

It has several other problems, besides. But the point I want to make is this: Why, when there are new indicators and new evidence of much more enriching theories and evident development of disciplines providing a more complete vision of economic phenomena, why, despite all this, do things continue unchanged and people remain enclosed within the confines of macroeconomic indicators? I like to assume that people on the whole act in good faith, so I am not saying that this is the result of premeditated perversity. I believe that what is happening is simply the result of ignorance and of unwillingness to learn about new situations and facts.

For example, suppose any of us were to organize a meeting to present new indicators from a discipline that is undergoing the most dramatic scientific advance in the world today: ecological economics, with its solid, hard, important evidence and biophysical indicators of what is happening and how to evaluate the processes under way. So I invite the authorities to a symposium or a congress and send invitations to Minister X and Senator Y. And what happens? Minister X arrives exactly five minutes before his turn to speak and having spoken leaves. The Senator does the same, so does the Representative. They never stay to listen to what others have to say. How many of you have experienced this? I have been through it innumerable times.

This is a sure sign of a wall that will be difficult to break through. There is an element of irresponsibility here. But there is probably a worse element: stupidity, the stupidity of not wanting to have any information that may alter what I like. This is a typical characteristic of economists and the military. When the military devise a strategy and become enamored of it, if it doesn't work, it's not because it was a bad strategy but because the enemy cheated. The same goes for the economic model we are talking about: it's a beautiful model and if it doesn't work, it's because reality cheats, and reality is there to be domesticated and adapted to the model. This is the function of reality, not the other way round. So if there is something that is going to cast a different light on my model, I find it tremendously disturbing.

This has led to the absurd situation in which, despite all the evidence (and I have only referred here to just a small portion of an overwhelming amount of evidence) the solution or answer still provided to problems is more of the same thing. But strange as it may seem, I feel optimistic, because the model has become so internally inconsistent that if it remains unchanged it is sure to collapse, though I cannot predict when. It is inevitably a doomed model. In my opinion therefore the urgent role of the heresy does not consist in attacking the model head on but in designing sound alternatives for when it collapses. That is where work needs to be done.

What will follow next? I think there will follow again a world with much a greater sense of community, which is one of the things that have been wiped out in today's world. The local aspect will become much stronger, with local economies providing once again protection against this globalization, which is not indefinitely sustainable. We have much work to do on the domestic front: it is pleasant work, and believe me that we are not alone in undertaking it. There are very many of us and I believe we are going to achieve a great many things.

9. A GLOBAL CRISIS OF CIVILIZATION: CHALLENGES AHEAD

Agnes Heller
Professor, New School for Social Research, New York

1

The phenomena that I will discuss under the preliminary heading global crisis , are not symptoms of an illness that can be remedied, but belong to the modus operandi of the modern world itself. These symptoms are not problems that could be solved if we only applied the best methods, or approached them with good will scientifically, or democratically. They are structural formations or, measured by the absolute yardstick of the values of freedom and life deformations. Yet they are not deformations in the strict sense, because they belong to the reproduction of modern life itself, so that they cannot be entirely eliminated, but are only (at best) handled in a way that they should not cause irreparable harm or irreversible global catastrophes. I am going to speak here about conflicts, threats, dangers, and dangerous phenomena that are produced and reproduced by modernity itself, constantly occurring and reoccurring facts and events that need to be kept under public control to the extent that they can kept under control at all.

My starting assumption is that by now the whole world has become modern. If we discuss global problems, then we speak of intrinsic features of modernity itself. As once upon a time *homo sapiens* emerged in Africa, yet mankind is not "African", as high civilization was born first in Asia, but high civilization as such is not "Asian", similarly modernity was generated in Europe, but modernity as such is, by now, neither "Western" nor "European". It became global.

This may sound odd, if one considers the immense differences between the various regions of our globe in economic resources, spiritual life, political organizations, and much else. (Not just similar, but far greater differences characterized all premodern ages).

There is a fundamental structural difference between all premodern civilizations on the one hand, and all the modern ones on the other. Premodern civilizations display the picture of an originary, life-determining, and seemingly immobile type of hierarchical stratification. Single men and women are born into particular social ranks, strata, estates, and this simple fact of birth determines in the main their whole path of life. The social hierarchy is all encompassing, there is no way to untie economic, social, political, and cultural positions. The function performed by the members of each and every rank are determined by their rank. The division of functions is thus deeply seated in everyday life. The whole edifice is based on the rigid allocation of day-to-day activities, such as customs, the use of things and that of language-use. This rigid hierarchical structure requires that one person or only a few persons should occupy the position at the top; one single man (the monarch) or a few single men. Pre-modern life was legitimated by tradition. Alternatives were absent, unless the repetition of a cycle can be termed an alternative, and if we disregard the interregnums between two different versions of fundamentally equally pre-modern arragements.

This pre-modern arrangement survived many thousand years, and it could have survived more. Its edifice became deconstructed in Europe, due to the unique coincidence of many contingent factors, from the late medieval period onwards till the twentieth century. This deconstruction process was so rapid that fundamental changes were registered by the selfsame generation; people have left their past behind with speed unheard of in Europe after the Roman civil wars. And the speed was constantly accelerated. At the beginning of the twentieth century the pre-modern world was not yet entirely deconstructed in Europe either; yet at the end of the same century the pre-modern social arrangement had been torn down all over the whole globe. There are no more traditional monarchies left. The not infrequent attempts at the restoration of traditional ways of life require an entirely modern kind of mass-mobilization. And for an ideologically underpinned mass-mobilization one needs a mass society first. Preference for a dense tradition plays here the role of ideology; it can perform this function precisely because it is a preference, it is no more taken for granted.

What is then the main characteristic of the modern social arrangement that began to take shape while the pre-modern was deconstructed? It is not a fundamental, all-encompassing, hierarchical stratification that determines the present functions men and women are expected to perform in life, but the other way around. It is in and through the performance of certain functions that they themselves define their situation in the social hierarchy of power, fame, and wealth. Wealth, power and fame will increasingly be determined by the position that men and women occupy during their lifetime within the hierarchy of the economic, political and cultural institutions. As a result, everyday life activities are thinning out. Which means that in principle men are born free, for they are born contingent: nothing is written on their cradle at the moment of their birth. In principle, again, their possibilities are unlimited. This means, that to be born free is to be born without determinations, freedom equals emptiness. This emptiness needs to be filled with content by the choices and the acts of modern men and women themselves. They have lost the tradition, at least so it seems; they have lost their sense of taken-for-grantedness, at least so it seems.

The modern social arrangement cannot be described as "progressive" in comparison to the pre-modern, for we have no single standard to perform the comparison. It is different, and it is ours. There is no way back to the pre-modern arrangement, if only for the simple reason that the traditional stratified society could not accomodate the sheer number of people who are now sharing our globe. The best thing to do then is to explore the optimal possibilities of the modern arrangement. For there is no third kind of social arrangement. Either the fundamental stratification determines functions or the other way around. The third possibility would have been a society wihout hierarchy altogeher, without division of labour. This was the project of Marx. It does not look only unrealizable, but one can also strongly doubt its desirability. Yet possibilities of essential change both to the better and to the worse are wide open within the actual modern arrangement. These are the issues that one must pay attention.

I said that in Europe the transformation was, by all historical standards, too rapid, although here at least this rapid change was fuelled by indigenous energies. By indigenous energy, I mean the dynamics of modernity.

The dynamics of modernity is something else than the modern social arrangement. This term refers to the way, or the mode, that modern institutions and forms of life are changed. The motivational forces add challenge that uproots and upturns well-established orders. Modern dynamics is characterized by constant negation and juxtaposition, by critique and idealization. For example: "This institution is unjust, another would be just, let us have another; this story is not true, it is a fiction, something else is rather true; this is not a virtue, there are no virtues at all just interests", and so on and so forth. This dynamics however, has not only contributed to the destruction of the ancient hierarchically structured social edifice, but it has also been accomodated by the new, modern social arrangement. Briefly, the modern world is not destroyed by, but maintained through, negation. It thrives on negation, for negation (and idealization) are the conditions of its reproduction.

I see here three serious questions arising. First, as to whether the modern social arrangement functions as well, or in the same way, in countries where the dynamics of modernity has not preceded its coming into being as in countries where it did. Second, whether it is indifferent or rather significant that this dynamics develops spontaneously, or is rather organized, and if organized, what (who) organizes it and how. Finally, whether the development or the maintainance of modernity through constant negation goes on without limits or may reach its limits. These questions lead me to the center of my topic: the global conflict zones of modernity. Next I will briefly reflect upon all three questions.

2

I have already mentioned the rapidity, the dramatic character of the process in which the ancient ways of life had been overturned and replaced by new ones in recent history. Such rapid transformations are traumatic experiences. The great transformation was traumatic even in Europe, the very place where modernity has originated. The least traumatic was the experience in the new world, on virgin soil, where no pre-modern arrangements needed to be deconstructed. Yet even here painful experiences took place. E.g., in the United States modernity was carried to final victory in the bloodiest civil war since the times of Marius and Sulla.

That the rapidity of development was traumatic already in Europe everyone familiar with the European cultural imagination will confirm. The nineteenth century was full of theories about the devastating results of the modern turn. Tönnies juxtaposition of society and community became influential because it could be used as the expression of nostalgia for the lost world order. The modern world was experienced as "mechanic" and contrasted to the allegedly "organic" structure of the old. The image of an organic kind of life was frequently associated with biological essences. But this was not always the case. The issue at stake was tradition: the loss of tradition, the loss of security, the loss of both the metaphysical and the empirical home. Marx said that the proletariat has neither fatherland nor religion; and Nietzsche spoke about the death of God. And although after the experience with totalitarianism, the cultural criticism of old days has lost its impact, its issues still remain. For example, the recent increasing ecological imbalance trigger very similar anxieties to those of the previous century. The threat seems even more acute because of the rapid transformation of everyday life experiences due to the intrusion of the ever-changing technology into the household, and even into intimate life. One has to change habits, ideas, creeds, and relearn practically everything three times in life. How much can one endure? How many times can a man or a woman change attitudes in life? How many times can a man or a woman change a profession in life? How many times can one re-orient oneself? Men and women feel that they are losing ground.

And in those parts of the globe where the modern social arrangement has been imported, willingly or unwillingly, from the West by the vehicle of the world market, through global communication and migration, the changes are even more rapid than in Europe. Yet due to the absence of original internal dynamics, the deconstruction of the pre-modern social arrangement resembles only very remotely the process of deconstruction as it took place in the West. It resembles more a collapse than a process of deconstruction. The house comes down, but its former inhabitants remain close to the ruins of the old, without finding real support in their walls which are no more. Contrary to the modern social arrangement, the dynamics of modernity cannot be imported. The danger of chaos looms large.

The ideology of the "Third World", the so called "third worldism" is, more than one way, a repetition of European social romanticism of the previous century. Here we encounter again the familiar juxtaposition of the organic and the mechanic, but this time those who allegedly represent the organic principle are seen as friends, and those who allegedly stand for the mechanic principle, as the foes. The accusations that Europe has infected and destroyed the healthy non-European countries remind me of the accusations that it was the atheists, the Jews or the Marxists that infected European cultures with the bacilli of modernity. It is far more realistic to admit that modernity is a steamroller. At first it has run down the pre-modern social arrangement in Europe, and without delay it continued to do the same in the whole world. At the present stage, no ideology can withstand this push. But romantic ideologies can still achieve several things. Some of them are dangerous, other dubious, yet a few of them make good sense and are of use as social/cultural brakes that can prevent chaos and protect against the sudden collapse of traditions.

Let me continue with the second question. Is there only one way to secure the dynamics of modernity that triggers the changes and is responsible for their continuity and rapidity? In fact, more than one way to accelerate this movement has been tried. Totalitarianism was (is) one amongst them. Totalitarianism was born in Europe, it is the ugly brainchild of modernity, it is absolutely modern. All kinds of totalitarianism have promised (and where they still exist they still promise) to undertake the total modern transformation (the revolution) faster and more radically than any other political regime. Yet they also promised that they will perform this great transformation without its social, personal, psychological price: collectivist modernity does not know contingency. The common idea was (and still is, where totalitarianism prevails) that the dynamics of medernity and the modern social arrangement can operate smoothly, or even better, without personal freedom and political liberty. But they can not.

Totalitarian states institutionalized constant social upheaval. This was particularly true about the Bolshevik type of arrangement which totalized culture and society in addition to the state. But it finally turned out that forced and centralized modernization, buttressed by the ideology of rapid and total change, does not enhance the dynamics of modernity. The project has worked insofar as both pre-modern and a few already modern institutions and these new ones, instead of promoting the dynamics of modernity, have brought it to a halt. To cut a long story short, it turned out that liberal democracy provides the optimal political conditions for the smooth operation of dynamics of modernity. For in a liberal democracy no institution is regarded as sacred, everything is open to change, everything can be "negated" and by everyone. Thus, a social-political arrangement that warrants personal freedom and political liberty can best accomodate the dynamics of modernity.

This seems now an obvious observation. But no Fukuyama-kind of conclusions follow from it. Even if liberal democracies accomodate best the dynamics of modernity, internal conflicts and malaises can constantly thwart it. Moreover, these malaises, similarly to computer viruses, can inhere in the dyamics of modernity itself. Whether or not history has arrived at its end is a fictitious issue which I will not address. One can admit that since there are only two models of social arrangement, the pre-modern and the modern, and since we cannot return, at least as far as we can see, to the pre-modern, and since liberal democracies warrant best the dynamics of modernity, the world may have arrived at a point of relative rest, that is, at a point where similar conflicts keep reccurring all the time. But then we have in mind an abstract and empty framework only. Modernity is a new social arrangement, we do not have even the faintest idea about its possibilities. One does not even know whether it can survive the next millenium. At least we could have learned from the devastating experiences under totalitarian regime that we have no privileged position in history, that moderns have no chances to know the future better than pre-moderns, perhaps even less. This is in itself a puzzling discovery, given that modernity is a future-oriented and not past-oriented social arrangement, and modern men and women are therefore more interested in embarking for a trip on the time-machine to cast a glance beyond our horizon.

Modernity is a great possibility and also a great burden. It develops too fast for humans to adjust. It offers the great possibility, particularly in liberal democracies, for everyone to participate in political decision-making and to become masters of their own life. Still not only in spite of, but also because of the rapidity of the transformation process, men and women have very little insight into the results of their actions. One is, perhaps, aware of one´s responsibilities for future generations in abstract terms, but one can hardly imagine the life of those generations. In a pre-modern world everyone could guess how their great-grandchildren are going to live, what they are going to do.

Now none of us knows that much about our children. To live in uncertainty is traumatic. To live in uncertainty about meaning and worth is even more so. A trauma has dangerous psychological and also social and political consequences. The modern trauma is not a happening but a state of affairs, it is continuous. One can expect that its symptoms will constantly emerge and reemerge. In our times, fundamentalism, the sad fact that fifty years after the demise of Nazism people speak the race-language freely and naturally all around the world, the emergence of biopolitics that contributes to the ferocity of local wars, all these will belong to those symptoms.

3

The deconstruction of tradition went hand in hand with the deconstruction of traditional ethical powers (*sittliche Machte*). I use the term *sittliche Machte* in a Hegelian understanding which, however, remains very close to the traditional interpretation. A social or political power can be termed *sittlich* if men and women living under the jurisdiction of this power are ready to sacrifice willingly their personal interests or well-being for it if they believe that this power stands above and beyond the pursuit of their personal interest.

I think that Hegel in his *Philosophy of Right*, suggested the best, although idealized, model of modern ethic al power and their interplay. The three main ethical powers are: the family, the civil society and the (*nation*) state; they stand for the communal, the corporative and the political ethical powers. But there is also a fourth ethical power, or perhaps, this should have been mentioned first: right itself. There are, again, three kinds of rights (*Recht*): statutory (legal) law, moral rights (there are three of them: the right for the pursuit of happiness, the right to develop our personality, and the right to our own conception of the good), and finally, right as embodied in the state, that is, in the Constitution.

This model is an "idealization", because it describes all ethical powers of modernity as integrated and as integrating. The model suggests that modern ethical powers — not in spite of having opened free space for the practice of the moral rights of single individuals but because of it— will, or at least can, maintain the unity, the cohesion of the modern world not just as successfully as the pre-modern powers maintained their own, but better.

I discussed briefly the Hegelian model of the balance of ethical powers in the modern state. Now I will ask the question whether the enumerated powers are still ethical powers or no more, and whether their ethical power, if they wield any, are still integrative, or rather divisive.

In Hegel, family wields the ethical power of community. But it is questionable as to whether the family can maintain its independent ethical power in a modern society for a long time. Empirical observation indicates that it does not. In the process of modernization, first the three generational (traditional) family has disappeared, and to date the nuclear family too is in a state of descomposition. The traditional socio-economic division of labour between the sexes in the family has no more foundation. The cachet of the modern social arrangement, its founding statement is that everyone is born free and equal. It was (or is) only a matter of time, and historically speaking of a very short time, that men and women will acquire de facto equal opportunity. In spite of setbacks and fundamentalist interventions, this development is unstoppable with or also without feminism, for it belongs to the modern transformation. The end of the traditional division of labour betwen the sexes leads, at least, to the total restructuration of the nuclear family type. Yet it does not lead necessarily to the dissolution of the family. At the present point however, it seems, that whether preserved or not, the institution "family" loses its might as an ethical power. There is no place here to discuss this matter. One important thing, however, needs to be emphazised. The family is, in Hegel´s model, a community, the sole community of modernity. Family is said to be the sole modern integration where the ethical power is related to immediacy, intimacy, the closeness of bodies and blood-relationship. This is the niche where traditional gestures survive in a post traditional world. Men and women do not start history from scratch. There is and remains the archaic need of community and for blood relationship, for bodily closeness, and for the warmth of the stable. It is not easy to get rid of them all. If the family as communal ethical power is in a state of decomposition, one can rest assured that substitutes will appear, for example thinking and speaking in terms of "races", forging a fictitious community as a fictitious body called the "race". In the United States, e.g. in this modern world par excellence, in the only traditional democracy with a stream of traditional racism, it became recently taken for granted (and even institutionally promoted) that real or fictitious ethnic groups integrate themselves alongside their alleged racial identity and speak the language of race. This development poses a serious threat for the modern world. The use of race-language is divisive within a state and also among the states. If alleged races will begin wielding high ethical power, we shall enter a world characterized by cruel and endless ethnic and civil warfare.

I first presented the model of the balance of ethical powers. Then I briefly discussed the situation of the family and of the intimate sphere. Now, briefly again, I turn to the private sphere. After the family, civil society is also the embodiment of relatively independent ethical powers. They are the positive "liberal" moral rights of the individual, and also the collectivistic, although not communalistic, kinds of rights and organizations (corporations, trade unions, etc.). Let me briefly look into the present status of those collectivistic ethical powers.

These ethical powers are ethical powers because their members, who join the institutions freely, take responsibility for the common cause. The pursuit of this cause is regarded as voluntary duty and such duty motivates attitude and behaviour. Such were the townships of America, the freely chosen or re-chosen religious congregations, clubs, and perhaps the most important among them, trade unions. By now, although most of the above institutions exist and some of them flourish, their ethical power has been strongly diminished. High mobility decreased, for example the ethical power of local communities. One of the ecological problems is also connected with this development. If people constantly come and go, if they have transitory dwelling places yet no homes, they will become indifferent to the natural environment.

All the ethical powers of modernity I have briefly discussed so far were related to work, and supported the value of work in one form or another. The modern social arrangement, contrary to pre-modern ones, put a premium on work. One was working for the well-being of one´s family, and men of profession with good work-morals were regarded as reliable members of corporations, and also as trustworthy citizens.

At this point modernity underwent drastic changes, and some of them might be detrimental to the survival of the ethical powers. Due to technological development, and also to the way that societies are nowadays organized, and further on to the human condition itself, the fate of work as one of the important ethical powers in the service of the great ethical powers, seems to be sealed. I can speak only in a telegramm style about this issue here. It looks as if in the near future societies will be divided into two unequal parts. First, a minority who will perform highly qualified professional work in sophisticated fields, who will learn much, know much, earn much, and work very long hours and will have no time to do anything else or to enjoy life, being anxious and neurotic, suffering from meaning-deficiency. And there will be the majority, doing inferior work in few hours or no work at all, earning little, learning little, knowing little, living in a state of disintegration, anxious, neurotic, dangerous. The dream of early socialism that due to the blessings of technology everyone will work no more than four hours daily and after work-hours will listen to the music of Beethoven or paint pictures or conduct philosophical conversations and the rest, proved to be highly utopian. It seems as if roughly the same or a similar percentage of a population would be interested in high culture and cultural activities, and that this number can only be relatively increased. But from this it does not follow that the extrapolation of the current trend would be the necessary outcome of modern development. There are always alternatives.

The same can be said about a similar bifurcation between the different regions of our earth. It is possible that in a minority of the regions, highly sophisticated work will be performed, whereas the majority of the regions will live in a state of dire poverty, on charity, without employment and in chaos. But, again, one must look for alternative solutions here too.

4

It is easy to imagine a modern world without ethical powers. Such a world would linger in the state of decomposition, chaos, disintegration. A world of total relativism, where nothing is worth living or dying for; where the low income groups live on crack and the high income groups on prosac. There are already people who live such a life.

But there is another possibility (or reality) which can equally lead to chaos and disintegration: namely the constant emergence and reemergence of divisive and hostile ethical powers. The nation-state as an ethical power was always divisive if it came to the issue of global integration of any kind. Now there are emerging again relatively strong ethical powers that are divisive within the states and for the states. Not just in Africa where the state has always been weak, but also in the Western world.

To avoid misunderstanding: divisive ethical powers are fruitful ingredients of any modern society. The limits of their fruitfulness cannot be formally defined. The question is how divisive they are, and on what ground they provide ethical substance to their following. From terrorist organizations to fundamentalist groups with their self-inflicted apartheid and strong enemy, there can be found a great variety of dangerous ethical powers that threaten global cooperation, regional alliances or the ethical order within a state. Some of them draw inspiration from certain interpretations of multiculturalism. Multiculturalism, however, is a real issue, and cannot be identified with its ideological use.

A variety of cultures share our globe. The coexistence of culturally diverse groups in the same area, or within the same political entity is put on the order of the day, and the world must learn to cope with it. But multiculturalism means frequently something else than, and sometimes even the opposite of, seeking mutual understanding between, mutual recognition of, and collaboration among, a great variety of cultures. Sometimes multiculturalism becomes the slogan for aggressive separatism, that penalizes multiple identity and commands absolute loyalty. This kind of divisive muticulturalists frequently prefer to speak the race-language (or gender-language). Are there now any strong and integrative ethical powers left?

In the United States, this model state of modern democracy, they will answer you, yes, there is one such power: the Constitution. The Constitution of the United States wields such a high ethical power. It is an integrative power. But it is questionable to what extent the force of this ethical power will be able to withstand the pressure of disintegrating relativism. Culture is perhaps the foremost ingredient of integration. And first of all legal culture, but a broader cultural framework in which a legal culture, too, is embedded.

Yet even if the Constitution could firmly hold its own ethical power in the United States, because it is their tradition, it is questionable whether in other countries this model could work. In the absence of democratic and liberal traditions, or in the presence of deeply rooted cultural traditions, this seems less likely.

5

The recognition of the plurality of ethical powers in the selfsame sphere (private and intimate sphere) implies the recognition of the plurality of identities.

I said that among ethical powers some are integrative ones, whereas others disintegrate and divide. Some of them are open to promote cooperation, others would lead their country or the world into a series of unpredictable conflicts of local warfare, ethnic and racial skirmishes, terrorism and the like. One stands for solidarity and strengthens social ties, the other brings about deviance, social chaos, dissolution. The problem is, however, that we speak about Dr. Jekyll and Mr. Hyde, we speak about the same powers.

One cannot conjure up one criterion to assess or evaluate the complex and often self-contradictory phenomena that are produced and reproduced in, and by, modernity. One can only point at some political conditions, under which it is more likely to keep the contradictions under control so that the beneficent face should appear instead of its dangerous Doppelgänger. I have in mind a kind of balance, the balance between political liberalism and democracy. I do not identify liberalism with negative freedom and democracy with positive freedom, but political liberalism with the advocacy of the rights of the single individual, and democracy with the claim to political equality and to majority rule, the conviction that the majoriy is always right. Both liberalism and democracy raise substantive claims (such as the freedom of the person, majority decision, the right of the individual, the right of the majority or minority). Both liberalism and democracy codetermine (in modern liberal democracies) the constituents of all the ethical powers, and so they are ethical powers on their own.

I now formulate my hypothesis: if one of these ethical powers is formalized whereas the other becomes substantive, all the ethical powers will get out of balance and modernity can destroy itself: yet if these two ethical powers are formalized to a roughly equal degree and preserve some substance, modernity has a good chance not just for survival, but also for progression wthin its own boundaries.

At the beginning of our century in Europe, liberalism became substantive yet democracy was formalized. This was an important condition in the emergence of totalitarianism. Now, it seems that (especially, but not only, in the United States) there is a tendency towards a formalization of liberalism and substantialization of democracy. The outcome is an increasing tolerance for violence and cold civil war in the name of "difference", and the contempt for minority rights in the name of the majority. The recognition of multiple identities on all levels of integration, and in relation to all ethical powers, is the minimal requirement for restoring the balance.

True, the proper balance between political liberalism and democracy does not remedy the *malaises* I have enumerated or briefly discussed. I cannot help but repeating, that they are not problems which can be solved. But if democracy and liberalism could be kept in proper balance not just within states but also within integrated regions, there might be a good chance for the survival of modernity on a global level. And modernity can survive now only if it survives on the global level.

10. STRUGGLE FOR KNOWLEDGE: A PERSONAL JOURNEY

Rajesh Tandon
Executive Director,
Society for Participatory Research in Asia (PRIA), New Delhi

ROOTS

I was born in an urban, lower middle class family, right after India became an independent country. My roots came from people who had actively participated in the freedom movement. A large part of my parentage had been educators and teachers. I was raised in a joint family, with values of sharing, cooperation and mutuality. I was encouraged to combine high quality schooling with participation in sports and cultural activities. While learning of languages and mathematics was especially valued in my family, reading of scriptures an other historical documents was particularly encouraged.

With such schooling, I got an opportunity to join an Institute of Technology, which was then recently created in cooperation with several American institutions. This was my youth, where I first experienced freedom in relation to what I could learn and how I could learn. Structured schooling was beginning to give space to options in relation to subjects, methods and initiatives.

This was also a period of great personal turmoil. My roots and my early upbringing was coming in conflict with my initiative to determine my own future. My family wanted me to join the Government service and therefore prepare myself to appear in necessary public service examinations. I was more inclined to have a professional background and an independent career. My personal choices in terms of education, friendship and intimacy came into conflict with tradition, family values, well established societal rules, etc.

I also learned the limits to obedience to authority. I was socialized to accept authority of elders, teachers, administrators, culture and tradition. I began to question the relevance and legitimacy of that authority in my contemporary pursuits. My active leadership of the student movement gave me the taste of rebellion and the implications associated with rejection of authority. It became obvious to me that the dominant system contained within itself seeds for its own transformation. I enjoyed obedience to authority as much as reveled in rebellion against it.

The late sixties were also a period of enormous national and global turmoil. Youth and student movements throughout the country and the world were erupting with almost similar challenges against systems of authority and subordination. Educational institutions were particularly targeted because knowledge, its dissemination and teaching had been organized in a highly authoritarian and top down manner. Rejection of the wider societal processes, in particular the top down models of State led intervention was also happening in different places. The violent Nazalite movement led by educated youth in the eastern part of India had a profound impact on many of my generation.

PROFESSIONALIZATION

This personal search for striking a balance between acceptance and rejection, authority and rebellion, tradition and modernity, intimacy and distance, absorbing knowledge available with others and creating one's own, continued to haunt me and ultimately began to clarify the directions of my professionalization. I began to look more closely at the phenomenon of change, social change in a wider societal context. But I also got curious about individual change, group change, organizational change. It is this curiosity which became the basis of my professional choice and my enrollment in a Ph.D. programme on organizational change.

I arrived in North America with a view to have a single minded pursuit of new knowledge. However my exposure to another culture, to another system, to another way of life produced fresh thinking in comparison with my upbringing and socialization. I pursued that programme with great vigor because it offered me the opportunity to develop competencies needed for action and not merely research. I enjoyed the opportunities created then and the preparations made for an interventionist role in individual, group and organizational change, an active intervener in the larger processes of social change and yet maintaining a learning orientation, a research and inquiry perspective.

In order for me to find a way to connect my new professional learning to my own reality back home, I returned to India with a view to participate in ways to improve the conditions of my people. I immersed myself in a rural reality to understand the problematic of rural development. This was a tremendous exposure, perhaps the most influential one year which shaped future directions of my pursuits. I experienced the extreme contradictions of the rural reality. I acknowledged the power and the distortions of the authoritarian State apparatus and I began to develop curiosity about voluntary development organizations as vehicles for empowerment of the powerless. From a model of top down delivery system I began to experiment with the idea of a bottom up acquisitive system organized around common interests of like minded have-nots.

In my pursuit of research towards my dissertation, I acknowledged that illiterate villagers seemed to know a lot more about rural reality and how to transform it, than me. I questioned the training I received as a researcher in transforming social realities.

The educational training interventions that I conducted with the rural poor: demonstrated the power of new learning opportunities in the hands of those who have otherwise been denied such access. I could see the twinkle in the eye of those who had discovered a new collective faith. I acknowledged to myself that knowledge for change is not only a professional pursuit but could also become a way of life. These were moments of critique and reflection which in my mind began to connect me with the relevance of discovering approaches to knowledge, linked to possibilities of social transformation. Social development not led from the top, but a social transformation built on the capacities of ordinary people. These were the beginnings of my connections with Participatory Research in the mid-seventies.

CHOICES

So, I ended up making certain choices about the nature of my work and life. The first component of the choice was to look at opportunities for an activist interventionist role in social transformation which relies on knowledge, learning, capacity building at organizational, group and individual levels.

The second choice I made was to position my interventions from the vantage point of the marginalized, the poor, the have-nots, those who have been excluded from the system. This gave me the strength to define "bottom up" strategies.

It became that this kind of choice required ways of relating to others which were more horizontal, less hierarchical and authoritarian. The early experience of building networks of participatory research in India and in Asia and linking up these networks with those in Africa, Latin America, North America, Europe provided an enormously valuable experience in how to work together, to share, exchange, learn and act. Working through informal collegial approaches was beginning to make sense as a congruent element of this package of choice. The linkage with the International Council for Adult Education (ICAE) at this particular moment of my history was extremely valuable, inspirational and productive.

My exposure to organizational frameworks and institutional mechanisms both professionally and personally continued to present other elements of the choice. I experimented with using an existing institutional framework to pilot alternative research and knowledge methodologies. I soon understood that philosophical underpinnings of an institutional framework are key to its impact. Clarity of vision and mission of an institutional framework must find consistency with the activities and programmes that it undertakes.

This recognition was perhaps the most important influence in my choice to build an alternative institutional framework which allowed me and others to pursue this approach of knowledge for social transformation in a professional, competent and serious manner which allowed for the possibility of elaboration of participatory research approaches and methodologies in different settings which enabled interventions aimed at strengthening individuals, groups and organizations, to practice countervailing force of power, promoting the ideals of an egalitarian, just and free society. This became the basis for the early thinking in founding PRIA (Society for Participatory Research in Asia).

GROUNDING

In that period of early 80's significant grounding was possible through a variety of opportunities, most significant of those came through the ICAE. The linkage between individual and collective learning, adult education and empowering processes was greatly clarified in my associations with the movement of adult education. The practice of learning for life and knowledge in self-managing individual and family health was clarified to me as I began to work on the project of primary health care and learning. The great strength of PR networks at that time was the ability to understand diverse socio-political contexts in countries of the South and yet the common threads that ran through this broad theme of knowledge for social transformation.

I found friends and co-travellers in Chile, Venezuela, Mexico, Kenya, Zimbabwe, Ghana, Philippines, Indonesia and Bangladesh during that period. This helped shape an identity of a Southern perspective, similar to the bottom up perspective of the excluded and the marginalized.

Yet, at the same time, I came in contact with and found the value of the work of several others, in North America and Europe. The Scandinavian movement of workers organizations and folk high schools had many elements which resonated with my own experience and hope. The practice of alternative education, grassroots research and empowering learning opportunities in Canada and North America made me realize the essential commonality of human endeavor throughout history, throughout the world. My visit to the Highlander Center in Tennessee and time I spent with Myles Horton gave me a sense of purpose and ideal for PRIA to aspire to.

In shaping the positioning of this alternative institutional framework of PRIA which was imbibed by the philosophy of Participatory Research, we began to practice and experiment with strengthening popular knowledge, articulation of existing knowledge and new learning opportunities for bottom up processes of social change. We focused on literacy and enjoyed the interaction with Paulo Freire. We discovered the enormous value of this perspective on issues of forest, land and water. How management of natural resources from the point of view of those who have done so for centuries, made contemporary ecological and scientific sense, even though they were excluded and rejected by the dominant State enterprise of Forest Departments and Land Development Corporations.

We experimented with understanding occupational health and disease in the workplace and recognized how significant the insights of workers were, not only in the organized shop floors of factories and mines but also in a wide range of work settings like homes, pavements, farms and wells.

In those early days of PRIA, we also had to count with the implications of positing an alternative view of knowledge, of research and inquiry and an institutional framework appropriate to that task.

One of the clear implications of this was rejection by the academic enterprise within the country and the region. Our pursuits were labeled as unscientific and our phraseology was seen as contradictory. Some academics would call the phraseology of Participatory Research, Popular Knowledge and Empowerment as a political ideology, while others would look at it as a Community Development tool. Our desire to link knowledge with participation of the excluded and the marginalized was challenged as they were seen as independent initiatives. Top down knowledge production that could be utilized for bottom up participatory processes was the message given to us in early 80's.

The alternative institutional framework of PRIA was challenged on several accounts. As an effort to make it a part of the wider, voluntary non-government movement in the country and the region, PRIA was seen as a different 'animal' because it was not engaged in grassroots work on its own. PR was promoting the idea of knowledge as a basis for social transformation. Learning was an integral component of organizing, and capacity building as a necessary step in bringing about a just and egalitarian order.

These ideas were new in early 80's and PRIA´s institutional framework appeared different from those of other voluntary organizations. The concept of a support organization as a vehicle to strengthen the learning opportunities at the grassroots and the articulation of their knowledge for wider social influence was an amazingly new idea, just fifteen years ago. We coped with this by developing methodologies which were immediately relevant to our partners at the grassroots.

Participatory training methodology became an enormously acceptable learning approach in preparation of field workers, trainers animators throughout the region. Participatory monitoring and evaluation methodologies began to gain acceptance even with the donors who were feeling frustrated with the non-use of evaluations and a resistant approach to monitoring of any grassroots interventions.

The idea that one could learn and change one's programmes and institutions while maintaining one's own control over it, seemed to be a revolutionary one in the mid-80's. We developed ways to strengthen collective functioning. Our interventions helped build teams, groups and organizations. We intervened in strengthening democratic, transparent and accountable ways of collective functioning through cooperatives, trade unions, voluntary organizations, community groups, women's associations, tribal collectives, etc. Thus group, team and organizational development interventions were integral in pursuit of our own choices.

MATURITY

It gives me a great deal of satisfaction to look back during these years with a sense of maturity. It is indeed heartening to see that ideas related to participation, empowerment, knowledge for social transformation, Participatory Research, learning and collective functioning in group and organizational development are today being utilized as common vocabulary among grassroots groups, professional practitioners, academic institutions, government agencies and international donor organizations.

So, in my stage of maturity I have recognized that the struggle for knowledge has to be taken forward. I have recognized that issues of participation, citizenship, empowerment, governance, collective initiatives are the essence of civil society. In our work we have begun to look at capacity building as a series of interventions which strengthen the intellectual, material and institutional bases of a variety of actors.

It has become clearer to us that social transformation is about creating a wide range of people's institutions, local institutions, community based organizations, intermediary actors, which enable the participation and empowerment of all sections of our people. The intellectual strength of such institutions is extremely important, just as their material, physical, financial aspect. How to organize, effectively manage, govern and promote the work of such institutions is in itself a struggle for knowledge. Learning opportunities, strengthening of capacities at individual, group and organizational level is a challenging pursuit.

In this maturity there is also a healthy aceptance of those big players, which have historically been the repositories of authority, power and control. The State institutions need transformation but they are not going to wither away. Corporate enterprises need accountability and social responsibility but their contribution to society cannot be wished away. Academic institutions will continue to produce and disseminate knowledge from the masters to the disciples, and yet they have a role to play in the larger society as well as in the production, reproduction and dissemination of knowledge. Therefore there is a need to engage these institutions of authority, power and control, which define legitimacy, which certify knowledge, which provide resources. Knowledge for transformation, therefore is also a struggle to engage these players of great power and authority in our societies.

FUTURE

It may appear that this is a stage of satiation. Maturity does not mean salvation. There is a huge and unfinished agenda in my own struggle for knowledge and I hope to pursue this in the remaining part of my personal journey. One of this relates to the growing omnipotence of the electronic media which in the present stage of globalization is promoting homogenization of cultures, lifestyles and value systems. This social homogeneity is undermining a great deal of social diversity and plurality which exists in human civilization and which provides the bedrock for civilizational survival and rejuvenation. I would like to find a way to understand how to engage this powerful media which in today's world have become a major producer and communicator of knowledge. Knowledge for social transformation requires contending with the role of media and media institutions.

Another component in the agenda is the new information technology. The Internet is a wonderful experience. The new information technology is providing cheap, easy and widespread access. It is able to pierce through boundaries of authoritarianism and control. It is able to reach to ordinary citizens in a world of inherent inequality, where nearly half of this new technology could, in fact, contribute to further equality in access to knowledge and tools of knowledge production.

Living in a country where computer software is produced for export and on a good bright day there is a fifty percent chance that telephones will work in Delhi, I am quite aware of the excitement that my colleagues in Europe and North America have about this new technology. But I do feel that its potential cannot be fully realized without intervening to transform those systems and institutions which obstruct and inhibit its access to vast majority of our people. How to influence the new information technology to serve the interest of bottom-up grassroots learning and empowering initiatives is a challenge.

Finally, how to move my struggle for knowledge forward such that it remains a healthy and positive experience as it has been in the first part of my life so far. This is so because advancing age and changing societal circumstances make mockery of the concept of struggle, which to me has been a personal and institutional knowledge for social transformation. It is indeed a struggle in individual, collective and institutional senses.

11. BEYOND "WHOSE REALITY COUNTS?" NEW METHODS WE NOW NEED

Robert Chambers
Institute of Development Studies, University of Sussex,
Brighton, United Kingdom

Activites called PRA (participatory rural appraisal) and its equivalents in other languages have evolved from a confluence, sharing and adaptation of methodologies, methods and participatory traditions. Synergies have generated new things to do and new ways to do them, including visual forms of analysis. A conjunction of conditions has produced an explosion of activities and applications, and spread to many countries and organisations: NGOs, government departments, and even universities, and raising questions of ethics and of sharing methodologies.

Coming from our different traditions, should we seek places of convergence and springboards for action? If so, could the concept of responsible wellbeing, and the question "Whose reality counts?" provide us with a common ground? They fit with eclectic pluralism, a celebration of diversity, and democratic reversals of dominance.

They raise shared issues of how we teach, learn, and construct realities, of dominant institutions and their cultures, and of personal power. They point towards responsible wellbeing for "uppers" being sought in empowering and privileging the realities of "lowers".

Do we now have a phenomenal opportunity? We have partici-patory methodologies which are powerful, popular and self-spreading. We have new space opened up by government and donor-agency policies for participation and poverty reduction. Rapid spread has brought much bad practice. At the same time, PRA and other participatory methodologies have also shown a potential to contribute to changes at levels which are policy-related, institutional and personal.

To make the most of these opportunities invites sharing methods and experience between different traditions, and inventing new methods. Five methodological challenges now (May 1997) stand out as points of leverage. These are how better to:

1. Enable the realities and priorities of poor and marginalized people to be expressed and communicated to policy-makers.
2. Enable trainers to facilitate attitude and behaviour change.
3. Make normal bureaucracies more participatory.
4. Build self-improvement into the spread of participatory methodologies.
5. Enable people with power to find fulfilment in disempowering themselves.

Could it be that effective repertoires for these could lead to much good change?

Could convergences and sharings of experiences and approaches among us contribute to such repertoires? Could we between us seize these opportunities in the new spaces which are opening up?

The past ten years have been a time of exhilarating innovation and discovery in participatory methodologies. Among these, those described as PRA (participatory rural appraisal) (Mascarenhas et al 1991; RRA and PLA Notes passim), now sometimes broadened to PLA (participatory learning and action), include many diverse practices. These have evolved and spread fast and wide, raising many issues and questions, and now opening up problems and potentials on a daunting scale. This paper asks whether those at this Congress can help in ways forward. It sets out to examine what has happened and where we are now, and to outline new methodologies we now need. In a pluralist spirit of self-doubt, it invites readers to share their experience and ideas, so that together we can try to do better.

PRA: WHAT HAS HAPPENED

PRA has flowed from a confluence and sharing of traditions and methodologies. The streams which have mingled and given it momentum have been many. Especially from Latin America, the inspiration of Paulo Freire (1970, 1974) and popular education and then of Participatory Action Research (e.g. Gaventa 1980; Fals-Borda 1984; Fals Borda and Rahman 1991) brought notably the idea that it is right and possible for poor and marginalized people to conduct their own analysis and take action. Research on farming systems and livelihoods brought the insights that resource-poor farming and other livelihoods are often complex and diverse, and that many farmers and poor people seek to complicate not simplify, and diversify not standardize, to reduce risk and produce more. Social anthropology brought understanding of insider-outsider interactions, of the importance of rapport, and of the distincion between emic and ethic, the view from inside and the view from outside.

This resonated with the post-modern understanding of multiple realities, and the recognition that professional realities are constructed differently from those of local people. Perhaps most creatively, agro-ecosystem analysis (Gypmantasiri *et al* 1980; Conway 1985) contributed from ecology the value of observation linked with mapping and diagramming, and of visual expression and analysis of local complexity. For its part, rapid rural appraisal (RRA) (KKU 1987) was the main antecedent of PRA, and brought alternatives to questionnaire surveys and to local "development tourism" (the brief local visit by the professional outsider). RRA stressed especially observation, semi-structured interviewing and focus groups. And the list can be lengthened, with parallels in and eclectic borrowing and adapting from other practical approaches-card sorting from VIPP (Tillmann 1993), role plays from theatre in development (Mda 1993), 3-D modelling and empowering through anonymity from Planning for Real (Gibson 1995, 1996). With the spread of PRA, different traditions have merged creatively, with synergies and inventiveness. Much of the spread has been South-South, through trainees from one country going to another. The sharing, borrowing and adapting have been very much in the spirit of this Congress, learning from one another without boundaries.

These traditions and methodologies have flowed together and inspired and supported innovations. Many of the early innovators were field staff in NGOs, at first mainly in India and Kenya. Methods and approaches evolved and spread with astonishing speed. Nothing may be new under the sun, but some methods and approaches have at least seemed new in form, emphasis, combinations and sequences, and in the way they have coalesced: the "discoveries" that "they can do it" that local people, whether they can read or not, can map, diagram, list, estimate, rank, construct and score matrices, and in other visual other visual ways present and analyze their complex realities; the advantages of visual over purely verbal analysis, especially with local complexity; the relative ease and utility of comparing rather than measuring; the synergies of analysis as a group activity and especially democracy of the ground, how differently we relate to one another when working on the ground, with less inhibition, and less verbal and physical dominance; the crucial importance of the behavior and attitudes of facilitators, not dominating, to keep quiet, not following a rigid routine but using their own best judgment at all times.

The result has been a growing and evolving family of approaches and methods, continuously discovered, invented, rediscovered, reinvented, and always experienced, variously known as PRA (parcipatory rural apprasial), PALM (participatory learning methods), MARP (méthode accélérée de recherche participative) (Gueye and Freundenberg 1991) and DRP (diagnóstico rural participativo); with other equivalents in other languages. To describe these and related participatory methodologies, the term PLA (participatory learning and action) has sometimes been used.

The scale and speed of the spread of these approaches are difficult to grasp. From small beginnings in the late 1980s, PRA related practices are now to be found in over 100 countries. PRA has spread from rural to urban, from countries of the South to countries of the North, from appraisal and planning to action and monitoring and evaluation, and from NGOs to government departments and even universities. In a research and data-collecting mode (which many feel should be described as RRA, not PRA or PLA) it is provided alternatives to questionnaires (Action Aid-Nepal 1992, Mukherjee 1995) and its methods are now widely used in graduate research (Attwood 1997). It has had many policy applications (Chambers and Blackburn 1996; Holland with Blackburn, forthcoming). In adult literacy, REFLECT (Regenerated Freirian Literacy through Empowering Community Techniques) (Archer 1995; Archer and Cottingham 1996a, 1996b; Fiedrich 1996) uses PRA visualizations, and after pilot testing in El Salvador, Uganda and Bangladesh, is now being implemented in over 25 countries.

There have been applications in almost every sector and practical domains of local development including agriculture, children, community planning and action, education especially girls education, emergencies and refugees, fisheries, forestry, gender awareness, health, land tenure and policy, livelihood analysis, livestock, older people, organizational analysis, participatory monitoring and evaluation, pastoralism, people and conservation, poverty programmes, sanitation, sexual and reproductive health (including HIV/AIDS), urban development, urban violence, water supply, watershed management, and women's programmes. Probably thousands of NGOs and hundreds of Government field organizations have sought to adopt PRA to some degree and in some form, and large organizations have tried to use it on a large scale.

In sum, a conjunction of conditions has produced an explosion of activities and applications, and much debate about the quality of practice (see e.g. Mosse 1993; Osuga and Mutarysa 1994; Guijt 1995; Guijt and Cornwall 1995; PLA Notes 25 passim). It is timely to take stock and ask what it is right to do now. What is right depends on who we are, where we are and what we can do. What we perceive as right depends on the traditions we work in and what we see as the ethical basis for action. It is a strength that we are all different, whether we can converge and share, learn from each other, and together do better.

CANDIDATES FOR CONVERGENCE: RESPONSIBLE WELLBEING, AND WHOSE REALITY COUNTS?

Agreement is not always necessary for action. Differences and dialogue can come first and lead to learning. Or action can come first generating experience. Similar actions and behaviors can generate similar experiences. These in turn can contribute to philosophy and theory. So it has been largely with PRA. People have done things, found what worked, and only then asked why. Common experiences have led to convergences. In a spirit of eclectic pluralism, sharing, borrowing and adapting, we can ask whether two of these can present a common ground.

The first candidate for convergence is a concept of responsible wellbeing. "Wellbeing" is the English word which best seems to encompass what local people often express when they cardsort individuals into piles or ranks in what used to be called "wealth ranking" (Grandin 1988; PRA Notes 15 passim). It is multidimensional and locally defined, referring to what are perceived as good or bad conditions, and good and bad quality and experience of life. Wellbeing encompasses much besides wealth or income.

"Responsible" qualifies wellbing, adding the social dimensión of relations with and effects on others, including unborn generations. The responsibilities of the rich and powerful are onerous, and responsible wellbeing is difficult for them to achieve. Responsible wellbeing is individually defined, and will differ much between individuals and cultures.

The second candidate for convergence flows from the question "Whose reality counts?" In puzzling how to reduce errors and do better in development, an issue in the late 1970s was "Whose knowledge counts?", and ITK (indigenous technical knowledge) was increasingly recognized and valued (IDS 1979; Brokensha, Warren and Werner 1980). Now the questions have elaborated and gone further to include:

Whose categories and concepts count?
Whose values and criteria?
Whose preferences and priorities?
Whose analysis and planning?
Whose action?
Whose monitoring and evaluation?

In sum, Whose reality counts? Is it reality "uppers", of those who normally dominate? Or should it be, can it be, increasingly that of "lowers", those who are normally subordinate?

"Whose reality counts?" fits with a theme of "reversals" (better expressed in the Italian inversioni), or turning things on their heads, upending the dominant and normal view. This has been an orientation of major religions and social movements. It belongs to no single tradition. Its implications resonate with eclectic puralism, a celebration of diversity, and democratic reversals of dominance. It raises shared issues of how we teach, learn, and construct realities, of dominant institutions and their cultures, and of personal power.

Could responsible wellbeing be sought in part through embracing the question "Whose reality counts?", and through "uppers" making what counts much more the reality of "lowers"? Could this be a common ground on which we converge?

A PHENOMENAL OPPORTUNITY?

This leads to asking whether the participatory development community may now, in 1997, at the time of this Congress, be facing a phenomenal opportunity. Having often been wrong before, I continually doubt my judgment in suggesting this. But there seems to be a conjuncture of two exceptionally favourable conditions.

The first is methodological. There have been many quiet convergences and sharings. We now have the potentials of participatory methodologies, including PRA, which are powerful, popular, versatile and self-spreading. Having evolved through borrowing and inventing, the ideal is that they should continuously evolve through more sharing without boundaries and more inventing, and be freely adopted, adapted and owned.

The second favourable condition is political. Donor agencies and national governments are on an increasing scale promoting participation, and often combining this with intentions to reduce poverty. Cynics will say that rhetoric is one thing, and reality another. But rhetoric opens doors, makes spaces, and provides points of leverage. Moreover, participation is being taken seriously in some of the centers of power. Under the leadership of James Wolfensohn, and following a prolonged internal learning process (see e.g. World Bank 1995), the World Bank is officially commited to participation: projects are monitored for it and some are participation flagship projects. An Interagency Group on Participation, of donor agencies with NGOs, has met three times. Governments have espoused participation: Bolivia has a Law of Popular Participation; others including India, Indonesia, Kenya, Nepal, Uganda and Vietnam have sought to go to scale with participatory approaches in government field agencies.

If we have both the methodologies and the political rhetoric for going to scale, do we have the vision, gut, creativity, flexibility and commitment to see and seize the opportunity, or will we mess up and miss the chance?

GOING TO SCALE

These two favourable conditions have combined to lead to requirements by governments and donors that PRA should be used on a large scale. In some places, all donors have required it in programmes. In both Nepal and Andhra Pradesh it has been said that the issue is not whether PRA will be used, but whether it will be used well. In India, PRA has been required in the very large national watershed programme, and over 300 trainers were trained in four months. In several countries, it is being used in local government, with training of elected leaders and staff. Most dramatically, the Indonesian Government in 1995 issued instructions that PRA should be used in over 60.000 villages, and that before the end of the financial year (Murkherjee 1996).

This list and these numbers are needed to force us to realize the scale of what has happened and is happening. Other methodologies introduced by governments on a large scale have usually had a more top-down orientation: the training and visit system of agricultural extension (Benor and Harrison 1997), and logical framework analysis and ZOPP (GTZ 1988; Foster 1996) are two examples. PRA differs from these by being in theory at least standardized, less routinized, more enabling, and intended to empower local people, to "hand over the stick", emphasizing changes in personal behavior and attitudes, and replacing domination and teaching with facilitation and learning.

Theory and practice are, though, never the same. Spread has presented many problems of quality. Cases have been common of the following. Methods have been stressed, neglecting behavior and attitudes. Visits have been rushed. Approaches have been standardized and routinized. Activites like mapping meant to be carried out by local people have been undertaken by outsiders. Appraisal has not linked with planning and action. Follow up has been weak. Local people have given their time and nothing has resulted. While these abuses are far from universal, and there has been some excellent practice, they have been widespread and have raised many questions of principles and ethics (Absalom et al 1995).

The PRA experience pitchforks us into the responsibilities of scale. We are exposed to implications of personal choice. Not to choose is a choice. Not to act is an action. The issue for trainers and practioners is at what scale and level to be involved or not involved. Three responses can be suggested (Chambers 1995): the small, secure and beautiful, limiting scale in order to maintain high quality; a middle range of engagement with a particular organization over months and years; and accepting trade offs in working with large organizations which go to scale rapidly. The temptations are either to hide in snug wombs of the small, secure and beautiful, or to be seduced by the importance and other rewards of going to scale. It is middle range, though, which is the most significant (Wagachchi 1995; Johansson 1995; Thompson 1995; Hagmann, Chuma and Murwira 1996; Blackburn with Holland in draft). Perhaps all three levels are needed, and engagement with each can be a responsible activity if complemented and informed by the others.

These conditions present huge opportunities. Bad practice is an opportunity to improve. Scale is an opportunity to have widespread impact. Potentials are not just for local level participation, but for changes at three levels: policy, institutional and personal. To seize those opportunities we have part of the means in existing methods and methodologies. But they are patently not enough. So the remainder of this paper asks for our own responsible wellbeing, what other methods or methodologies do we now need to seek, invent, use and spread?

THE FUTURE: NEW METHODS WE NEED

As new spaces open up and the frontiers move fast, five methodological challenges now (May 1997) seem to present points for innovation and leverage.

1. How better to enable the realities and priorities of poor and marginalized people to be expressed and communicated to policy-makers

Political organization and power is the usual means for securing action to benefit poor and marginalized people. That will always be vital. But beyond that, it has become more evident that the realites and priorities of poor people often differ from those supposed for them by professionals and policy-makers. The challenge is to enable poor and marginalized people to analyze their conditions and identify their priorities in ways which freely express their realities, generate proposals which are doable, and are credible and persuasive to policy-makers.

Two approaches have begun to be developed and show promise:

(i) *Participatory poverty assessments(PPAs)*. PPAs using PRA approaches and methods have been pioneered in Ghana (Norton, Kroboe, Bortei-Dorku and Dogbe 1995; Dogbe 1996), Zambia (Norton, Owen and Milimo 1994). South Africa (Attwood 1996, May 1996, Murphy 1995, Texeira and Chambers 1995), and most recently in Bangladesh (UNDP 1996), using a variety of processes (for reviews see Norton and Stephens 1995, Robb 1996, Chambers and Blackburn 1996, Holland with Blackburn in draft).

Insights and priorities have included, for example, the importance of all-weather roads for access to curative medicine during the rains, the need to reschedule the timing of school fees aways from the most difficult time of year, and how rudeness by health staff deters poor people from seeking treatment. In Bangladesh, where the focus of analysis by poor people was on "doables", differences in priorities between men and women, urban and rural, were highlighted. The first doable priority of urban women was drinking water, and the second private places to wash themselves. A widespread desire of poor people was enforcement of the anti dowry laws. A better understanding of sectoral priorities, for example between health and education, has also resulted.

(ii) *Thematic investigations*. Thematic investigations using PRA approaches and methods have illuminated local realities in a range of contexts. Examples of insights are:

- Area stigma: how living in an area with a bad reputation for violence makes it difficult to get jobs (from Jamaica, Moser and Holland 1997).
- How a quarter of girls of school age were "invisible" to the official system (from the Gambia, Kane, Bruce and O'Reilly De Brun 1996).
- How the problems and priorities of women differ not only from those of men but also between women depending on their access

to basic services and infrastructures, and their social background (from Morocco, Shah and Bourarach 1995).

- How wide the gap was between policy and practice with exemptions from healthcare charges for the destitute and those with infectious or chronic diseases (from Zambia, Booth 1996).
- How indigenous people's threatened land rights coincided with areas of greatest biological diversity (from Honduras and Panama, Denniston with Leake 1995).
- How an official belief that indigenous tenure systems no longer existed was wrong, and how diverse and crucial they were (Freudenberger 1996).
- The ability of local peoples to define sustainable management and conservation practices for themselves (from India and Pakistan, Gujja, Pimbert and Shah 1996).

There are methodological challenges in further developing these methods.

Perhaps now, though, a larger challenge is finding how the insights they generate can effect changes in policy, both policy-in-principle and policy-in-practice. As part of political process, there are questions here about how findings are analyzed and by whom, how they are presented and to whom, and how they are followed up. Some options and issues are:

- Modes of analysis and categories.
- Forms of presentation, especially maps and diagrams.
- Videos taken by and with local people.
- Poor people meeting policy-makers face-to-face in central places.
- Policy-makers meeting local people face-to-face in local places

Have you experiences and suggestions to share?

2. How better to enable trainers to facilitate attitude and behaviour change

In the PRA experience, attitude and behaviour change among facilitators and trainers has been recognized as more important than methods. An international South-South Sharing Workshop held in South India in 1996 described attitude and behavior change as the ABC of PRA (Kumar 1996), as perhaps it should be the ABC of all participatory methodologies. Learning to unlearn, and learning not to put forward one's own ideas, not to dominate, criticize, interrupt or talk too much, not to rush or be impatient, these negatives, together with positives such as show respect, embrace error, ask them, and be nice to people (personal communication, Raul Peresgrovas), have proved key to good facilitation of analysis by others. Many professionals have been socialized into behavior that is the opposite of these. As facilitators, then, they are disabled at the start. The concern then has to be for programmes of rehabilitation to liberate them (us) from the prisons of their (our) conditioning.

There is now a wealth of experience, and a repertoire of approaches and techniques for training for ABC (see e.g. Pretty, Guijt, Thompson and Scoones 1995; Kumar 1996; Roy, Chatterjee, Yadav, Mukherjee and Bhattacharya 1997). The opportunity is further to develop and spread three sets of methods. These are for the following practices:

Exercise and sequences for use in training. Some exercises and sequences are already widely used in PRA training, for example: in role plays like "dominator" and "saboteur", leading to those words becoming part of the joking culture of a group; sequences like "what would you do if?" leading to group formation and group contracts.

Staying nights in communities. Again and again, in PRA training, there has been resistance to spending nights with communities, again and again the experience has been formative. UNDP staff have together spent days and nights with communities in India as a training experience. World Bank staff are now required to spend a week of immersion in a village or slum as part of their executive training. The significance and potential impact of this practice could easily be underestimated.

Training of trainers and styles of training. The very word "training" is a problem here, implying as it does teaching and the transfer of knowledge. Learning to improve as a trainer, largely experiential through sharing, example, and fieldwork. A basisc principle is that such training must itself be participatory and experiential. Training has to become not teaching, but helping one another to experience and learn. A trainer of trainers is then herself or himself a participatory facilitator.

Going to scale demands many more trainers in participatory methodologies. The temptation and tendency is then for "cascade" training, in which trainers train trainers, or even train trainers of trainers. The ideal training, which is experiential and interactive with people in communities, is to be in some central institutes to organize. So the initial trainer is liable to be in some central place, classroom based, with lectures. This then is the imprint and culture which is passed down the cascade.

The challenge is to add to the exercises, sequences and types of experience, and to develop and spread participatory styles of training.

Have you experiences and suggestions to share?

3. How better to make normal bureaucracies more participatory

A repeated experience with PRA has been tension and contradiction between topdown bureaucratic cultures and requirements, tending as they do to standardize, simplify and control, and demands and needs generated at the local-level, tending as they do to be diverse and complex and to require local-level discretion. Participation at the grass-roots level requires participatory procedures and culture in facilitating organizations. Where these do not exist, field-level participatory processes are liable to be fragile, vulnerable and damaged by dominating modes of interaction.

The changes needed are personal, procedural and systemic (Blackburn with Holland in draft). At the personal level they include: ability to listen; reflexivitty; capacity to facilitate and engage in dialogue and mutual learning; and capacity for vision. Procedurally, they include moving from product to process, new incentives for participatory behavior, and multiple feedback mechanisms including participatory monitoring and evaluation. Systemically and structurally, they include decentralized budgets and replacing targets with trust. The changes sought correspond with those advocated by some of the gurus of management, for example Tom Peters in *Thriving on Chaos* (1987) and Senge in *The Learning Organization* (1990).

In the field of development, considerable experience has been gained and analyzed (see e.g. Uphoff 1992; Thompson 1995; Leurs

1996; Adhikari *et al* 1996; Blackburn with Holland in draft), and strategies recommended. But the task remains enormous and intimidating. Where progress with bureaucratic reorientation occurs, regression to the "normal" often seems to follow. Sometimes corruption may be a part of this, where participation would mean lower incomes for government officials. So there remain daunting methodological challenges. Three in particular are the following:

1. How to conduct and report on research which identifies what really happens, especially with "rent seeking behavior" (corruption). Unless this is known, many obstacles to participation may remain hidden and ignored, with a potential for preventing change. How to archieve some of the more commonly advocated actions and conditions for change within bureaucracies, for example:

- Continuity of commitment to participation.
- Networking with allies.
- Starting small and slow, and resisting pressure to scale up too fast.
- Funding flexible without the punitive orientation of targets.
- Accountability and transparency based on trust.
- Training, encouraging and supporting grass-roots staff.
- Accommodating diversity of activites at the field level.
- Incorporating participatory monitoring and evaluation, and multiple feedback channels.
- Incentives to reward participatory behaviour in-house and in the field.
- Easy access to information to foster learning across organisational units.

2. How to archive more rapid grassroots spread of participatory approaches, as often required by donors and governments, with acceptable trade-offs between quality and scale. Options to explore include lateral spread of grassroots innovations, and the routinized insertion of benign genes with self improvement built in.

    Have you experiences and suggestions to share?

4. How better to build self-improvement into the spread of participatory methodologies

Of these questions, this may appear the most way out. It is whether in PRA and other participatory methodologies it is possible to sow seeds of change which will work away improving performance over the months and years. This question crosscuts the others.

The metaphors are genes and viruses. Genes are part of the core composition of an organism, reproducing similar characteristics wherever the organism develops. There is a genetic code or script which is largely unalterable. For their part viruses spread on their own, penetrating organisms that already exist. So the question is whether, either as genes inserted at the start, or as viruses spread later, there can be elements in participatory methodologies in general, and PRA in particular, which will mean that however badly things start, they will get better.

Three clusters of genes or viruses exits and could be strengthened, as follows:

1. *Field Experience.* One cluster in PRA methods and experiences. In themselves, they have a capacity to transform the mindsets, behaviours and attitudes of professionals. Here is an illustrative account, from a PRA training: "I felt that the methods were not relevant, interesting or rigorous. Then we went to the field and in the village we agreed to have positive attitudes and respect for the community. My problem was not in respecting people. I just wanted to know what we would gain from respecting people and using stones and so on. I was invited into the hut of a poor agricultural labourer in the most marginalized part of the village. We asked the old man in the hut to show the village in a sketch map and gave him some chalks. This was the turning point of my life. He started sketching the village, showing the poorest huts the only ones he knew. I was amazed to see the professional expertise with which this illiterate man used seeds and chalks. I was also impressed with the wealth of information and how he was enjoying telling people his story. I got many answers to my questions from that one day in the field". (Neela Mukherjee in Kumar 1996:20).

The PRA methods which empower local people to present and analyze their realities do, again and again, surprise them with what they find they can do, and change the way outsiders see them and behave towards them. Thus a villager in Sinthiane, Senegal, after completing a historical matrix said: "This is just astonishing. We know each of these pieces because they are parts of our existence. But we have never thought of it all put together like this. This is our life and our history". (Quoted in K. and M. Schoonmaker Freudenberger 1994:128).

Or a Tembomvura woman, Zimbabwe, who said to Ravai Marindo (Ranganai 1996:88) after PRA modelling and diagramming: "And we thought we were so foolish because we could not write. Yet look, we had all this information inside us".

And as a facilitator, John Devavaram has written (Mascarenhas et al 1991:10), "one doesn't get bored repeating field work. It is always interesting".

2. *Reflexivity.* If PRA has a tablet of stone, it is the non tablet "Use your own best judgment at all times". To the extent that it is a system, it is self-organizing. In the spirit of Richard Forsyth's (1991) idea that each of us can design our own religion, so any practitioner can, in this ideal, evolve her or his understanding through reflection on experience. Reflexivity has been part of PRA as of other methodologies. It could, though, be more stressed and practiced, through activites like keeping diaries, reflection on experience, and sharing reflections and learning. And new forms of reflection and learning using PRA methods could be devised.

3. *Behavior and attitudes training.* The prime candidate gene is ABC-attitude and behavior change. In PRA, behavior and attitudes matter much more than the methods. But PRA training still usually stresses the methods. Often in a routinized manner. The question here is whether a core of a few ABC exercises, relatively unthreatening and easy to implement, could be identified and made a standard requirement, and embedded in PRA training for going to scale.

Such top-down standardization conflicts with PRA philosophy. But it may be a question of trade-offs. The issue is whether such a cluster of genes might work away on the trainer/facilitator as well as those trained/facilitated, with better long-term effects than other approaches.

All three clusters of genes or viruses are already there, but not yet all fully developed or used. All present scope for innovation. In itself, one cluster may not be enough.

With bad facilitation, the fulfillment and fun of field experience do not manifest themselves, and PRA can be variously rushed, rigid, routinized, and explotative. With only reflexivity, personal dominance might not be confronted. Behavior and attitudes training without reflection might allow defences to inhibit learning and change. But together there might be a powerful synergy.

Where new training is undertaken, inserting these genes may be feasible. It is likely to be more difficult to spread them where there is already bad practice. At least partial solutions may be trainers' retreats to share experience, and general recognition that training and change should never cease.

Have you experiences and suggestions to share?

5. How better to enable people with power to find fulfillment in disempowering themselves

Perhaps the methodological challenge is to find good ways to enable powerful people to gain from disempowering themselves. For the realites of "lowers" to count, "uppers" have to hand over the stick. Changes in dominant behavior entail having respect, standing down, shutting up, and facilitating, enabling and empowering. This is the key to many changes, professional, personal and institutional.

Zero-sum thinking misleads here. We talk of giving up power, abandoning power, surrendering power, and then of gaining power, as though it were a commodity of which more was better and less worse. The reality is often different . Personal disempowerment can be a gain in several ways as follows:

- *Liberation and peace of mind.* Participatory styles and management are liberating. Centralized control of more than the minimum is stressful. Disempowerment spreads responsibility and diminishes stress. Decentralization decreases punitive management and fear. Disempowerment reduces the deceptions of "all power deceives" (Chambers 1997 ch. 5). Openness, honesty and realism make for peace of mind. When responsibility is shared and dispersed, the strain of centralized work overload and of

doing badly are diminished; the main responsibility for development is removed from overburdened shoulders, and conflict
reduced by permitting and promoting local diversity.
- *Effectiveness*. Disempowerment offers new roles and new
  effectiveness. To facilitate participation is practical. It works.
  Uppers can gain from the instrumental success of the approach.
  There are fewer errors of standardization and control.
- *Collegiality*. Power on a pinnacle is lonely. In a participatory
  mode, a boss is not isolated, but a team member. Relationships
  are more equal, with mutual learning and partnership.
- *Fullfilment*. Disempowerment and participatory styles and
  management can be fulfilling. One learning from the PRA
  experience is how satisfying it can be to facilitate participation.
  This is not new; it is a rediscovery, a reaffirmation. Losses are
  more than compensated by gains. Indeed, the self importance
  and control that are "lost" are often liabilities anyway.
- *Fun*. Faced with the horrors of war and extremes of cruelty and
  deprivation, talk of fun seems frivolous. But fun (creativity, play,
  laughter, shared pleasures) are part of what most people value
  and wish for themselves and for others. Repeatedly, PRA
  experiences have been enjoyed by participants who conduct
  their own analysis, make their owns maps and diagrams, add
  detail, and are creative; and have been a delight for facilitators
  who do not dominate but act as catalysts and find satisfaction
  in discovering what local people know and can do.

The key understanding is that reversals need not be threatening
for uppers. Uppers who lose in one way can gain in others.
Reversals of roles like "handing over the stick", enabling others,
and disempowering oneself as an upper are means to responsible
wellbeing , fulfillment and fun.

The challenge is to find use of more and better methods to help
powerful people realize these gains. PRA has some, including field
experiences. Others could be the self-improving genes. What else?

Have you experiences and suggestions to share?

QUESTIONS AND CHALLENGES

Is all this stuff of the real world or fantasy? Could a good repertoire of methods in any one of these domains have a huge impact? Could convergences and sharing of experiences and approaches contribute to such repertoires? Can we between us seize these opportunities in the new spaces which are opening up? Immediately and practically:

Other priorities. Are these other methological domains with bigger potential which should take priority?

Practical help. Can you contribute ideas and experiences which will help in a practical way?

Development and spread. How could methods best be found, developed, shared and spread?

Future action. Should we try to take things forward? If not, peace. But if so, how?

FINAL REMARKS

It is a defect of this paper, for which I apologize, that it does not relate directly to other papers in this symposium. All of us are following different paths and have different preoccupations. I hope that in a spirit of pluralist convergence we will find common ground and mutual learning in our discussions.

In this paper methodology refers to a system of principles and methods. Method, refers to a way of doing something. PAR, agro-ecosystem analysis, and PRA are examples of methodologies. Semi-structured interviews, transects and matrix scoring are examples of methods.

The question of labels is difficult. PRA and its equivalents in other languages are still the terms most commnly used. So PRA is used in this paper. RRA Notes was renamed PLA Notes (participatory learning and action) in 1995 to reflect the range of approaches and applications (including urban) in contributions received. PAMFORK, the Participatory Methodologies Forum of Kenya, and some others, are using PMs (participatory methodologies) to embrace an even wider range.

I feel bad suggesting this as point of convergence, since I have written a book with this title. It is a "can't win". It is arrogant for me to put this forward. At the same time, it would be wrong not to do so if it really could provide common ground. In the spirit of the one-sentence manual, "Use your own best judgment at all times", let me urge any reader to be critical, to make up her or his own mind, and above all to make better suggestions to help us forward.

For a more detailed exploration of responsible wellbeing, please see *Whose Reality Counts?* pp. 9-12, which includes equity, sustainability, capabilities and livelihoods as components of and contributors to responsible wellbeing. Examples of other experiences with going to scale are badly needed. I would appreciate sources of information on this. The Community Development movement of the 1950s ought to provide relevant lessons. There must be others, even if they have not so centrally had to confront the issues of personal behavior and attitudes, and institutional cultures.

In an earlier draft I said "We can be safe as ostriches hiding our heads in sand, avoiding the issue, or as giraffes with a lofty view, pontificating far from the ground. Or we can be vulnerable as a gazelle, committed to the middle ground and exposed to predators." The analogies do not fully work, but I did not want to lose them completely. The danger in this paper, and the temptation to be feared in the milieu of the Congress, is posturing as a grotesque ostrich-giraffe hybrid.

Examples of the differences between the realities and priorities of local people and those supposed for them by professionals can be be found in *Whose Reality Counts?* (Chapters 2, 3 and 8, 174-183).

Participatory monitoring and evaluation could well have been a separate methodology for development. It has a potential for closing the participatory project cycle, referring back to and reinforcing participatory baseline analyses. See the IDS Participatory Monitoring and Evaluation Pack (Mebrahtu et al 1997). Oddly, there is much writing about the concepts of participatory monitoring and evaluation but rather little actual experience reported. Priorities would seem to be writing and sharing accounts of this type in practice, and further field experimentation and development, rather than more academic and theoretical writing on the subject.

REFERENCES

Absalom, Elkanah et al 1995. "Participatory Methods and Approaches: Sharing Our Concerns and Looking to the Future". *PLA Notes* 22 pp 5-10.

ActionAid-Nepal 1992. *Participatory Rural Appraisal Utilization Survey Report. Part I. Sindhupalchowk*, ActionAid-Nepal. PO Box 3198. Kathmandu, July.

Adhikari, G.B. et al 1996. "Sharing Our Experience: an Appel to Donors and Governments", in Kumar ed *ABC of PRA: Attitude Behaviour Change* pp 41-44.

Archer, David 1995. "Using PRA for a Radical New Approach to Adult Literacy". *PLA Notes* 23 pp 51 55, June.

Archer, David and Sara Cottingham 1996a. *Action Research Report on REFLECT: the Experience of Three REFLECT Pilot Projects in Uganda, Bangladesh, El Salvador,* ODA Education Papers No. 17, ODA, London, March.

Archer, David and Sara Cottingham 1996b. *The REFLECT Mother Manual Regenerated Freirean Literacy Through Empowering Community Techniques.* ActionAid, London, March.

Attwood, Heidi 1996. *South African Participatory Poverty Assessment Process: Were the Voices of the Poor Heard?* Paper for the PRA and Policy Workshop, IDS. Sussex, 13 and 14 May 1996.

Attowwod. Heidi 1997. PRA Research, *PRA Topic Pack*, IDS, University of Sussex. Brighton, UK.

Backhaus, Christoph and Rukman Wagachchi 1995. "Only Playing with Beans? Participatory approaches in large-scale government programmes". *PLA Notes* 24 pp 62-65.

Benor, Daniel and James Q. Harrison 1977. *Agricultural Extension: the Training and Visit System,* Worl Bank, Washington.

Blackburn, James with Jeremy Holland eds. (in draft). *What Changes? Institutionalizing Participation in Development,* IDS, Sussex.

Booth, David 1996. *Coping with Cost Recovery: a sectoral policy study,* paper for the PRA and Policy Workshop, IDS Sussex, May 13 14 1996.

Brokensha, David. D. Warren and O. Werner and O. Werner eds. 1980. *Indigenous Knowledge Systems and Development,* University Press of Amercia, Lanham, Maryland.

Chambers, Robert 1995. "Making the Best of Going to Scale", *PLA Notes* 24 pp 57-61, October.

Chambers, Robert 1997. *Whose Reality Counts? Putting the First Last,* Intermediate Technology Publications.

Chambers, Robert and James Blackburn 1996. *The Power of Participation PRA and Policy, Policy Briefing*, Institute of Development Studies, University of Sussex, Brinton, UK.

Denniston, David, with Andrew Leake 1995. "Defending the Land with Maps," *PLA Notes* 22 pp 36-40.

Dogbe, Tony 1996. "The one who rides the donkey does not know the ground is hot", Paper for the PRA and Policy Workshop, IDS, Sussex, May 13-14 1996.

Fals-Borda, Orlando 1984. "Participatory Action Research", Development: Seeds of Change, reprinted in *Development: Forty Years in Development: The Search for Social Justice*, Vol 40 no 1 pp 92-6.

Fals Borda, Orlando and Mohammad Anisur Rahman eds. 1991. *Action and Knowledge: Breaking the monopoly with participatory action research*, Intermediate Technology Publications, London.

Fiedrich, Marc 1996. *Literacy in Circles?*, Working Paper Number 2, ActionAid, Hamlyn House, Macdonald Road, Archway, London N19 5PG, December.

Forster, Reiner ed 1996. *ZOPP marries PRA? Participatory Learning and Action A Challenge for Our Services and Institutions*, Deutsche Gesellschaft fur Technische Zusammenarbeit (GTZ) GmbH, Posfach 5180, D 6236 Eschborn 1 bei Frankfurt am Main, Germany.

Foryth, Richard S. 1991. "Towards a Grounded Morality", Changes, vol 9, no 4, December pp 264-278.

Freire, Paulo 1970. *Pedagogy of the Oppressed*, The Seabury Press, New York.

Freire, Paulo 1974. *Education for Critical Consciousness*, Sheed and Ward, London (original edition Editora Paz e Terra, Rio de Janeiro, 1967).

Freudenberger, Karen Schoonmaker 1996. *The Use of RRA to Inform Policy: Some Personal Observations*, paper for the PRA and Policy Worshop, IDS Sussex 13-14 May 1996.

Freudenberger, Karen Schoonmaker and Mark Schoonmaker Freuden-berger 1994. "Livelihoods, livestock and change: The Versality and Richness of Historical Matrices", *RRA Notes* 20 pp 144-148.

Gaventa, John 1980. *Power and Powerlessness: Rebellion and Quiescence in an Appalachian Valley*, University of Illinois Press, Chicago.

Gibson, Tony 1995. "Showing What You Mean (Not Just Talking about It)", *RRA Notes* 21 pp 41-47.

Gibson, Tony 1996. The Power in Our Hands: *Neighbourhood based World shaking*, John Carpenter, Charlbury, Oxfordshire OX7 3PQ, UK.

Grandin, Barbara 1988. *Wealth Ranking in Smallholder Communities: A Field Manual*, Intermediate Technology Publications, London.

GTZ 1988. ZOPP (*An introduction to the Method*). Deutsche Gesellschaft fur Technische Zusammenarbeit (GTZ) GmbH, Pstfach 5180, D 6236 Eschborn I bei Frankfurt am Main, Germany.

Gueye, Bara and Karen Schoonmaker Freudenberger 1991. *Méthode Accélérée de Recherche Participative*. IIED, London.

Guijt, Irene 1995. Rhetoric versus Practice: *Reflections on the Challenges Facing the Spread and Development of PRA,* Paper prepared for Uganda National Worksop "Taking PRA and other participatory techniques forward", May 11 and 12 1995.

Guijt, Irene and Andrea Cornwall 1995. "Editorial: Critical Reflections on the Practice of PRA", *PLA Notes* 24, pp 2-7.

Gujja, Biksham, Michel Pimbert and Meera Shah 1996. *Village voices challenging wetland management policies: PRA experiences from Pakistan and India,* paper for the PRA and Policy Worshop, IDS Sussex, May 13-14 ,1996.

Hagmann, Jurgen, Edward Chuma and Kudakwashe Murwira 1996. "Improving the Output of Agricultural Extension and Research Through Participatory Innovation Development and Extension, Experiences from Zimbabwe", *European Journal of Agricultural Education and Extension*, Vol 2 no 3, March 1996.

Holland, Jeremy with James Blackburn eds in draft. *Whose Voice? Participatory Research and Policy Change*, IDS Sussex.

IDS 1979. Whose Knowledge Counts? *IDS Bulletin* Vol 10 no 2, Institute of Development Studies, University of Sussex Brighton, UK.

Jones, Carolyn 1996. *Preliminary Behaviour and Attitudes Pack*, PRA Topic Pack, IDS, University of Sussex, Brighton, UK.

Johansson, Lars 1995. "Reforming donor driven projects and state bureaucracies through PRA", *Forests, Trees and People Newsletter* 26/27, April pp 59-63.

Kane, Eileen, Lawrence Bruce, Haddy Sey and Mary O'Reilly-de Brun 1996. *Girls' Education in The Gambia,* paper for PRA and Policy Workshop, IDS Sussex, 13-14 May 1996.

KKU 1987. *Proceeding of the 1985 International Conference on Rapid Rural Appraisal, Rural Systems Research and Farming Systems Research Projects,* University of Khon Kaen, Thailand.

Kumar, Somesh ed., 1996. *ABC of PRA: Attitude Behaviour Change.* Report of the South-South Workshop pn PRA: Attitudes and Behaviour, Bangalore and Madurai, organized by ActionAid India and SPEECH, 1 10 July 1996.

Leurs, Robert 1996. "Current challenges facing participatory rural appraisal", *Public Administration and Development,* Vol 16, pp 1-6.

Marindo-Ranganai, Ravai 1995. "Diagrams for Demographic Data Collection: Examples from the Tembomvura, Zimbabwe", *PLA Notes* 22 pp 53-61.

Mascarenhas, James, Parmesh Shah, Sam Joseph, Ravi Jayakaran, John Devavaram, Vidya Ramachandran, Aloysius Fernandez, Robert Chambers and Jules Pretty eds., 1991. Proceedings of the February 1991 Bangalore PRA Workshop, *RRA Notes* 13, August.

May, Julian 1996. *Kicking Down Door and Lighting Fires: Participating in Policy,: the SA-PPA Experience,* Paper for the PRA and Policy Workshop, IDS, Sussex 13 14 May 1996.

Mda, Jacques 1993. *When People Play People: Development Communication through Theatre,* Witwatersrand University Press, Johannesburg and Zed Books, London and New Jersey.

Mebrantu, Esther with Heidi Attwood and John Gaventa 1997. Participatory Monitoring and Evaluation, *PRA Topic Pack,* IDS, University of Sussex. Brighton, UK.

Moser, Caroline and Jeremy Holland 1997. *Urban Poverty and Violence in Jamaica.* World Bank Latin American and Caribbean Studies. Viewpoints.

Mosse, David 1993. *Authority, Gender and Knowledge theoretical reflections on the practice of Participatory Rural Appaisal* ODI Network Paper 44, ODI, London.

Mukherjee, Neela 1995. *Participatory Rural Appraisal and Questionnaire Survey: Comparative field experience and methological innovations,* Concept Publishing Company, New Delhi 110059.

Mukherjee, Nilanjana 1996. "The Rush to Scale: Lessons Being Learnt in Indonesia" paper for the Workshop on Instituonalising Participatory Approaches, IDS Sussex.

Murphy, Carol 1995. *Implications of Poverty for Blank Rural Women in Kwazulu/Natal,* Report for the South African Participatory Poverty Assessment, Institute of Natural Resources, P Bag Xo1, Scottsville, South Africa 3209.

Nelson, Nici and Susan Wright eds., 1995. *Power and Participatory Development Theory and Practice,* Intermediate Technology Publications, London.

Norton, Andy, Dan Owen and John Milimo 1994. *Zambia Participatory Poverty Assessment:* Report 12985 ZA, Southern Africa Department, The World Bank, Washington, November 30, 1994.

Norton, Andy, David Kroboe, Ellen Bortei-Dorku and D.K. Tony Dogbe 1995. *Ghana Participatory Poverty Assessment Consolidated Report on Poverty assessment in Ghana Using Qualitive and Participatory Research Methods: Draft Report, AFTHR,* World Bank.

Norton, Andrew and Thomas Stephens 1995. *Participation in Poverty Assessments*, Environment Department Papers Participation Series, Social Policy and Resettlement Division, the World Bank, Washington, June.

Norton, Andy and Dan Owen 1996. *The Zambia Participatory Poverty Assessment: Notes on the Process and Lessons Learned*, Paper of the PRA and Policy Workshop, IDS Sussex, May 13 14, 1996.

Osuga, Ben and David Mutayisa 1994. *PRA Lessons and Concerns: Experiences in Uganda*, Uganda CBHC Association, P.O. Box 325, Entebbe, February.

Peters, Tom 1987. *Thriving on Chaos handbook for a management revolution*, Alfred A. Knopf.

Pretty, Jules, Irene Guijt, John Thompson and Ian Scoones 1995. *A trainer's Guide for Participatory Learning and Action*, IIED Participatory Methodology Series, IIED.

Robb, Caroline 1996. *Participatory Poverty Assessment: Key Issues*, Paper presented at the PRA and policy Workshop, IDS Sussex, May 13-14 1996.

Robinson Pant, Anna 1995. *Gender and PRA, PRA Topic Pack*, IDS, University of Sussex, Brighton, UK.

Roy, S.B., Mitali Chatterjee, Ganesh Yadav, Raktima Mukherjee and Prodyut Bhattarcharya 1997. *Group Sensitisation and Participatory Rural Appraisal: Process Documentation of Training for Indian Foresters*, Inter-India Publications, D-17 Raja Garden, New Delhi 110 015.

RRA Notes 1-21 subsequently PLA Notes 22-28 continuing, International Institute for Environment and Development, 3 Endsleigh Street. London WCIH ODD (and issue 15 on Wealth Ranking).

Samaranayake, Mallika 1994. *Institutionalizing Participatory Approaches*, paper presented at the "Dare to Share" Fair, Participatory Learning Approaches in Development Cooperation, 20 21 September 1994, GTZ, Eschborn, Germany.

Senge, Peter 1990. *The Fifth Discipline: the art and practice of the learning organisation*, Doubleday, USA (1992 edition Random House, London).

Shah, Meera Kaul and Khadija Bourarach 1995. *Participatory Assessment of Women's Problems and Concerns in Morocco*, Report submitted to the World Bank, first draft, February.

Teixeira, Lynne and Fiona Chamambers 1995. *Child Support in Small Towns in the Eastern Cape*, Black Sash Advice Office, Port Elizabeth, October.

Thompson, John 1995. "Participatory Approaches in Government Bureaucracies: Facilitating the Process of Institutional Change" *World Development* vol 23 no 9 pp 1521-1554, September.

Tillmann, Hermann J. 1993. VIPP: *Visualisation in Participatory Programmes: A manual for facilitators and trainees in participatory group events*, UNICEF, P.O. Box 58, Dhaka 1000, Bangladesh.

UNDP 1996. *UNDP's 1996 Report on Human Development in Bangladesh: A Pro-Poor Agenda*. Volumen 3 Poor People's Perspectives, UNDP, Dhaka.

Uphoff, Norman 1992. *Learning from Gal Oya: Possibilities for Participatory Development and Post-Newtonian social science*, Cornell University Press, Ithaca and London.

World Bank 1995. *World Bank Participation Sourcebook, Environment Department Papers*, The World Bank, June.

12. Action Research and the Management and Systems Sciences

Robert L. Flood
Center for Systems Studies
University of Hull, United Kingdom

In this paper I explore the possibility of a complementary relationship between action research and the management and systems sciences. Action research has many strengths, for example, in the way it develops relationships between social science research and the concerns and needs of people in society. The management and systems sciences also have many strengths, for example, in the way they promote necessary efficiency and effectiveness in organizational processes and structure. Although establishing different platforms for change, the two do share a common endeavor of organizational and societal improvement. Thus, establishing some kind of complementary relationship between the two platforms might broaden action/management and deepen research/sciences, making change and "improvement" more likely.

Traditionally, although not exclusively, the two "disciplines" have enjoyed a less than a respectful relationship. Action research has viewed much of what goes on in the management and systems sciences as instrumental in serving the needs of experts and decision takers who are divorced from the concerns and needs of people in society. Rational thinking, hypothetico-deductivism and empirical analytical studies separate the means of study from a subject to be studied, even when the subject is people who are also the means. On this score, the management and systems sciences have been little impressed by action research's deep involvement of the researcher in that being researched, arguing that it leads to sophistry rather than objective rational science. Substantiated repeatable observation, it is argued, is reduced in action research to inductive, partially transferable, ephemeral social theories. Crucial technical issues are neglected. Even worse, theory is written up in the first person which is mere assertion and opinion.

These disagreements are of an epistemological nature. Action research does not easily accept the validity of knowledge generated by the management and systems sciences and viceversa. Attempting to harmonize their epistemologies is barely feasible and no way desirable. A more productive avenue hypothesized here is that strengths in each discipline may be harnessed by referring them to an holistic epistemology.

Tangential literature helps set the scene. A sample of two is considered. In order of presentation they are Checkland(1) from the systems sciences and Levin from action research(2).

Checkland consistently presents his work on soft systems methodology as a form of action research. In a section called Understanding Rational Intervention In Human Affairs-Checkland (4) notes that with purposeful human action there is always the question of what intellectual framework makes the action meaningful. Linking ideas and their use in action distinguishes a basic set of ideas from a process for applying those ideas in an organized way. There are some linked ideas in a framework F, a way of applying these ideas M, and an application area A. After employing M there is reflection on what learning has been acquired, learning about all three elements F, M and A. This, Checkland argues, is a very general model of the organized use of rational thought and is a form of action research. In the management and systems sciences, he suggests, M has begun to change becoming more an interpretive process, as in soft systems methodology (3,4).

Soft systems methodology through this brand of action research has invited further consideration. Reflection on F, M and A, where M is soft systems methodology, has offered only tenuous interest in problematising the controlling position of experts and decision takers (e.g., 5,7). A new strand to research in the management and systems sciences, called critical systems thinking, emerged that fostered a new F by problematizing knowledge-power dynamics (e.g., 5 8, and under the name critical systems thinking, 9-11). Where F in soft systems methodology explored interpretive theory, F in critical systems thinking began to explore emancipatory theory.

Levin (2) inquired into the possible relationship between critical systems thinking and action research. He declared the task difficult since he sought commensurable variables in two traditions that hardly refer to each other. There was almost no common ground established through using the same literature, Levin observed. He thus developed a set of variables by which to advance comparison. Through an analysis of the relationship among theory, people and practice, Levin came up with three central questions that both address in the meaning construction process:

- Is theory understood and based on people's interests?
- Are research questions relevant for people?
- Are people emancipated to act in their own interest?

Levin thus concluded that action research and critical systems thinking "are carved out of the same log". They share a similar F, M and A, using Checkland's terminology. Yet there remains a notable variance between the two that is uncovered below.

It is possible to identify three themes that run through critical systems thinking (10): critique, emancipation and pluralism. These are summarised by Schecter (12) roughly as follows:

- Critical systems thinking began by constructing critiques of extant approaches to management and systems science, examining their theoretical foundations, their history, assumptions embedded in them and who they serve.
- Critiques led to increasing awareness of coercive contexts, those characterized by perpetuation of patterns of social relationships through knowledge-power plays. Very few critiqued strands of management and systems science had much to say on this score. Because of this, critical systems thinkers sent out a call for an explicitly emancipatory approach with the aim of transforming such relationships.
- Critical systems thinking developed vigorous and healthy critiques on extant forms of management and systems science, but did not advocate replacing or subsuming them just because of a growing interest in emancipatory practice. Instead, critical systems thinking made a further commitment to a complementarist path, where the potential of each approach is determined in action contexts.

Levin's three core questions, that both traditions address, cluster most obviously under critical systems' themes of critique and emancipation. The variance (mentioned earlier) is that critical systems thinking also has a commitment to investigate possible complementarity between different Fs an Ms, a commitment that is not obviously at the forefront of action research. That is not to say that action researchers are unaware of the issue, as evidenced by Whyte et al.(13) who stress, "The complexity of the world around us demands the deployment of a variety of techniques and strong intellectual and methodological discipline, not a commitment to the hegemony of a single research modality". It is just that action research has not as yet explored in detail this issue.

The remainder of this paper looks into critical systems' interest in complementarity as such, and through this investigates a possible complementary relationship between action research and the management and systems sciences. In so doing it develops a possible F and M, leading to a particular perception of A. In fact, it proposes an holistic perpective of F, M and A.

PURPOSES

To start, it may be instructive to explore a range of different purposes P, that action researchers and management and systems scientists pursue. What purpose P do these researchers/scientist assume in action A, driven by a methodology M that reflects an intelletual framework F? To facilitate this exploration some form of categorization is inevitable. The categorization adopted herein mirrors four main research strands, or purposes, that can be located in one or both of action research and the management and systems sciences. There are four purposes named in the following categorization: efficiency of systems of processes, effectiveness of systems of meanings and achieving fairness in knowledge-power plays. Each main purpose is probed below in the order just given.

Systems of processes are commnly the core interest of management and systems sciences. Methodology is constructed to guide action with the purpose of making processes more efficient. Efficiency here means to work without any unnecessary waste in time or resources. The exact nature of the purpose may differ however. For example, quality management, represented by Kaizen (14) seeks continuous incremental improvement in efficiency.

Meanwhile, business process reengineering (15-19) searches for possible radical improvement in efficiency. There is, then, a spectrum of purposes from incremental improvement to radical improvement.

Interestingly, business process reengineering is said by some commentators to have replaced quality management in the 1990s. A complementarist position, however, assumes that each one pursues a purpose that may have some relevance. It is a matter of encouranging people to explore and to interpret each purpose in aech action contex and to make an informed decision in this way about the relevance of each one. This avoids control through universal decisions of external commentators about what efficiency means.

Systems of structure are another focus of the management and systems sciences. Structure is often discussed in terms of competing models. Methodology can be extrapolated from models, for example, in the way Stafford Beer did with his viable system model. The viable system model (20,21) is translated into organizational effectiveness. Effectiveness here means relevance in structure that facilitates achievement of choices.

There are many optional structures discussed in the literature of the management and systems sciences and organizational analysis. Bureaucracy offers a form of hierarchy built with systems of procedures that aim to be comprehensive and seamless (23-25). Democratic hierarchy modified the procedures of bureaucracy, building in a circular element to enable people to be directly involved at three levels: the one in which they work, the one above and the one below (26-28). This encourages greater democratic involvement of people in issues that affect them. Much stronger reactions to bureaucracy have given rise to larger scale modifications and to new forms of structure. Viable system organisation (20-22, 29-30) establishes a new ideal form of recursive model for structure with its own as free as possible whilst maintaining viability procedures. Adhocracy (24) relaxes on formal procedures and hence considerably loosens structure. Postmodernism, perhaps the strongest of all reactions, is antagonistic toward procedures and cohesive, solidified structures, yet ironically implies "freeing" procedures of its own hopefully to help people become procedure free (cf. 31-35, 60). A spectrum of purposes seems to characterize these modifications/transformations, from procedure free to procedure bound structures. Versions of structure have mushroomed at points on this spectrum. Again, a complementarist position suggests that it is a matter of encouraging people to explore each purpose in the action context and to make an informed decision in this way about the relevance of each one and how to proceed.

We have explored so far systems of processes and systems of structure. The purposes associated with these approaches are technically oriented. These approaches are termed fuctionalism, associated with mechanistic and biological metaphors and a naively objetive view of things. Emerging from a critique of which they may use conversation to engage with one another, this gives some meaning to the concept and practice of debate. With postmodern debate, however, everything is provisional. Cautions are continually raised about the possibility of assimilation. The purpose is to maintain tensionful toleration between systems of meanings.

Approaches reviewed above that explore systems of meanings, aim to come to a considered decision with the purpose of achieving some kind of understanding that enables choices for action to be made. The spectrum of purposes here ranges from consensus through accommodation to tolerance. Complementarism informed decision in this way about the relevance of each one.

A phenomenological inspiration was behind the development of a number of approaches inspired by critical theory (modernist and postmodernist) that are concerned with emancipation. Emancipatory approaches are directed at systems of knowledge-power plays with the purpose of bringing about fairer practice.

There are several members of the family of action research approaches that direct attention to systems of knowledge-power plays. One of these is called collaborative inquiry (51-53). Collaborative inquiry is a way of training individuals and developing communities toward a consciousness of future participation. Co-inquirers present knowledge and ideas that they have as well as the view of the purpose of the inquiry. This involves problematizing power. Co-inquirers then engage in a set of agreed actions, recording and interpreting the process and the outcomes. This is followed by further engagement with preconceptions. Co-inquirers reassemble, reconsider their original propositions and consider modifications and further questions that are raised. Action and reflection continue, ideally until questions are fully answered in communities. Tension, caused to a considerable extent by the problematization of power, contributes to the development of both. The purpose is a desire to discover better (fairer) ways for people to live together.

Another member of the action research family is self-reliant participatory action research (54-56). It is meant for members of society who are disadvantaged. The idea is first to stimulate awareness of the capacity to transform the relations of knowledge as a priority, the consciously shift patterns of power that are buttressed by forms of knowledge creation. The process involves subverting top-down forms of knowledge relationship. Self-development begins by engaging in socio-economic activities that help to transform relations of knowledge production. This involves challenging the way in which support is received from, for example, state bodies. The purpose is defense of multiple and cherished ways of life and, thus, resistance against homogenization.

Examples of approaches relevant to this argument but not covered here in discussions that have questioned whether complemantarity is theoretically feasible or not. I will expand on this concern below.

Each category in Figure 1 can be thought of as a paradigm offering different Fs and differents Ms. Complementarity assumes people are able to move between different Fs and different Ms. Academic debate on this matter has generated two theses, a commensurability thesis and an incommensurability thesis. Recently a third option has been formulated, an (in) commensurability thesis (60). These theses are summarized below.

Commensurability promises to hold in the frame many different Fs and Ms. How can choice be made between different Fs and different Ms? This will depend on the meaning ascribed to commensurability. Commensurability is often thought to mean measurement by a common standard; or, in other words, the reconciliation and integration of different Fs and different Ms according to some given P. Reconciliation and integration, however, carry more than a suggestion that Fs and Ms must end up denatured, surely being reduced in meaning to comply with the P of the measurement standard.

Incommensurability on the other hand means that there is no common measurement standard, no meaningful way of comparing different Fs and different Ms. They are fundamentally different and that is that. Action in A following choice of F and M, therefore, can result in only one thing to avoid contradiction. The result of choice appears to be nothing more than an arbitrary adherence to a preferred P. Both commensurability and incommensurability therefore tends to reduce to one P.

The third thesis is that of *(in)commensurability* (60). This adds an important proviso. Tension between different Fs and different Ms, as modes of knowing and intervening in organizational and societal affairs, needs to be kept in consciousness and radical differences acknowledged. Keeping radical differences in consciousness allows us to reformulate the relationship between the apparently incomparable Fs and Ms they equip people with. The term (in)commensurability, therefore, is useful only insofar as it allows people to keep in consciousness diversity and the radical differences in P, which opens up a wide set of choices. To highlight this feature of choice-making brackets are placed within the word (in)commensurability. In doing this, emphasis is placed in equal amounts on experiential knowledge (experience through action in A), practical knowledge (how to do things in the form of Ms) and propositional knowledge (theories as different Fs).

PROCESS

The (in)commensurability thesis introduced above suggests that holistic action follows tensionful processes of knowledge generation. A potentially useful realization of this is the reflexive process of critique, choice and action (cf. 61). A process can be extended into three parts:

- Boundary critique, choice and action, in which an action context is temporarily created by the act of bounding.

- Issue/dilemma critique, choice and action, in which the action context temporarily bounded and the boundary are explored and issues/dilemmas are surfaced.
- Approach critique, choice and action, in which the four spectrums of purposes are explored in the action context established by "boundary" and issue/dilemma critique and choice, yielding a thoroughly informed unfolding methodology design in action.

Each of these three interrelated processes of critique, choice and action, are now discussed in the order presented above.

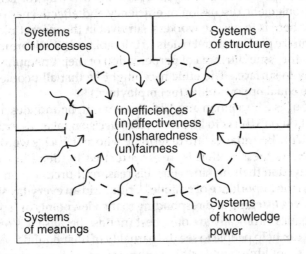

Figure 1

BOUNDARY CRITIQUE, CHOICE AND ACTION

Boundary critique, choice and action is the process in which reality is temporarily created in the form of an action context by the choice of a boundary (refer to back discussion around Figure 1). Churchman (62-65) criticized the traditional systems view that boundaries exist in the natural order of physical, biological and social things, arguing that they are mental constructs. Mental constructs determine what is in view and to be taken account of, and what is out of view and therefore excluded from consideration.

Boundary setting will therefore determine issues/dilemmas of concern and purposes to pursue in defining an action context. Ulrich (66) suggested that power may be the drawing force in boundary setting. Power may have more or less insidious explanations.

The drawing of boundaries indicates both an ethical stance and values being pursued. Choice of boundaries therefore is ethical and value-laden even when they are not purposely etched out. Midgley (67) presses home this point making reference to unemployed people. Drawing a boundary that excludes unemployed people from organizational analysis opens up the way for seemingly unproblematic discussion of efficiency and effectivenes. A likely ethic here is to ensure workers' survival in the market place or to maximize profit to shareholders. If unemployed people are included, then the issue/dilemma of perpetuation of their unemployment is likely to surface. The ethic here might be that all people should have equal opportunities for employment.

So, as Churchman and Ulrich point out, boundaries declare a position on who is to be involved as decision taker, as expert and as client. Boundaries also determine who, in Ulrich's words, are to be the witnesses, that is, those affectted by decisions but not involved in their making. For this reason Churchman and Ulrich stress the importance of critique. Critique in an everyday situation involves listening and responding to the viewpoints of "enemies". "Enemies" ironically are our best friends because it is only they who can help people to see the partiality of their boundary choices. Or, as Gouldner (68) put it, we are informed if we listen to "bad news" that does not conform to our bounded rationality.

The dilemma with "dilemmas", of course, is that they are insoluble. That is not to say people should be gloomy and slip into free lives of experiences in which we do nothing with dilemmas, as if this is a meaningful choice. Free living, ironically, can easily succumb to existing knowledge-power plays. Dilemmas, then, are reduced and controlled in this way. Researchers can try and do something about this by encouraging deeper exploration of dilemmas and ways of sensitively managing them.

"Boundary" critique, choice and action, begins this process since, as we have seen it is a process that problematizes ways of bounding dilemmas, drawing out possible ways of thinking about them. Discussion in the next section on "approach" critique, choice and action, problematizes ways of managing dilemmas, accepting their insoluble nature.

APPROACH CRITIQUE, CHOICE AND ACTION

"Approach" critique, choice and action explores purposes to be pursued in the action context established by "boundary" and "issue and dilemma" critique, choice, and action, yielding a thoroughly informed methodology design for action. Choice does not mean selection of one or more methodology. Choice does mean design of methology in action. Methodology design unfolds through a process called triple loop learning (60). The three loops circle around the four spectrums of purposes generating a discourse of critique, choice and action.

The first loop of learning circles around technical issues/ dilemmas of (in)efficiency of systems of processes and (in)effectiveness of systems of structure. Discourse evolves around process-based approaches and their purposes as well as a range of structural proposals that suggest structural arrangements which processes flow. The center of learning asks, Are we doing things right ? The question is, How should we do it?

The second loop of learning circles around issues/dilemmas of (un)sharedness of understanding in systems of meanings. Discourse evolves around possible interpretive-based purposeful action. Interpretive-based action is a reaction to an obsession, for example, with finding processual and structural solutions that preclude the intersubjective-debate processes necessary to meaningfully define efficiency and effectiveness. Interpretivism recognizes that definition of process and structure is problematic because there are many different viewpoints on what is perceived to be relevant. A new center of learning is therefore a set that asks, Are we doing the right things? This specific question in other words is, what should we do?

The third loop of learning circles around issues/dilemmas of (un)fairness systems of knowledge-power plays. Discourse evolves around the purpose of fair(er) practice. The reaction here is to the obsessive foci of design-based and debate-based action. Definition of purpose from How? -type learning is considered to be problematic because it runs the risk of definition production yielding results that are unfair to some, if not many people. Definition of (in Ulrich's view) the critical and systemic ideas are inadequate without each other. The critical idea is that any assumption made in boundary setting must be open to question thus facilitating airing of all viewpoints. The systemic idea is that boundaries provisionally have to be drawn so that meaningful critique may be conducted. Critique without the systemic idea is expansionary. The systemic idea without critique takes ever hardening boundaries.

Secondary boundary setting is an important recent development (69). The argument is that boundaries are never clear cut giving black and white vision. Between what is in view and what is not in view is a grey area that can be thought of as a marginalized zone. Marginalization in boundary setting is the use of more than one boundary. There are primary and secondary boundaries.

Critique of boundaries involves making the secondary boundary explicit and making choices between boundaries. There are two recurring options here. The first is to choose a primary boundary and deal with marginal issues/dilemmas in relation to it by choosing a secondary boundary and, possibly, to choose a new secondary boundary.

The process of secondary boundary choice must be sensitized to a new issue. Marginal elements can be thought of as "sacred or profane" (69). Sacred means valued, whilst profane means devalued. This phenomenon may have its roots in culture. Culture is an intersubjectively produced system of meanings. Relevant features of culture include myths and metaphors, rights and rituals, saying and stories and, consequently, relevant issues/dilemmas for debate. For example, Midgley emphasizes rituals in systems of meanings and the danger that they determine the sacredness or profanity of issues/dilemmas and hence perpetuate a power over marginalized people or things.

The example given by Midgley (67:6) of unemployed people, mentioned above, is elaborated on later in his paper (67:13-15). The customer is introduced into the discussion, i.e., the boundary is redrawn. Midgley talks about the profane status of the marginalized unemployed people within the mainstream of society and the most often sacred status of marginalized customers (as traditionally defined). The status of marginalized elements, as sacred or profane, significantly influences the relevance of issues/ dilemmas for debate relating to those elements and, subsequently, purposes that might be chosen and acted upon.

With boundary critique and choice, in summary, "We should always remain critically aware that we live within what we describe as a dynamic web of boundaries, marginalizations, ethical conflicts, and value judgements." (69:13). If we are critical about this then we may recognize the extent of partiality in our choices, for example, of issues/dilemmas that we decide to act upon. The scene is here set for issue and dilemma critique, choice and action.

Purpose from-What? type learning is considered to be problematic because debate is easily distorted by, say, coercive forces, meaning that debate is not open and free, is not participative, and decisions made are not fair on those who are coerced. A new center of learning is required that asks, Is rightness buttressed by mightiness, and/or mightiness buttressed by rightness? This specific questions is, Why should we do it?

Clearly, there can be much conflict over what is considered to be "the right" center of learning to adopt. Advocates of each loop may attempt to win people over by "demonstrating" its superiority. One complementarist attempt to overcome this conflict that reflects the (in)commensurability thesis introduced earlier is triple loop learning (60).

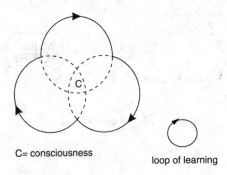

C= consciousness

loop of learning

Figure 2. C= Consciousness

Triple loop learning wants to generate discourse from all three centres of learning, the purposes they pursue and to preserve the diversity each one brings forward. It does this by bringing together the three questions from the three loops into one overall awareness: Are we doing things right, and are we doing the right things, and is rightness buttressed by mightiness and/or mightiness buttressed by rigthness? There is a new reflexive consciousness as interventionists continually loop between the three questions (Figure 2). The looping helps people to become widely informed, especially as the discourse is related to issues/dilemmas that they face in their lives. Triple loop learning then manages the diversity of purposes in the centers of learning through purposeful methodology design in the action context, that in turn enhances management of the diversity of issues/dilemmas to be dealt with. In this way triple loop learners operate intelligently and responsibly. Their whole consciousness becomes more than the sum of its parts.

The reflexive process of critique, choice and action (focusing on boundaries, issues/dilemmas and approaches) it is suggested, is an holistic process (see Figure 3). Such a notion begs the question of what, fundamentally, is implied here by holism.

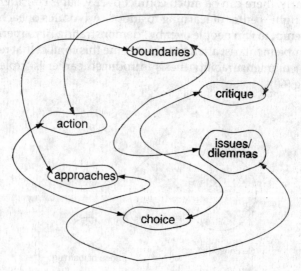

Figure 3

HOLISM

We people "bear the universe in our beings as the universe bears us its being. The two have a total presence to each other and to that deeper mystery out of which both the universe and ourselves have emerged (70:132)"; quoted by Reason after he had noted that the human race is "not an alien species set on earth out of nowhere" (52:15). Because of this, "phenomena as wholes can never be fully known for the very reason that we are part of them, leading us to acknowledge and respect the great mystery that envelops our knowing" (52:13). In other words, knowledge will always be bounded, partial and subjective, and for that reason alone our lives will be always surrounded by mystery.

This way of thinking contrasts with the dualist consciousness that currently characterises Western thought. Western thought separates science from life and thus sees the researcher as an outside observer of a world of separate physical, biological and social objects. Science studies phenomena as entities that can be identified as separate, real wholes, operating through causal relationships. "The scientific way separates intellect from experience, so that knowledge that comes in propositional form is valued more highly than intuitive, practical, affective, analogical or spiritual knowledge (52). It also leads to immediate conscious purpose being valued more highly than systemic wisdom. This reinforces the tendency to think in terms of parts rather than wholes, things rather than processes" (52:12), problems rather than issues/dilemmas, solutions rather than ongoing tension, and favored purpose rather than optional purposes.

The scientific way, however, does bear considerable although not necessarily total relevance to the physical world. That part of the whole labelled "non-living things" is demonstrably well characterized as physical relationships of cause and effect. Propositional knowledge of this sort has made possible new ways of living molded by technological developments that are at the same time impressive and oppressive. Most of us are impressed, in one way or another, by the long-haul Boeing 747-400s that transport non stop passengers from continent to continent, or by powerful computer hardware and software reproducing virtually what knowledge we have about our universe as well as (and in the guise of) make believe worlds, or by the electronic highway that brings millions of people together without them having to budge an inch. But many of us are oppressed by changes in biological and social behaviour coupled to these technological developments. Oppression is primarily a result of science and technology becoming an obsession of planners and decision takers who have lost touch with other people and themselves. They have lost touch with systemic wisdom.

Obsessive science has thus led to an artificial duality that, whilst helping to characterize the physical world, often has been damaging when applied to biological and social worlds, where order is better characterized as patterns of relationships. The scientific duality has fragmented these worlds. It has alienated the parts from the patterns of which they are a part and which are part of them. The richness and mystique of the biological and social worlds are reduced to a mindblowingly limited model of the type "a caused b".

Obsessive science has led human beings to value the biological world from a "distance yet have little idea, and no felt experience, of the damage that (technologically stimulated) patterns of consumption and waste continue to have (in it)" (52:12). This is doubly concerning because, "The body and the natural world are deeply connected: our body is that piece of wilderness that we carry around with us all the time, a living ecology which provides a home to many creatures and life events, which may be in balance or out of balance" (52:13). We are damaging ourselves in damaging the biological world. This implies the urgent need for a participative mentality in the sense that "civilized life depends directly on the balance of natural living processes, and (participation will) take us back to experience of body and of the wild" (52:13).

Obsessive science has also had a dramatic and direct impact on social behavior, "if we start from a notion of an individual autonomous self, we must from body, masculine from feminine: the whole fragmentation of Western epistemology can be seen as starting from the establishment of self" (52:11). "The separation of knower from known implies a separation of self from other and researcher from subject" (52:11), and purpose from people. This leads to "alienation, the split that characterizes modern experience" (52:10). We isolate ourselves through obsessive science. This highlights, Reason says, the urgent need for a reflexive mentality to heal the alienation and to make things whole again.

The overarching purpose of holistic thinking is to bring together in our thoughts and actions the physical, biological and social worlds, as parts of a whole. Characterizing the physical world in terms of causal relationships, then, is a legitimate part of this endeavor only for as long as it does not concretize causality and duality in all thoughts and actions. Equally, characterizing the social world in terms of experiences and differences is also a legitimate part of this endeavor for as long as it does not concretize relativism in all thoughts, and implies the need for a standard of choice with a mentality that falls neither to absolutism of obsessive science nor relativism of free living.

A standard that suits such a reflexive mentality is, "the chances people have to make widely informed and locally contingent choices in the process of managing issues/dilemmas that characterize organizational and societal affairs" (60).

So, what does all this imply when it comes to gaining knowledge of the world, that is, when it comes to epistemology? Here I return to Reason (52) and his extended epistemology. Knowledge has much to do with experience. People experience the physical, biological and social worlds, giving rise to experiential knowledge. People also have practical knowledge about how particular things can be done in those worlds, consolidated in skills and competencies and knowledge about purposes and how they may be pursued. And then there is propositional knowledge in the form of statements and theories about the physical, biological and social worlds. The link between experiential knowledge and propositional knowledge is made by presentational knowledge (71), which suggests we first order "our tacit experiential knowledge of the world into spatio-temporal patterns of imagery, and then symbolize our sense of their meaning in movement, sound, color, shape, line, poetry, dream and story" (52:52).

Knowing and indeed acting, then, can be understood by way of an epistemological process whereby four types of knowledge interplay: experiential, practical, propositional and presentational knowledge. There is no hierarchical order in which the epistemological process introduces these knowledges. Each type of knowledge is of equal importance. This is holism at a most fundamental level.

CONCLUSION

Action research and management and systems sciences might usefully come together to provide a potent force in a common endeavor of organizational and societal "improvement". One place to begin investigation of this possibility is by surfacing the purposes that each one has generated. In doing this, four possible spectrums of purposes can be located: continuous through to radical improvement in efficiency of systems of processes; procedure bound through to procedure free systems of structure seeking improvement in effectiveness; consensus through accommodation to tolerance in/between systems of meanings; and might through to right as ways of achieving fairness in the face of knowledge-power plays. These purposes as a whole encourage systemic appreciation of issues/dilemmas to be managed and, through methodology, possible ways of managing them. A sense of (in)commensurability between them may be achieved for as long as these purposes are kept in mind in a tensionful way, suggesting a possible means of managing organizational and societal affairs. This means avoiding bias sometimes found in management and systems sciences toward propositional and in particular practical knowledges. Equally, it means avoiding bias sometimes found in action research towards experiential knowledge. A possible complementary relationship between action research and the management and systems sciences is proposed in this way that hangs on Reason´s extended epistemology, which has holism as its essential quality.

The argument of this paper is now consolidated through a blend of Checkland's (19) terminology and Reason's (52) extended epistemology.

• F, linked ideas in a framework, propositional knowledge in the form of statements and theories. Phenomena can never be known fully because we are a part of them. Life therefore will be surrounded by mystery. Life as mystery is meaningfully approached through systemic wisdom. Systemic wisdom means thinking in terms of wholes whilst keeping awareness of their bounded, partial and subjective nature. Awareness comes through a reflexive mentality.

- M, a way of applying F practical or instrumental knowledge about purposes to pursue and how they may be pursued by employing methodology. There is a number of possible things to do to apply F. These involve critique, choice and action in boundary judgments, issue/dilemma surfacing and exploration of purposes to pursue realized in unique methodology design.
- A, application area experiential knowledge is acquired that is ordered in the form of presentational knowledge that presents tacit experiential knowledge to propositional thought. Experiences relate (at least) to (in)efficiencies of systems of processes, (in)effectiveness of systems of structure, (un)sharedness in/between systems of meaning and (un)fairness coming from systems of knowledge-power plays.

If nothing else, this paper highlights potential advantages to all in developing a complementary relationship between action research and the management and systems sciences. Advantages may come through and improved choices for action/management and research/sciences. By definition, this paper invites further action/management and work on research/sciences to be done in the pursuit of an adequate, workable complementary relationship between the two disciplines brought into focus herein.

REFERENCES

1. Checkland P.B. 1985. From optimizing to learning: A development of systems thinking for the 1990s. *Journal of the operational Research Society*, 36, 757-767.
2. Levin M. 1994. *Action Research and critical systems thinking: Two icons carved out of the same log. Systems Practice*, 7, 25-42.
3. Checkland P.B. 1991. *Systems Thinking, Systems Practice*, Wiley, Chichester.
4. Checkland P.B. and Scholes J. 1990. *Soft Systems Methodology in Action*, Wiley, Chichester.
5. Thomas A.R. and Lockett M. 1991. *Marxism and systems research: Values in practical action.* In Flood R.L. and Jackson M.C. (eds) *Critical Systems Thinking: Directed Readings*, Wiley, Chichester. Originally published

1979 in Proceedings of the 23rd Annual Conference of the International Society for General Systems Research.

6. Mingers J. 1980. Toward an appropiate social theory for applied systems thinking: Critical theory and soft systems methodology. *Journal of Applied Systems Analysis*, 7, 41-49.

7. Jackson M.C. 1985. *Social systems theory and practice: The need for a critical approach. Journal of General Systems Theory*, 10, 135-151.

8. Flood R.L 1990. *Liberating Systems Theory*. Plenum, New York.

9. Flood R.L. and Jackson M.C. 1991. *Creative Problem Solving: Total Systems Intervention*. Wiley, Chichester.

10. Flood R.L. and Jackson M.C. eds., 1991. *Critical Systems Thinking: Directed Readings*. Wiley, Chichester.

11. Flood R.L. and Jackson M.C. eds., 1996. *Critical Systems Thinking: Current Reaserch and Practice*. Wiley, Chichester.

12. Schecter D. 1991. Critical systems thinking in the 1980s: a connective summary. In Flood R.L. and Jackson M.C. eds., *Critical Systems Thinking: Directed Readings*. Wiley, Chichester

13. Whyte W.F., Greenwood D.J. and Lazes P. 1991. *Participatory Action Research*. Sage, London.

14. Imai M. 1991. Kaisen. McGraw-Hill, Singapore.

15. Hammer M. and Champy J. 1993. *Reengineering the Corporation: A Manifesto for Business Revolution*. Nicholas Brealey, London.

16. Born G. 1994. *Process Management to Quality Improvement*. Wiley, Chichester.

17. Cheryl Currid and Co. 1994. *Reengineering Toolkit*. Wiley, Chichester.

18. Obelensky N. 1994. *Practical Business Re-engineering*. Wiley, Chichester.

19. Ould M.A. 1994. *Business Processes*. Wiley, Chichester.

20. Beer S. 1979. *Heart of Organisation*. Wiley, Chichester.

21. Beer S. 1981. *Brain of the Firm*. Wiley, Chichester.

22. Beer S. 1985. *Diagnosing the System for Organisations*. Wiley, Chichester.

23. Gouldner A.W. 1954. *Patterns of Industrial Bureaucracy*. Free Press, New York.

24. Mintzberg H. 1979. *The Structuring of Organisations*. Prentice Hall, Englewood Cliffs, NJ.

25. Weber M. 1947. *The Theory of Social and Economic Organisation*. Oxford University Press, New York.

26. Ackoff R.L. 1994. *The Democratic Organisation*. Oxford University Press, New York.

27. Lartin-Drake J.M. and Curran C.R. 1996. All together now: the circular organisation in a university hospital. Part I Planning and design. *Systems Practice*, 9, 391-402.

28. Lartin-Drake J.M. and Curran C.R. and Kruger N.R. 1996. All together now: the circular organisation in a university hospital. Part II Implementation. *Systems Practice*, 9, 403-420.

29. Espejo R. and Harnden R. eds., 1989. *The Viable System Model: Interpretations and Applications of Stafford Beer's VSM*. Wiley, Chichester.

30. Espejo R. and Schwaninger M. eds., 1993. *Organisational Fitness: CorporateEffectiveness Through Management Cybernetics*. Campus Verlag, New York.

31. Feyerabend P. 1975. *Against Method. Outline of an Anarchistic Theory of Knowledge*. New Left Books, London.

32. Foucault M. 1984. Interviews. In Rabinow P. (ed), *The Foucault Reader*. Random House, New York.

33. Foucault M. 1986. Disciplinary Power and Subjection. In Lukes S. (ed) *Power*. Basil Blackwell, Oxford.

34. Foucault M. 1990. *Interviews and other Writings, 1997-1984: Politics, Philosophy, Culture*. Edited with an introduction by Kritzman, L.D., Routledge, London.

35. Lyotard J.F. 1984. *The Postmodern Condition: A Report on Knowledge*. Manchester University Press, Manchester.

36. Whyte W.F. 1991. Introduction. In Whyte W.F. (ed) *Participatory Action Research*. Sage, London.

37. Whyte W.F. 1991. *Social Theory for Action*. Sage, London.

38. Whyte W.F. 1996. Emancipatory practice through the Sky River Project. *Systems Practice*, 9, 151-158.

39. Kingel S. and Martin A. eds., 1988. *A Fighting Chance: New Strategies To Save Jobs and Reduce Costs*. ILR Press, Cornell University.

40. Argyris C. 1973. *Double Loop Learning in Organizations*. Harvard Business Review, September-October.

41. Argyris C. and Schon D. 1974. *Theory in Practice*. Jossey-Bass, San Francisco.

42. Argyris C. and Schon D. 1985. *Strategy, Change and Defensive Routines*. Ballinger, Cambridge, Mass.

43. Argyris C. and Schon D. 1991. Participatory Action Research and Action Science Compared. In Whyte W.F. (ed), *Participatory Action Research*. Sage, Newbury Park, Ca.

44. Whyte W.F. 1991. Comparing PAR and Action Science. In Whyte WF (ed) *Participatory Action Research*. Sage, London.

45. Mason R.O. 1969. A dialectical approach to strategic planning. *Management Science*, 15, B403-14.

46. Mason R.O. and Mitroff I.I. 1981. *Challenging Strategic Planning Assumptions*. Wiley, New York.

47. Ackoff R.L. 1974. *Redesigning the Future*. Wiley, Chichester.

48. Ackoff R.L. 1981. *Creating the Corporate Future*. Wiley, New York.

49. Ackoff R.L. 1993. Idealized design: creative corporate visioning. OMEGA, 21, 401-410.
50. Magidson J. 1992. Systems practice in several communities in Philadelphia. *Systems Practice*, 5, 493-508.
51. Reason P. 1994. The Co-operative Inquiry Group. In Reason P. (ed) *Human Inquiry in Action*. Sage, London.
52. Reason P. 1994. Human Inquiry as Discipline and Practice. In Reason P. (ed) *Participation in Human Inquiry*. Sage, London.
53. Moggridge A. and Reason P. 1996. Human inquiry: Steps towards emancipatory practice. *Systems Practice.*, 9, 159-175.
54. Fals-Borda O. and Rahman M.A. eds., 1991. *Action and Knowledge: Breaking the Monopoly With Participatory Action Research*. Intermediate Technology Pubs / Apex Press, New York.
55. Fals-Borda O. 1996. Power/knowledge and emancipation. *Systems Practice*, 9, 177-181.
56. Rahman M.A. 1991. The Theoretical Standpoint of PAR. In Fals Borda O. and Rahman M.A. eds., *Action and Knowledge*. The Apex Press, New York.
57. McKay V.I. and Romm N.R.A. 1992. People's Education in Theoretical Perspective. Loongman, Cape Town.
58. Ulrich W. 1983. *Critical Heuristics of Social Planning: A New Approach to Practical Philosophy*. Haupt, Berne.
59. Ulrich W. 1988. Systems thinking, systems practice, and practical philosophy: a program of research. *Systems Practice*, 1, 137-164.
60. Flood R.L. and Romm N.R.A. 1996. *Diversity Management: Triple Loop Learning*. Wiley, Chichester.
61. Flood R.L. and Ulrich W. 1990. Testament to conversations on critical systems thinking between two systems practitioners. *Systems Practice*, 3, 7-29. Reprinted in Flood R.L. and Jackson M.C. eds., 1991. *Critical Systems Thinking: Directed Readings*. Wiley, Chichester.
62. Churchman C. West 1968. *Challenge to Reason*. McGraw Hill, New York.
63. Churchman C. West 1968. *The Systems Approach*. Delacorte Press, New York.
64. Churchman C. West 1971. *The Design of Inquiring Systems, Basic Concepts of Systems and Organisation*. Basic Books, New York.
65. Churchman C. West 1979. *The Systems Approach and its Enemies*. Basic Books, New York.
66. Ulrich W. 1988. Churchman's Process of Unfolding, its significance for policy analysis and evaluation. *Systems Practice*, 1, 415-428.
67. Midgley G. 1992. Pluralism and the legitimation of the systems sciences. *Systems Practice*, 5, 147-172.
68. Gouldner A.W. 1973. *The Coming Crisis of Western Sociology*. Heinemann, London.

69. Midgley G. 1992. The sacred and profane in critical systems thinking. *Systems Practice*, 5, 5-16.
70. Berry T. 1988. *The Dream of the Earth*. Sierra Club, San Francisco.
71. Heron J. 1992. *Feeling and Personhood: Psychology in Another Key*. Sage, London.

Editor's Note: The journal *Systems Practice* has been expanded of scope from the first issue of Vol. II, 1998 and its new title is *Systemic Practice and Action Research*, directed by Robert L. Flood.

PART III

THEORETICAL AND PRACTICAL EXPERIENCES

Orlando Fals Borda
Drawing on working-group speakers, rapporteurs and coordinators.

The formal invitation to the Congress on Participatory Convergence, distributed in 1995, identified three related dimensions of this idea: knowledge, space, and time, as factors of change for the advancement of peoples.

On the first day of the Congress, after Immanuel Wallerstein's exposition on the social invention of "geopolitical and transformational TimeSpace" as the basis of knowledge, those three dimensions were immediately and swiftly synthesized, and the revision then began to be reflected in the working-group discussions. Further reflections were presented by the other five general speakers (Heller, Max-Neef, Tandon, Chambers and Flood) and also by President Cardoso of Brazil, whose ideas have clear theoretical and practical implications for the responsibility we have as scientists and professionals to improve the sorry state of our societies and induce an urgent transformation of nations and the world at large.

Of course, the main motivation of the Congress continued to be to further the economic and political advancement of base communities in every country, meaning those groups exploited or oppressed by dominant systems, particularly by globalizing capitalism. We repeated the classical review of the links between theory and practice, considered this time from the perspective of participatory research. We admitted that deterioration of the world situation allowed of no delay, and this became apparent by comparing the discussions at the Congress with those that took place at the First Symposium in 1977. Old demons reappeared before us in new and more appalling guises, and were identified and denounced by the delegates: violence and paramilitarism, developmentalism and neoliberalism, media manipulation and dissimulation, breakdown of morals and laws.

It seemed logical therefore to steer towards a vademecum of participatory research for socio-economic, political and cultural action. Fortunately we did not, for it would have proved a counterproductive and chaotic exercise. Instead, as the event proceeded, clarifications were offered calmly on theories, concepts, experiential situations and fieldwork methods that we brought up in formal working-group discussions or in corridor conversations; they could be said to represent the ideal of conceiving a new humanism.

In the following sections (and footnotes) I go on to summarize and comment on the most significant points I consider to have been made about theory and practice in the general presentations and group discussions. I do so on my own responsibility and by way of reviewing "the state of the art" of participatory research in today's world.

13. THEORETICAL FOUNDATIONS

Almost from the inception of our movement in the seventies, Husserl's phenomenology, or existentialism, was identified as the seminal source of our orientations.[1] From Husserl, through José Ortega y Gasset, we inherited the idea that the phenomenon is a given, in terms of a "lived experience" or *Erfahrung*, and is not concealed but expressed in nature. To reach the essence of things we rely on actual description and hermeneutics, and recover the intentionality of acts. From that source we derived also an emphasis on ethics and commitment in research and politics; this emphasis was reaffirmed by the Cartagena Congress.

CERTAIN PREMISES

1. We were greatly aided on these capital points by our colleagues the philosophers in the working group coordinated by Guillermo Hoyos.[2] They insisted on relying on *practical reason* as a matrix that generates arguments for intervening in reality, especially the reality of our democracies, and on continuing to "think on the countries" in a fruitful dialogue moderated by philosophy as a *theory of communicative action* —the philosophy proposed by Jürgen Habermas. Practical reason continues to be reason, claiming as it does the capacity to present arguments on ethical and political matters that lend themselves to agreement and consensus being reached about minimums.[3]

2. This group also reviewed conceptions about holders of the types of knowledge that are built through daily experience and common sense. Recalling Gramsci and his famous remark that "all men are philosophers", the group gave its blessing, in his fashion, to the participatory proposition of the seventies on the

sum or *conjunction of academic and popular knowledge*, which may become an element of the new scientific paradigm.[4] Such academic knowledge would not be the elitist, segmented type usually found in academic departments but another, less arrogant, *multi-and inter-disciplinary knowledge*. It would include historical, social and cultural dimensions and relevant aspects of the "hard" sciences, based on the study of specific "problems" of either a structural or everyday nature.

3. With regard to participatory research itself, presentations at the Congress employed the phenomenological expedient of breaking up the asymmetric Subject/Object relationship, to shape a *horizontal participating felt experience, or Subject/Subject "dialogical relationship"*, for investigation and action. This was viewed as a fundamental theoretical principle that had long been in force.[5]

4. The *breaking of this asymmetry* conceptually and in practical and existential terms began to be recognized as providing a creative potentiality for investigation and social, economic and political organization, for it required a profound change of personality and culture, something akin to a rebellion against routine, egoism and manipulation. We called this process *"existential commitment"*. Alejandro Sanz de Santamaría, a Colombian economist and rapporteur at the Congress (drawing on Davydd Greenwood of Cornell) concluded that this involved attending to a "spiritual dimension in research" which made us look within ourselves and thus helped us to go beyond the "fraudulent procedures" of conventional social research. Such symmetrical commitment to people's beliefs and wishes was also considered to be important in bringing about essential transformations for the benefit of their communities. During the Congress this idea of a horizontal, existential commitment was repeatedly mentioned as an ideological beacon and guiding light for discussion and action in building a *"countervailing power"* or "people's power".

5. Generally speaking, the conviction grew in Cartagena that we were right to rebel against what Thomas Kuhn defined as "normal science" and the "dominant paradigm" as pursued in established institutions. These are the working rules of logical

empiricists, positivists and functionalists, derived from the imitative influence that the "hard" sciences have exercised on social disciplines since the nineteenth century, and include the principles of objectivity and neutrality. We recalled that, starting from the brilliant works of Galileo, Newton and Descartes, the Enlightenment's reaction against scholasticism and superstition had, despite its merits, also led to continuation of another type of intellectual subordination and exploitation, represented this time by the elitist, oligarchical monopoly of knowledge. Indeed, it became necessary to dominate nature and civilize diverse "backward" peoples, and for the purpose the select, objective, neutral "advanced" investigators —always few in number and arrogant in their preferred ivory towers or as members of power groups—, had to place themselves outside and above the processes investigated and their "objects" or "targets".

As these attitudes of Cartesian dominance, idealized objectivity and value-neutrality in science had been rejected in our previous congresses and in countless works already published or in progress[6], no time was lost criticizing them anew in Cartagena. We felt that enough punishment had been inflicted on positivists by many of us as social scientists, non-linear quantum physicists, and chaos theorists. Instead, we reviewed possible radical alternatives that could lead us to another type of science inspired by a "holistic" or extended cosmology, based on "equivalent participation" or "symmetrical reciprocity".[7] That was the origin of a *holistic or extended epistemology* useful for our work. According to Peter Reason, a Congress rapporteur, holism is expressed by four kinds of interacting knowledge: experiential, practical, propositional and presentational knowledge.[8]

6. The reasons for adopting a holistic approach are well-known. Conducting participatory research means accepting that the research shall be in the nature of a *communicating interaction*, in which the researcher and researched learn from each other and build mutual trust through a process of dialogue. In this process the traditional division between objective and subjective knowledge no longer applies; standard guidelines for measuring and analyzing reality are fine-tuned or extended to include new criteria; the external observer's theoretical interests are balanced

by the local actors' desire to transform everyday practice; and an interdisciplinary approach is used. The result turns out to be as reliable and legitimate as any adduced for traditional research. And since the researcher is a part of the reality being investigated, he is involved as a committed actor who is in turn subject to self-analysis and being analyzed by others.

HERESY, SUBVERSION, LIBERATION: TOWARDS AN ALTERNATIVE ETHOS

1. The current homogenizing tendencies in the world, which paradoxically tend to create an ethos of uncertainty, call for integrity and originality in facing up to these problems to try and build a different world on a sound ethical basis or by articulating an *alternative ethos* through a new humanism. Manfred Max-Neef, recalling what we had read in G.V.S. De Silva, maintained at the Congress that with such aims in mind we had to become *heretics* and act like a swarm of mosquitoes (see Chapter 8). But as latter-day heretics we needed to learn the dominant languages, other codes and new technologies to foster "countervailing power" and succeed in our endeavors in the postmodern age. It was remarked by some that rather than thinking in terms of mosquitoes, which are liable to be dispersed by ventilators or killed off by insecticides, we could usefully emulate viruses, which operate even under the rhinoceros's hide.

2. The idea of exercising "countervailing power" within and under given systems or institutions led to re-emergence of the concept of *"moral subversion"*, introduced in the sixties by the personal contributions of Camilo Torres Restrepo and Ernesto Che Guevara. With reference to the recently published self-subversive essays of Albert O. Hirschman on economics[9], the controversial concept of moral subversion was touched on again during the Final Panel discussion, to remind us of the obligations we assume as participatory investigators to bring about changes for social justice in our struggle against uncertainty. We also reviewed this issue in discussing the negative tendencies in recent years to coopt Participatory Action Research (see Chapter 15).

3. In this connection, the Italian philosopher Giulio Girardi invited us in Paper 32 to reflect on the relationships between PAR and *liberation theology*. This recent major historical component, which has been losing prominence in some places for ecclesiastical reasons, continues to be valid according to many. Girardi asserted that participatory methodology should be a part of an alternative culture that was at the same time liberating. It was therefore essential to return to liberation theology's propositions of commitment.

4. Unlike what had occurred at the First Symposium in 1977, no strong Marxist arguments were heard on historical materialism or dialectics, although *Marx* continued to be revered for his undeniable contributions to our strivings. Statements were made in recognition of Gramsci and the concept of "organic intellectuals". *"Praxis"* was brought up again, but tied to the Aristotelian concept of *"phronesis"*, to prevent it from running loose with a headlong or unreflecting dynamism, and ensure it is undertaken with a sense of moral responsibility, good judgment and practical wisdom (see below). Current "normal" research was almost universally defined as just another piece of merchandise.

5. Discussion of the concept of *"participation"* as such followed along the lines indicated by Carole Pateman drawing on Rousseau, Owen and Mill, with additions from the anarchists Proudhon and Kropotkin and the educationalist John Dewey. It was always radically conceived of as a struggle against political and economic exclusion from exercising control over public resources. And rejection was expressed of liberal definitions such as that given by the political analyst Samuel Huntington, who reduces participation to a simple manipulation of the masses to obtain support for government proposals designed to maintain the status quo[10].

6. Freire's concept of *"consciousness raising"* was transmuted to a *"popular education"* that employs postmodern pedagogical techniques of communication inspired by philosophers such as Habermas ("communicative action"). The aim of consciousness raising, subsequently reassessed by Paulo Freire himself, has come to be social organization and intellectual training to

investigate and induce transformations beyond the school itself
but within the community. Its underpinnings would be the
propositions put forward by the English educator L. Stenhouse
in 1975 on starting the *"educator as investigator"* movement, which
has since spread vigorously throughout the world[11].

7. Besides the theorists mentioned above and much earlier ones,
   and those who fortunately were present in Cartagena in 1997,
   the *intellectual heroes of this rebellious, heretical, liberating
   countervailing power* are well-known. Frequent reference was
   made to some of them at the Congress: Gregory Bateson, H.G.
   Gadamer, John Elliott, Clifford Geertz, Fritjof Capra, Anthony
   Giddens, P.B. Checkland, Ilya Prigogine, Tzvetan Todorov,
   Michel Foucault, Paul Feyerabend, Humberto Maturana, Eric
   Hobsbawm, Norberto Bobbio. References to the physicist
   Werner Heisenberg showed that participatory research might
   be closer to modern physics than to traditional sociology, as
   Wallerstein recalled on referring to the "social scientization" of
   physics; they also suggested that the relations between the
   natural and social sciences needed to be redefined —a recurrent
   theme at the Congress.

We felt assured therefore that our search for scientific theories
on participation was neither a solitary nor ignored effort, and that
we were on the right road and in good company towards
developing an alternative ethos. There was a feeling that we were
moving in the direction of a new science with those travelling
companions already mentioned, as with postmodernism, post-
developmentalism, post-colonialism and post-capitalism. Current
scientific advances are positive and favorable to the development
of participatory research; and societies themselves now have a
greater need of such research than they did before to induce
processes conducive to social change.

CONTRIBUTION OF THE SCANDINAVIAN SCHOOL

This feeling of intellectual maturity combined with the hope of
change found confirmation in the interesting presentation, by some
of its co-authors, of the recently published book *Beyond Theory*,
edited by Stephen Toulmin and Bjorn Gustavsen[12]. The book

describes a large-scale participatory research study conducted among Swedish industrial workers, on the basis of theoretical considerations for improving work procedures and results in factories. The general theses of the study can be summed up as follows:

a) Participatory-research work is at once discovery and creation, thus unfolding in an *epigenetic space*. Its style is historical and anthropological. It seeks not only to explain but also to improve or reform situations (as in clinical medicine). That is why in its holistic epistemology **what is** can only be defined in the context of *what should be*. (Pages 179, 199, 210)

b) Participatory research derives its rational basis from the Aristotelian concept of *phronesis*, which, unlike the concept of episteme and the Platonic tradition, does not seek to justify knowledge by an accumulation of abstract and universally valid facts, but by sound judgment or practical wisdom in understanding the specific, current and concrete. Participatory method cannot therefore be the same method as is employed by logical empiricists; it must develop its own techniques. (Pages 207, 210)

c) The relation between an epistemic subject A and an empirical object B in a social-research situation X is, as we have seen, characterized by the fact that the object is at the same time the subject. The ABX structure becomes an *observable constituent system*, as was maintained also by the systems theorists at the Congress (see the following section). In the minds of those participating in the system, the structure becomes "pox" (the person, the other and x). This situation resembles that postulated in quantum physics for uncertainty relations. (Pages 181, 188)

d) The ABX/pox system involves the *double hermeneutics* proposed by Giddens: one for everyday or ordinary language, and the other for technical language, the two languages to be interpreted through dialogue in order to achieve understanding and create new languages; the quality of communication between A and B also depends on this. The mechanism or cement linking this system in practice is *everyday language*. (Pages 183-185, 190)

e) Two *classes of reality* are found in participatory research: an experiential and a representational reality, each with its respective type of knowledge, the former's arising from the very act of doing, and the latter's associated with different aspects of the context of the act. (Page 187)

f) The interplay between experiential and representational reality calls for mutual responsibility, which makes *participatory democracy* an essential condition and intrinsic element of participatory research, in society at large as well as in institutions and companies. And participatory research, in turn, will induce advancement of democracy. (Pages 196, 224)

CONTRIBUTIONS FROM SYSTEMS THEORISTS

The group of systems and management methodologists from Hull University (England) and Los Andes University (Colombia), headed by Robert L. Flood (Chapter 12 and Paper 14) and Ernesto Lleras, found that a common holistic epistemology, such as that suggested by Reason and Morten Levin, would bring the systems sciences productively closer to participatory research and other disciplines. This complementary closeness, by broadening action and management, would facilitate change and improvement in organizational efficacy and lead to fairer practices in society.[13]

Indeed, the methodologists recalled that one of the leading systems theorists, P.B. Checkland, presented his work as a form of "action research", in which three elements came into play: the framework of the action (F), the method (M) and the area of application (A). Critical systems scholars added the dynamics of knowledge/power to F, which led them to consider "emancipatory theories" in which the everyday interests of peoples were of essential importance. In fact they wondered how to transform narratives of resistance to change into narratives of liberation, rightly regarding society as a system whose structure and evolution are determined by multiple interacting and interrelated factors, rather than by simple linear chains of cause and effect.

There were also a number of practical concerns. The traditionally esoterical, mathematical or mechanistic task of engineering, for example, could be led towards an interdisciplinary approach to consider the social contexts in which specific projects are carried out, and to take into account inputs from the knowledge and experience of the communities involved. In this way dramatic errors and failures could be avoided in designing and executing public works, such as roads and bridges, where natural resources would be affected. The contexts —social systems and cultural complexes— should be taken into account.

The variety of approaches and methods covered by the umbrella of Participatory (Action) Research has brought about a fragmentation of languages and interpretations of knowledge that needs to be lessened. Intercommunication between types of knowledge may become possible and desirable, but the ways and means of bringing it about are not yet clear. In Cartagena systems theories were said to be potentially very useful for this purpose.

Since the systems involved are open systems, like the triadic ABX/pox scheme developed by the Scandinavian school, a spectrum of purposes can be envisaged, ranging from consensus to compromise and tolerance. But the systems will be strategically and humanly comprehensible only if they are bounded. One of the main elements in setting such boundaries to systems is, precisely, power; other factors to be taken into account are values, significance and ethics.[14]

The revelation of mutual conceptual support between Checkland, a systems theorist, and Reason and Levin, participatory theorists, resulted in one of the most important theoretical advances at the Convergence Congress.

DIALOGUE, COMMUNICATION AND ART

1. Some participants pointed out rightly that the essence of participatory research did not necessarily lie in action, as definitions emphasized, but in the nature and content of the *language used in the experience lived*, that is, in the information, dialogue and modes of intersubjective contact in the creative process. Because the knowledge involved is a social construction, as explained by Tandon in his presentation (Chapter 10) and discussed by Horton and Freire in their book cited above. Some delegates went so far as to maintain that when information leads to action it becomes power.

2. This classical issue, which in the Western tradition started with Plato, is a problem experienced everyday in *cultural transmission* between generations. The Cartagena working group coordinated by Jesús Martín Barbero considered the matter extensively, and reminded us not only of the origins of concepts ("from palimpsest to hypertext", see Paper 156) but also of the present impact of specialized telecommunications media. In contrast, they pointed out how, for their part, unstable groups in diaspora create specialized media to counteract homogenizing cultural tendencies. Great emphasis was also placed on the influence of television media in schools, and on the new possibilities —and risks— of the Internet.[15]

3. It was striking that in these discussions the participants did not dwell on Chomsky's or Saussure's formal semiotics, which deals with the origins of composition and rules of speech, but on the broader orientations of Mikhail Bakhtin and Ludwig Wittgenstein, with their emphasis on the *mechanisms of socialization*, symbolic languages, and knowledge that is produced in daily life and action itself. Paulo Freire and his dialogics also dwelt on these things for the modern school and participatory research. We know that it is only through these mechanisms of language —everyday, symbolic and mathematical language— that new knowledge is produced or the interpretation of realities is modified.

4. We saw that the effectiveness of such mechanisms of communication depended greatly on *feelings and esthetics*, elements that have received little formal treatment by researchers.[16] Hence the special attention accorded to them in Cartagena, not only at the plenary sessions by splendid writers such as Eduardo Galeano, David Sánchez Juliao and Rodrigo Parra, who occasionally referred to "thinking-feeling" people, but also at performances by minstrels, singers and dancers. Their examples and performances produced or reinforced communication techniques based on diverse styles.[17] To be thinking-feeling or "sentipensantes", they said, synthesized what participatory research was all about. If the style makes the man, we have here a broad field of reflection for determining the effectiveness of messages transmitted under the PR label, and the ways in

which culture is created or re-created by enfolding science in art. For it seems to be more productive to marry the two sisters, as the poet said, than to go on loving them separately as though they were enemies.[18]

5. At the Congress there were also demonstrations of the game of *language of the arts*, with three types of expression that went beyond the intersubjective dialogical level to the collective: music, song, ballet and painting. These artistic expressions were seen to carry a participatory significance by inducing among performers and audience symmetrical relations that overcame differences of class, gender and age. Thus performances were given in which music was combined with messages of commitment to popular participation, for example Colombian *"vallenato"* protest songs from the seventies and "songs of struggle" from the Cauca Valley; and the syncretic music of the Yothu Yindi people of Australia, which has served them to regain their dignity. Ethno-religious conflict between Kosovo's Serbs and Mohammedans was reported to have been alleviated in some measure by a love of pop music among the young, who gathered together to dance to it without any qualms. Forgotten provincial composers of merit who had found inspiration in vernacular themes were remembered, and a concert was given of works of one such composer, Adolfo Mejía (Sincé, Colombia) by the Symphony Orchestra of Barranquilla, the largest city on Colombia's Atlantic coast (see Video 4).

The *ludic element* was provided by the ballet "The Bridge", performed at St. Francis's Cloister, which was connected with defense of life and solidarity with colleagues killed by political violence. Traditional Caribbean dances were performed in other locations by the Catalina de Carrillo Ensemble (Córdoba, Colombia), which has been using participatory techniques of social and historical research. Huge wall-hangings jointly painted by workers and participative researchers from Pereira (Colombia) adorned the Convention Center's entrance hallway, and transmitted to all passers-by the emotions of struggling against exploitative institutions of domestic or international origin. Many delegates used the facilities provided in the hallway to paint their own posters with messages for the final session, which they displayed at that session.

6. A *reading room*, containing about a thousand volumes on topics discussed at the Congress, was provided by the Luis Ángel Arango Library, which belongs to the Banco de la República (Colombia's central bank). It was used by many participants, for example, for having photocopies made of new materials. The reading room was one of the most striking technical innovations for events of this kind.

Such theoretical-practical, informative, artistic and ludic elements have an obvious influence on the methodological conceptions and performance of participatory fieldwork, on formal and informal education and on business management, as we shall see in the following chapters.

DEFINITION PROPOSAL

Given these theoretical inputs, participatory research may usefully be said to combine at least two observable elements that distinguish it from other forms of scientific or investigative work: 1) an evaluative or ideological structure, with critical attitudes to knowledge and its use, social context, and cultural patterns undergoing or in need of improvement and change; and 2) an array of combinable multidisciplinary survey techniques derived from a single immanent logic of scientific research and from a holistic or extended epistemology, as explained above.

Accordingly, on the basis of findings at Cartagena, participatory research may be defined as a method of study and action that goes hand in hand with an altruistic philosophy of life to obtain useful, reliable results for improving collective situations, particularly for the popular classes. It requires that the researcher base his/her observations on living with the communities, from which he/she also also obtains valid knowledge. It is inter- or multi-disciplinary and applicable in continua ranging from micro- to macro-universes studied (from groups to communities and larger societies), but never losing its existential commitment to the life-philosophy of change that characterizes it.[19]

CLARIFICATION ON THE ACRONYM PAR

Soon after the First Symposium in 1977 a discussion arose over our movement's acronym, PAR (Participatory Action Research), as distinct from PR (Participatory Research) chosen earlier by a group of Canadian educators, one of whom, Budd Hall, acted as a rapporteur at the 1997 Congress. The "A" was included to stand for action. We were concerned at the time to lay stress on committed existential action, and to clarify the social participation orientation to dissociate it from liberal or reactionary influences. However, without taking us into account, Kurt Lewin's earlier psychologistic, experimental Action Research school -of a different flavor from ours- remained active at the same time, with the result that doubt and confusion arose with regard to our stance.

Time has moved on and in the aftermath of the 1997 Congress it may now be appropriate to segregate PAR clearly from the classical, positivistic, psychologistic tradition it emerged from twenty or more years ago, as has been demanded by some critics. We can therefore discard the "A" and call ourselves PR, or to make the transition easier, P(A)R, as in this book.

This summary has been facilitated by a wealth of studies on symmetrical participation in different contexts and cultures, which naturally include, as a component, action consistent with its commitment. This was taught us in 1985 by the economist Mohammed Anisur Rahman of Bangladesh.[20] Moreover, a number of general analyses of our field have been published[21] that help to delineate and configure the "participative family" we have been building, in which we feel better placed than with the Lewinians. We have accordingly proposed that the abbreviations PR or P(A)R be used interchangeably from now on to identify our work better. And recommended that Hall's good example be followed again (Paper 13).[22]

NOTES

1. O. Fals Borda and M. Anisur Rahman, *Action and Knowledge*, New York: Apex, 1991, pp. 10-12; cf. E. Husserl, *La crisis de las ciencias europeas y la fenomenología trascendental*, Barcelona: Crítica, 1991. Categories were also derived from Marxism and Hegel, see O. Fals Borda's *Por la praxis:*

El problema de cómo investigar la realidad para transformarla, Bogotá: Tercer Mundo, 1980.

2. The speakers in this (philosophy) group were: Patrice Vermeren, Ángela Calvo de Saavedra, Oscar Mejía, Daniel Bonilla, Eric Lecerf, Mauricio García, Nilce Ariza, Lelio Fernández, Francisco Cortés Rodas, Carlos Thiebaut, José L. Villacañas, Juan Carlos Velasco, Alfonso Monsalve, Francisco Colom G., Rodrigo Romero, Angela Uribe and Federico Gallego, besides Guillermo Hoyos.

3. Cf. Jürgen Habermas, *Theory and Practice*, Boston: Beacon Press, 1973, although the author unjustifiably expresses the reservation that action-research is incompatible with data-collecting techniques in the field (page 11); this has been disproved in practice and by historical time. In Cartagena we lacked the French School's contributions on practical reason and theories of action, by Pierre Bourdieu ("habitus") and Alain Touraine ("intervention"), to study similarities and differences between them and the participatory schools. The recent publication of Bourdieu's *Razones prácticas: Sobre la teoría de la acción*, Barcelona: Anagrama, 1997, translated from the original in French (1994), drew attention and comments; it deals with subjects discussed at the Congress, such as "social space", "power" and "art".

4. This central element, which I shall return to below, was also discussed by the working groups on social movements, PAR histories, local government, popular education, poverty, and literature and society, as well as by the panels on schools and methods, and popular leaders.

5. H.G. Gadamer, "The Phenomenological Movement", in *Philosophical Hermeneutics*, Berkeley: University of California Press, 1976, 130-181. Fals Borda and Rahman, cit. 12, 197. The Subject/Object dichotomy, which is Kantian, was intellectually resolved long ago by Schopenhauer by means of the concept of "representation" (Vorstellung) as "the first act of consciousness", we are reminded by Allan Janik and Stephen Toulmin in their fascinating book, *Wittgenstein's Vienna*, New York: Simon and Schuster, 1973.

6. Regarding the apparent "neutrality" of purists, attention was drawn in Cartagena to the interesting exchange between Myles Horton and Paulo Freire in *We Make the Road by Walking*, Philadelphia: Temple University Press, 1990, 102-105, and to the need for sincerity in stating the purposes of an action.

7. Terms introduced by Agnes Heller, "From Hermeneutics in Social Science Toward a Hermeneutics of Social Science", in *Theory and Society*, 18, No. 3 (May 1989), 304-305. These participatory attitudes in the sciences should do away with disoriented old practices, such as the use of "experts" and "expertese" by international institutions and many NGOs.

8. Peter Reason, *Participation in Human Society*, London: Sage, 1994;
    Morten Levin, Action Research and Critical Systems Thinking, *Systems Practice*, 7 (1994), 25-42. It is curious that Goethe, in his theory of colors, managed to move away from Newton's technical reductionism and adopted holistic explanations, as recounted by James Gleick in *Chaos: Making a New Science*, New York: Viking, 165, 197. Cf. Rajesh Tandon and Peter Park, who provided similar frameworks at the Congress in Papers 92 and 155, respectively. These authors, as many others, have found inspiration in Fritjof Capra's works like *Belonging to the Universe*, New York: Harper Collins, 1992, xi, 83. The speakers in the working group on "knowledge building" were: L. David Brown, Roberto Gutiérrez, Gerard Rademeyer and Luis Barraza, besides Tandon and Park.

9. Albert O. Hirschman, *Tendencias autosubversivas*, México: Fondo de Cultura Económica, 1996, which brings to mind Gunnar Myrdal's classic critical positions, with new conceptual tools such as "voice", "way out" and "loyalty" for understanding conflict.

10. On the subject of "control over resources and institutions", a valuable contribution was made by Andrew Pearse, Mathias Stieffel and Marshall Wolfe in the Series on Participation published by UNRISD (Geneva, Switzerland) in the eighties, which provided us with considerable orientation.

11. Wilfred Carr and Stephen Kemmis, *Becoming Critical: Knowledge, Education and Action Research*, London: The Falmer Press, 1986, 18. Kemmis was a principal rapporteur at the Cartagena Congress.

12. Stephen Toulmin and Bjorn Gustavsen, eds., *Beyond Theory: Changing Organizations through Participation*, Amsterdam: John Benjamins Publishing Co., 1996. Presentations were made in Cartagena by co-authors B. Gustavsen, O. Babüroglu, O. Palshaugen and Y. Josefson, as well as by Morten Levin and Davydd Greenwood. This book confuses "action research" with PAR, but if you self-correct for this it is very useful reading, upholding as it does the primacy of participation. It contains a study on national participation in Turkey, which is valuable because participatory research has so far very rarely reached the macro level. This same group of authors began in 1996 to publish *Concepts and Transformation: International Journal of Action Research and Organizational Renewal*, under the editorship of Hans van Beinum at Halmstad University.

13. Besides Flood and Lleras the speakers were: Norma Romm, Néstor Valero-Silva, Mónica Escobar, Mohammed Emadi, Guangming Cao, Brian Lehaney and Steve Clark. This highly inter-disciplinary position is shared, as a "new philosophy of science", by scientists such as the biologist Ernst Mayr, *Toward a New Philosophy of Biology*, Cambridge:

Harvard University Press, 1988, 21, in advocating a greater recognition of stochastic processes, pluralism of causes and effects, emergence of non-anticipated properties, and the internal cohesion of complex systems.

14. Cf. Peter Park, "Participatory Research, Orders of Change and Paradigm Shift", Congress Paper 155. Park writes: "Groups, organizations or other collective entities can be conceived of as systems that learn to modify their acts. This systemic learning is distinct from learning by isolated individuals within the system. ... The problems lie in the way the system is organized and operated." According to Bourdieu, cit., 147, human behavior "is carried on inside game spaces" and game theory could be applied, but without any postulated "strategical intention" because social agents seldom expound it, though they admit to needing it. For Mayr, cit., 14, 19, biological systems are open systems with homeostatic mechanisms, which only leads to probabilistic prediction, without the classic criteria of validity adopted by purists.

15. The speakers in the working group on communications were: Martin Hopenhayn, Phaik-Loh Kin, Hermann Herlinghaus, Guillermo Orozco, Rosa María Alfaro, Magola Delgado and William F. Torres, besides Martín Barbero. Publication of *Escenografías para el diálogo: Comunicación, política y cultura* by the Popular Communications Network of the Latin-American Adult Education Council (CEAAL), Santiago de Chile: CEAAL, 1997, was very timely. It contains contributions by Alfaro, Germán Rey, Raúl Leis, Gabriel Kaplun and other colleagues. In this connection it is relevant to recall the controversy over ordinary language that Wittgenstein's criticism of philosophy provoked with Norman Malcolm, Gilbert Ryle and Stanley Cavell, cf. V.C. Chappell, ed., *Ordinary Language*, New York: Dover, 1964.

16. It is odd that greater emphasis has not been placed on the link between science, esthetics and art, as postulated by Ernest Mach, for it has stimulated the creativity of great men, according to their own testimony. A telling case in point is Einstein's development of his theory on relations between mass and energy, in which he resolved the question of equilibrium as a matter of esthetics and formal congruence, cf. Banesh Hoffmann, *Albert Einstein, Creator and Rebel*, New York: New American Library, 1972, 81, 176, 217.

17. The members of the working group on literature, history and society, coordinated by Máximo Alemán, were Eduardo Galeano, David Sánchez Juliao, Rodrigo Parra, Alfredo Molano, Gabriel Restrepo, Luz Mery Giraldo and Azriel Bibliowicz.

18. As in the case of the Peruvian poet and Indigenist José María Arguedas, who was remembered at the Congress. In connection with such

creative convergence, special mention should be made also of David Sánchez Juliao's novel, *San Fernando de Cumbé*, Madrid: Grijalbo 1997. This novel combines a rich literary style with participatory methodology, inspired precisely by the places and events that gave birth to this methodology in Colombia in the seventies. In this way he transforms my *Historia doble de la Costa* (1979-1986) into a delightful production. See also Paper 154 by Carlos Arboleda González on this significant novel (perhaps the only one of its kind), which surpasses the García-Marquean trend.

19. This definition may be compared with the very similar one presented at the Cartagena Congress in Paper 150 by William H. Whyte, eminent professor and pioneer in these endeavors: "PAR involves members of an organization or community under study to take part fully with the researchers in designing the project, obtaining data, and carrying out the actions resulting from the process. One of the underlying aims of any PAR project is that the members of the lower classes become sufficiently empowered to participate actively in running their organization or community".

20. Mohammed Anisur Rahman, "The Theory and Practice of Participatory Action Research", in O. Fals Borda, ed. *The Challenge of Social Change*, London: Sage, 1985, 107-109.

21. Peter Reason, "Three Approaches to Participative Inquiry", in N.K. Denzin and Yvonna S. Lincoln, eds. *Handbook of Qualitative Research*, London: Sage, 1994, 324 ss. Cf. D.P. Dash, "Problems of Action Research-As I See It", Working Paper No. 14, Lincoln School of Management, University of Lincolnshire and Humberside, England, 1997: Harry Coenen, "Action Research: The State of the Art", paper presented at the Conference on Quality in Human Inquiry University of Bath, March 14-17, 1995. For our Congress, Reason also contributed interesting reflections on Complexity theories (Paper 15).

22. Changes in acronyms or labeling are also being made in sister schools, towards greater simplification. For example, the University of Sussex's school of Participatory Rural Appraisal or PRA (formerly Rapid Rural Appraisal or RRA) now tends to call itself Participation, Reflection, Action, or Participatory Learning and Action, thereby approaching PAR. See Paper 4 by Robert Chambers or Chapter 11 of this book.

14. METHODOLOGICAL GUIDES

In Cartagena we heard with natural concern the old, almost universal, chorus on P(A)R's failures in methods and techniques, its lack of demarcation from other schools of investigation, its weakness in rigorous scientific criteria, validity and replication, and similar complaints, often justified but sometimes explainable by many participatory researchers' characteristic negligence in communication. It was paradoxical that, with the proliferation of hard-working field groups across the five continents since the seventies, their field-research procedures had still not become any clearer and no serious attempt been made at an overall assessment of what was happening.[1]

The Cartagena meeting was at last a great opportunity for a comparative review. The analyses carried out before and during the Congress provided presentable evidence from which the state of the art in this field can now be deduced. The main findings on methods, summarized in this chapter, provide evidence of significant advances that, we feel, cannot be ignored by observers from our own or other disciplines. These advances will certainly further the progress of our fieldwork, to make it even more efficient and useful in the social, economic, political and cultural contexts in which it is performed, in a manner consistent with the philosophical framework inspiring it.

CALGARY'S ELECTRONIC EXCHANGE

In connection with the Congress, Timothy Pyrch of Calgary University in Canada organized a prior exchange between eleven colleagues from different participatory tendencies in the world. As an experience in travel through cyberspace with the scientific and technical preoccupations referred to above, this exchange was fascinating, significant and highly useful to the event. The eleven participants were:

Robert Chambers (Participatory Rural Appraisal, PRA, Sussex)
Robert L. Flood (Critical Systems Theory, Hull)
Davydd Greenwood (Action Research, Cornell)
Morten Levin (Action Research, Scandinavia)
Yvonna S. Lincoln (Constructivist Research, Texas)
Robin McTaggart (Action Learning, Australia)
Peter Reason (Cooperative Research, Bath)
Maruja Salas and Timmi Tillmann (PAR, Germany/Peru)
Michael Schratz (Action Research, Austria)
Rajesh Tandon (PAR, India)
Timothy Pyrch (PAR, Canada)

The e-mail exchange between these colleagues allowed them to learn more about what each was doing in his respective milieu, with his own research tools, and to determine not only what united them but also how they differed. The findings reinforced the idea that we truly belong to the same participatory intellectual family, and that the same immanent critical epistemology and methodology was used at least in each one of the schools or tendencies that took part in the exercise.[2]

There were two dimensions to the exercise: 1) a recounting of the participants' personal experience in these endeavors, and 2) a technical exchange in the form of contributions and papers for the Congress, which are available in published form.[3]

A fruitful discussion, ranging from the emotional to the rational, was carried on also to understand the writers' clear break with the academic elitist tradition they all had belonged to, and to review the most pressing methodological propositions.

Great consideration was given by the participants both to the nature of the bond established in the field, and to the links between theory and practice in empirical work. Regarding that bond, it was no easy task to establish a relationship of trust and respect with the people but it was highly possible to do so and brought great personal satisfaction to both sides. Regarding those links, it was inadvisable to limit research to either practice or theory, rather they should be balanced according to an integral vision of the situation created.

Since the aim was to enhance and expand scientific as well as practical knowledge for the purpose of resolving concrete situations and/or problems and creating countervailing power, it was advisable to recognize the limitations of all the actors involved in the research experience. It was therefore important to impart theoretical knowledge to the field staff who were going to remain in the communities they belonged to and continue the research and practical work once the external activists had departed. Such continuity in work was considered indispensable, although the need remained to adapt techniques and procedures as the conditions of the process changed. Because participatory research's long duration made it vulnerable to the changes inevitably imposed by life.

The external researcher would not as a rule be expected to replace local co-researchers in their roles or positions, particularly as regards politics. To do so had been seen to cause unnecessary confusion in both the research process and the relevant action, and was contrary to the aim of helping communities become more independent and better able to manage on their own. Such was the testimony of some participants in the exercise, and it was confirmed by the panel on the history of participatory movements, coordinated by Budd Hall (Canada).

The panel emphasized also what it called the "holistic and spiritual" aspect, by recommending qualitative procedures, a transdisciplinary approach, and observation of non-fragmented realities. There was concern for "interventions in processes for a long-term action" on communal self-management infrastructures, and for indicators that expressed not only the holistic/spiritual aspect but also the tenor of local life in the cultural, economic and political domains. These proposals were taken up by other panels and working groups, and more especially at the final session organized by Carlos Brenes (Costa Rica) and Timmi Tillmann (Germany), when allusive posters and drawings made by dozens of delegates in the draped hallway were paraded around in an extremely long roll, which was finally placed all around the great hall of the Convention Center. These spontaneous, valuable expressions of the participants' views and knowledge eased the inevitable stiffness of the formal sessions, led to hugs and other collective gestures of friendship, to singing in chorus ("Pueblito viejo" from Colombia, "We Shall Overcome" from the US, among others), and to attention being drawn to aspects ignored in the general list of topics. Many of these ideas of the Congress participants are taken into account in the following section, which presents guidelines for our work in the field.

If there was more affinity than expected both among the eleven prior participants and the Congress audience, it may be interpreted as reaffirmation of the orientations described above regarding the values and philosophies of participation. The differences, limited in every case, were attributable to various specific factors: institutional social-policy requirements, cultural conditioning, literacy levels and mass-communication facilities, limitations caused by poverty, and particular ecological characteristics and use of natural resources.

Given such similarity of values and methodologies, the panel discussion by researchers at the plenary session of the Congress was calm, generous and to a certain extent consensual. There were no mutual disqualifications, dogmatic rejections, or underrating of the position of others, as might have occurred if the ground had not been prepared sufficiently in advance. In fine, discussion was characterized by professional maturity and a broad scientific outlook.

GENERAL GUIDELINES FOR WORK

Place and mood invited fraternal recognition of a generally applicable common methodological task, rather than personalistic assertions as to "who was first or best" or "who cited whom". As a result, several forms of work were made known explicitly or implicitly that can be regarded as providing indicative guidelines for the ordinary or common endeavors of participatory research. These guidelines could be summed up as follows:

a) It is otiose to look for or determine general *social laws* in our field (or in others such as biology, according to Mayr, cit., 19). There will be foreseeable developments limited as to time, place and culture and producing effects determined by various specific factors, which are not necessarily unilinear or irreversible. This does not mean that it is unjustified to take reasonable measures through economic and social policy, nor does it limit the scientificity of the research experiences themselves. But it does deny authenticity to *absolute prediction*, because of the plurality of intervening causes and factors.

b) The logical empiricists' traditional requirements for demarcating scientific fields and looking for objective universal laws serve above all to define *two poles* within the spectrum of the sciences: one a cosmological, abstract pole; and the other a pole comprising participatory local projects concerned with current circumstances and imbued with values.

c) The *rigor of research* cannot be judged solely by *quantitative* measures, though these may be necessary for describing and explaining the results. Measurements have to be blended with relevant *qualitative* descriptions, which are equally valid and necessary. So it is not advisable in our field to continue to blindly imitate research procedures that are appropriate only for the natural sciences. Our work is made more difficult by this and therefore needs to be performed with greater competence, reliability and sense of responsibility than in other fields of knowledge.

d) The natural fluidity of social, cultural, economic and political phenomena calls for greater scope to take in several series of *interpretations and reinterpretations* of the same phenomena studied, that is, they must be regarded as historical processes subject to hermeneutic analysis.

e) All scientific *methods and techniques* may legitimately be applied in participatory research, provided that doing so is compatible with the *frame of reference agreed on* by a joint decision taken within the ABX system on the basis of participatory philosophy; the initiative for the decision should preferably originate from the grass roots. Open surveys, semistructured interviews, group and community work, information triangulation, and collective workshops have proved to be appropriate techniques for obtaining satisfactory results in the field.

f) *Empathy and participant observation* (as in psychoanalysis and ethnography) are the most suitable techniques for investigating the intimate or hidden nature of situations that are of interest in participatory research and the experiences it offers; they are particularly suitable for problems of anomy, conflict, violence, drug addiction and other symptoms of social pathology.

g) *Validity* criteria for P(A)R rely, not on evidence of an internal correlation of "objective" or quantifiable variables or exercises, but on inductive/deductive examination of results determinable by practice, by empathetic development of processes felt amidst the actual realities, by the considered judgment of local reference groups, and by common sense. Even children may take part in evaluation sessions, as has been successfully tried at Barefoot College in Tilonia, India (see Bunker Roy's abstract in the book of *Congress Abstracts*, 90-91).

h) Results are not necessarily *evaluated* at the end of a given or prefixed period by the familiar reflection-action cycle, as though one were dealing with a unilinear or unicausal banking procedure in the hands of planners. Rather, the evaluation may be performed during the actual course of the fieldwork, as a stimulus to action. The necessary inspiration for carrying on with the job is "fractal", that is, a random, accidental or spontaneous product of many factors, including intuition and feeling in everyday activity. (Of course, both this and the preceding guideline raise the hackles of experts and academics, who see their institutions and simplistic procedures threatened. Their resistance may be expected to grow).

i) The diversities and contradictions encountered in the real world and best observed by focussing on dependent or varying attributes, make it necessary for the *values, goals and commitments* of participatory researchers —in contrast to those of planners and logical empiricists— to be transparent and explicitly stated in the frames of reference and in the actual fieldwork.

j) There is no room here for *experimentation* in the manner of the natural sciences, with repeatability of phenomena in controlled contexts: there is just a margin for comparative forms of *induction and deduction* subject to given SpaceTimes. Hence, neither can there be "typical cases" or "pilot projects" in P(A)R, only theoretical-practical interpretations likely to be generalizable.

k) Breaking up the researcher/researched dyad to eliminate asymmetry and *horizontalize the relationship* does not imply intellectual predominance of the one or other pole. Rather it provides the possibility of respectfully making mutually fruitful contributions through evidence and facts that can be checked against one other, since neither the common people nor the professionals (addressed as "doctor" in Latin America) are right all the time.

l) On receiving and considering without bias expressions of *popular wisdom and common sense*, interdisciplinary academic knowledge can, by critical assessment, provide a fuller, essentially descriptive, and holistic understanding of reality and thus enrich and simplify forms and styles of communication with the communities under study.

m) In certain circumstances it is advisable to distinguish between investigative and political *rationality* and not mix them up indifferently. In these cases each person shall contribute to the research process what he is most competent to provide or what satisfies him most as an individual or citizen.

n) Demonstration techniques employed in *extension practices*, or to induce structural changes, are limited by economic factors or lack of perseverance. As participatory processes are mostly of medium- or long-term duration, the institutions involved (such as universities and NGOs) and the relevant formal arrangements should be adapted to this, rather than the other way round-as still occurs.

o) If the fieldwork leads to macro levels of political, social, economic and/or cultural *mobilization*, for example, in the form of "countervailing power" or popular movements, it is important to proceed from the *bottom* up through the social structures, and/or from the *periphery to the center* of the systems involved.

p) Analytically, participation's move in scale from the *micro* to the *macro* can not only be accomplished but also calibrated and related to the emergence of social movements, organizational networks, and domestic or international policies, making sure first that these are not manipulative.[4]

q) Objectivity and subjectivity may coincide in the art, sensory images, and literary and esthetic expressions of scientific work. This fact justifies the creative incursion of *imagination and expression* in participatory research (see the previous chapter); and their use is becoming a sort of hermeneutic technique.

SOME HERMENEUTIC TECHNIQUES[5]

1. *Relative Truth*. It is inadmissible and dangerous to construct one truth, for there is not just one truth. According to Agnes Heller, in the social sciences a truth may consist in the agreement between a researcher and his research participant, because knowledge is constructed socially. All the same, facts and information need to be verified by means of triangulation, documentation and filing techniques.

2. *Plausibility and Meaning*. Looking for plausibility in a series of verifiable items of knowledge may reveal the meaning of real-life processes. This brings understanding of the action by giving a meaning and context to objects of study, such as the testimonies of living or dead witnesses, diaries, photographs, maps and materials from (family) "trunk archives".

3. *Historical Retrieval*. Where there are official or unilateral versions of facts and events, it is justified to make a critical retrieval of the history on the basis of family (trunk) archives, interviews with lucid elderly people who have a good memory, and cross-referencings to complement or correct observed biases. This technique is associated with the principle of interpretation/reinterpretation referred to in point (d) of the previous section.

4. *Restitution or Return of Knowledge*. This technique implies respect for the groups that were the source of the information obtained. It involves adopting styles and forms of communication, such as illustrated booklets, radio magazines, videos and social dramas, suited to their language and literacy level so that the information being returned to them will be properly understood. (In this and the next technique the technical jargon used in learned circles has to be abandoned.)

5. *Symmetrical Communication*. This is carried out through information checking, dialogue or horizontal conversation

between researchers and the participants being researched, to reach a plausible consensus.

6. *Communication Structure.* In the social sciences the (written or audiovisual) product is composed of two interrelated elements that need to be in balance: a core or skeleton, and a cortex or envelope. The core consists of information from authorized, verifiable sources. The cortex is an elaboration of the same information from particular viewpoints, in which imagination is circumscribed by cultural matrices or imputations are made to personalities; it is the channel for introducing interpretative originality, innovation and striking description. This is the logos-mythos technique, which allows writers to present their messages and deal with history in strikingly effective ways (see Video 12 for an example from the Uruguayan writer Eduardo Galeano). It can be used to combine the novel and social science, a combination treated at the Congress by a dynamic working group coordinated by Rodrigo Parra and Luz Mery Giraldo.[6] It is also possible with this technique to construct multivocal or "stereophonic" works, like the *Historia Doble de la Costa* written in two separate streams each in a distinct style but presented side by side (see Note 5).

7. *Communication Balance.* Where the core of a work or a communication is more highly developed than the cortex, the communication becomes a nomothetic exercise, or merely technical and informative, and unlikely to arouse much interest. But if it is the cortex that is overdeveloped, the work done may turn out as fiction or ideology, rather than science as such or credible knowledge. The necessary balance between the two elements is obtained through a sense of proportion derived from phronesis, experience in applying sound judgment, and practice in communication.[7]

Notes

1. Almost at the same time as the Congress, Robin McTaggart (Deakin, Australia) completed his extensive project of publishing P(A)R histories from Colombia, India, Austria, Australia, Venezuela, United States, England, Spain, Thailand and New Caledonia: *Participatory Action Research: International Contexts and Consequences,* Ithaca: State University of New York Press (SUNY), 1997.

2. A very valuable contribution was Robert Chambers's recently published book *Whose Reality Counts? Putting the First Last*, London: Intermediate Technology Publications, 1997, which was distributed at the Congress. The author enriched our event with his reflections, set forth in the book, on Participatory Rural Appraisal and "paradigmatic evolution from things to people". In his Paper 4 (164 in Spanish), included as Chapter II of this book, Chambers deals specifically and constructively with institutional methods and support.

3. Published in the review *Studies in Cultures, Organizations and Societies*, 5, No. 1 (Summer 1998). Note was taken of "Action-Science" and the important trend introduced by William Torbert, who could not unfortunately be present at Cartagena. P.B. Checkland, too, was absent; he had been the keynote speaker at our World Congress in Brisbane (1992), where the "process management" school so successfully promoted by Ortrun Zuber-Skerritt had been highlighted.

4. Michael M. Cernea's contribution on this issue of scale at the World Bank deserves particular mention. Thanks to books such as *Putting People First*, Washington: World Bank, 1995, and articles such as "The Sociological Action-Research of Development-Induced Population Resettlement", in the *Romanian Journal of Sociology*, World Bank Reprint Series No. 480 (1995) and others published over the past fifteen years, Cernea and his Working Group on Participation have brought about relevant modifications in the Bank's policy. The World Bank delegate, Anders Rudqvist made a successful presentation on the matter, though there were protests from skeptics who expected to see greater participatory results in the actual management of the Bank's major projects. Cf. Chambers observations in Chapter 11 (Paper 4) on problems of scale in our fields.

5. *Cf.* Agnes Heller's comparative article on these techniques published in *Collaborative Inquiry* (Bath) 18 (1996), and O. Fals Borda (*Historia doble de la Costa*, Bogotá: Valencia, 1978-1986, 4 volumes). A huge contribution has been made in this domain by the *Handbook of Qualitative Research*, a monumental work edited by Norman K. Denzin and Yvonna S. Lincoln (London: Sage Publications, 1994), particularly Part V, "The Art of Interpretation, Evaluation and Presentation". On truth and verisimilitude see Capra, cit., 144-162.

6. The speakers in this group were Colombian and foreign writers highly reputed for their originality, imagination, style and concern for social questions: Azriel Bibliowicz, J.E. Pardo, Karl Kohut, Claude Fell, Oscar Collazos, R.H. Moreno Durán and Rubén Sierra, besides Parra and Giraldo. The group has announced the forthcoming publication of a book containing the essays prepared for the Congress.

7. *Cf.* David L. Altheide and John M. Johnson, "Criteria for Assessing Interpretive Validity in Qualitative Research", in Denzin and Lincoln, *cit.*, 485-499, on meta-narratives, style, reflective ethnography, rhetoric and discursive analysis.

15. COOPTATION AND THE NEW SCIENTIFIC PARADIGM

Two major, possibly interrelated, issues were extensively discussed in Cartagena. They were: cooptation of P(A)R and of the idea of participation by the Establishment and dominant institutions; and conformation of a paradigm for us to use in place of the present one of "normal science", to respond to the needs we are beginning to feel as participatory investigators and men and women of science with experiential commitments. This chapter deals with these two topics.

COOPTATION OF THE IDEA OF PARTICIPATION

The 1997 Congress, recalling that twenty years before academic circles had dismissed participatory research as unscientific and unreliable for not following positivist canons, took note of the strong tendency that had emerged since then to assimilate or coopt this methodology[1]. PR's adoption has been particularly noteworthy in that, from 1989 on, all the regional congresses of our great family have been organized at universities and attended by representatives from international organizations, government departments and NGOs.

Actually, participatory research and the quasi-ideological concept of participation began to be incorporated into official policies by governments, international organizations and academic institutions some decades ago. Many delegates from such entities were conspicuously present in Cartagena, and one of them (Anders Rudqvist, of Sweden) ran the risk of organizing a working group, on the World Bank's participatory macro-projects, in the Congress's Garden of Proposals. This presentation also received positive input from Robert Chambers and his central paper (Chapter 11).

What is the reason for this cooptation? There are certain signs pointing to it. For example, it is evident that the large economic-development projects sponsored by the aid agencies have not worked satisfactorily (except for the oligarchies), and that developmentalist policies have not been equal to the task of meeting people's needs, for the reasons discussed by the working groups (see Chapter 17). The lifeline is promotion of popular participation and P(A)R, increasingly seen to be convincing. However, there is doubt about the authenticity of enthusiastic claims by many institutions and non-governmental organizations that they are applying PAR when they are not really doing so, having become, as someone said, bureaucratic "bag" entities that monopolize resources in their offices instead of letting them flow properly to the base communities. This explains the recent wave of rejection of NGOs by such communities. In addition, risks are seen in vertical (top-down) experiences that are also labelled as participatory and show poor technical quality. Hence the need to look for convincing solutions, like the successful initiatives of our authentically participative family that were presented and reviewed in Cartagena; and the need to be clear about (and, it is hoped, have control over) the processes of assimilation of our idea by institutions in danger of sinking.

Current cooptation of PAR, PRA (Participatory Rural Appraisal) and sister techniques is therefore understandable but must be watchfully observed. Ample evidence of positive cooptation is provided by hundreds of social and political movements and NGOs associated with these ideas in the Third World and also in the First.[2] Presentations at the Congress thus showed that the different forms of social, cultural and economic participation stimulated by our trends have been institutionalized without too much watering-down but are in danger of being adulterated.

To sum up, in conclusion: where our endeavors are recognized as "emancipatory" or liberating efforts rather than applications of "expertise", that is, recognized as successful attempts to redress unbalanced and/or unfair processes of social change, alienation and ecological devastation, as efforts to improve educational techniques and devise better forms of communication, planning and systems theory, and as stimuli for developing more satisfactory and humane functions of business administration and management, there will be less risk of negative cooptation and a greater possibility of crowning these endeavors with a new paradigm commensurate with our aspirations and capabilities. According to the consensus generated in Cartagena, this is the golden rule we should apply to defend the authenticity of participation and ensure that P(A)R is employed in a manner consistent with its implicit ideological and philosophical commitments, according to the frames of reference described above.

TOWARDS A NEW PARADIGM

On the basis of these facts it is not surprising that the skepticism expressed at the 1977 First Symposium about a new scientific paradigm (despite Heinz Moser's prophetic paper)[3] should have given way, twenty years later in Cartagena, to prudent acknowledgement of a possibility of building it.

In fact, authorized opinions like William H. Whyte's were heard at Cartagena about the need to break away from "the hegemony of a single research modality that precludes comprehension of the complexity of the world."[4] It was suggested that a likely non-hegemonic paradigm should above all combine the praxeological with the ethical; it would articulate academic knowledge and popular wisdom, the rational and the existential, the regular and the fractal, but as an open project of ongoing research, not one fenced in by a self-complacent intellectual elite acting as watchdogs of knowledge, as occurs today with the dominant paradigm.

An emerging paradigm for us would also be inspired by the concept of "otherness", which recognizes and values the other's knowledge. Rejecting dogmas and absolute truths, it would favor: learning to live with differences; knowing how to communicate and share what is learnt; introducing perspectives of gender, popular classes, and multi-ethnicity into projects; and many other positive, altruistic and democratic approaches. An emerging paradigm for us would bring about an articulation of science with conscience, and of the heart beating in time with reason. All this would make it something unique in the history of science, by linking it to lived and felt experience or existential *Erfahrung*.

With a paradigm reconstructed in this fashion, the social values of the actual work performed in participatory research could not be hidden or disguised, as some purists assert, but would be openly recognized and incorporated into the frames of reference. Thus Cartagena Congress rejected once more the precepts of so-called "objective science" and "internal validity", and agreed that in participatory research the gathering of knowledge should not be governed by value-neutrality but by clarity of purpose in the work being performed.

Of course, dilemmas continue to exist in the construction of an alternative paradigm. This point was discussed by Fernando Henrique Cardoso, who is a sociologist and the President of Brazil (Chapter 2). Cardoso said that, since it was impossible to walk away from an unfair reality, it was necessary to learn what relations existed between the logic of a rigorous knowledge of society and the logic of action in a political project. To define such relations no monopoly could be held over truth or morality by either academics or public figures. It would be best, Cardoso maintained, to engage in debate and dialogue to strike a balance between the ideal and the possible, between conviction and responsibility, between the technical and the ethical, so that political decisions might at least be "enlightened" by thought. Cardoso thus transcends Hegel's old injunction to politicians and philosophers not to attempt to act and learn at the same time without allowing for the reverse effect of theory on praxis.[5]

For his part our Colombian colleague Alfredo Molano in recollecting the 1977 Symposium acknowledged that by then P(A)R, with creative skepticism, had already discarded Marxist dogmatism and the commonplaces of functionalism, with the idea that commitment and militancy could be "serious scientific tasks". This was part of the paradigm search. However, Molano saw a continuing crisis in work centered on analyzing conflicts such as those arising from violence or postmodernity; in this work, efforts by investigators to explain or resolve the conflict often proved suicidal. (See Chapter 1)

Despite such weighty reservations, other participants felt that the new scientific paradigm of open searching would help in three ways to improve the working of institutions and the life of communities. One way was to focus on the shaded areas of overlap between the formal boundaries of our arts and disciplines, this being one of the major challenges facing science today. The second way was to shake up the tardy, tedious and routine-bound academic world that is rejected by demanding students and professors, and put these people in touch with the real life of problems of communities, as a necessary condition for reviving the academic world. The third way was to break down the intellectual isolation created by technical jargon, and bring freshness and clarity to the language and style of communication of the disciplines. This was explained and demonstrated at the Congress not only by communicators, writers and invited artists, with their deep insight and creative imagination, but also by civil engineers concerned with the human aspects and the social system that have a bearing on their particular tasks.

In Paper 155, Peter Park states that the new paradigm for PR should enrich the values of the naturalistic paradigm (consistency, simplicity, scope, certitude and productivity) by supplying other values such as altruism, sincerity, trust, autonomy and responsibility. According to him, these values are the machine that may constantly rejuvenate society via participatory research —they should be taught to our community of practitioners .

Construction of this new, more feeling, open paradigm may be a preferred task for the younger generations, who came to Cartagena with overflowing enthusiasm. It will be their historical responsibility to continue and persevere in this work. We the older participants expressed our full confidence in them at the Congress.

Notes

1. There has been little treatment of this tendency. See the analysis I presented in 1991, in Fals Borda and Rahman, cit, 43-45. *Cf.* D. Greenwood's points of view in Paper 17.

2. These facts lead us to reject imputations that our position is ambiguous over developmentalism, *cf.* Majid Rahnema and Victoria Bawtree, eds., *The Post-Development Reader*, London: ZED Books, 1997, ix, 388. These authors provide highly respectable data and arguments against "development", and so does Wolfgang Sachs, ed., *The Development Dictionary*, London: ZED Books, 1992. The development institutions' inertia in this matter is amazing but partly explicable by the vested interests surrounding them. To disguise "development" by attaching

to it adjectives such as "participatory" and "sustainable", which contradict the noun, is a clumsy way of coopting participation and participatory research. See reference to Arturo Escobar's important contribution in Chapter 17.

3. Heinz Moser and Helmut Ornauer, eds., *Internationale Aspekte der Aktionsforschung*, Munich: Kösel Verlag, 1978. These viewpoints have been reinforced by Capra, cit., 81-162 by proposing five criteria for a new paradigm, namely, from the parts to the whole, from structure to process, from objective to epistemic; from building to network, and from truth to approximate descriptions.

4. W.F. Whyte, D.J. Greenwood and P. Lazes, "PAR Through Practice to Science in Social Research", in Whyte, ed., *Participatory Action Research*, London: Sage, 1991.

5. *Cf.* Habermas, *Theory and Practice*, cit., 139, 182, containing viewpoints convergent with Cardoso's.

16. IMPLICATIONS FOR SCHOOLS AND COMPANIES

Important contributions were made on the subject of participatory research by educators and businessmen who came to Cartagena to take part in the working groups on popular and adult education, and systematization of business and environmental management.

SCHOOLS AND UNIVERSITIES

Educators attending the Congress, such as Budd Hall, Stephen Kemmis, Robin McTaggart and Arlés Caruso, considered many of today's educational institutions to be vacuous and in a serious crisis, for having turned instruction into exploitable merchandise. They therefore recommended changing the form and substance of teaching, improving the techniques and contexts of communication, motivating teachers, and generally combatting the deadening routine of schools and universities. On Colombian education, Gabriel García Márquez, winner of the Nobel literature prize and a promoter of the Congress, has said: "Our irrational violence is to be blamed largely on a formalistic, repressive and stultifying education, which bears no resemblance to us at all (considering our creativity)."

1. The teachers concurred in recommending "action-learning", "educational-leap" and "*the-teacher-as-researcher*" campaigns, introduced some years before and essentially designed to bring formal teaching back into touch with informal instruction, from which it should never have been separated, for the latter represented the realities of communal life.[1] They also urged that academic structures and curricula should give greater attention to the complex issues we have inherited, to provide

an understanding of them and establish order among them, using participatory research for the purpose; this urging was vociferously supported by the students present, worried about the uncertain future professional life offers them nowadays.

2. Stress was laid on the need to promote urgent work such as implanting an early respect among schoolchildren for *human rights* and responsible citizenship, and defending *peace* and tolerance in dealing with public or private issues. It was generally agreed that *children* and their rights and creative abilities should be valued, and that much still remained to be done in this respect.

3. We recognized, as taught before by De Schutter, that there should be communicating vessels between participatory research and education, with educators boldly and resolutely taking on the participatory *research work* needed to learn more about the realities of school and community life, to involve and motivate students of all ages to the point that they become managers of their own learning, and also to strengthen the teachers' role in providing leadership and collective orientation. Budd Hall is very illuminating on these issues in Paper 95.

4. A possible aim would be to turn the classroom into an articulated system of communication, investigation and knowledge-building between its different strata, and in this way establish a kind of *integral educational community*. The conversation between Horton and Freire at the Highlander Center was considered highly relevant contribution on this point.

5. The working groups on formal and information pedagogical experimentation, led by John Gaventa and Sue Thrasher,[2] focussed on these topics, discussed many concrete cases presented by participants, and identified other issues arising in the institutions concerned, particularly with regard to gender and popular education, training of educators, and participatory evaluation of learning and teaching.

   Women, it was seen, tend to be more numerous and persevering than men both in seeking education and in educational administration. Yet, male-chauvinist or androcentric tendencies continue to exist in philosophical-pedagogical concepts and prevent a greater expansion of the different perspectives that would be provided by an educational policy more balanced in this respect. Women continue to play a central role in introducing and spreading the principle of educational participation.

The *training* of educators remained routinized despite the unmistakable beginnings of a search for better communication techniques and group dynamics in the classroom and the surrounding community. Participatory *evaluation* of learning and *teaching* (also described as "eye-witness", "interactive", "emancipatory", etc.) often came up against the contrary aims of the mercantile conceptions of teaching imposed by prevailing models and by government policy, for example, formation of "human capital" and competitivity, The Congress thought it would not be easy to reach a congruence of evaluation factors, though it agreed that it was highly desirable socially and culturally to do so.

6. Interest was shown in learning about *heterodox educational experiences*, such as the "Barefoot College" in Tilonia, India, which was designed as a self-reliant solution to specific problems in the waste lands of Bihar. According to the College's founder Bunker Roy, it is often necessary "to unlearn what has been learnt" and "undo normal science" in order to assimilate local knowledge and talent, which are more effective for solving problems. In these conditions degrees and diplomas are of no use; only qualifications acquired through local experience serve any purpose. Such rejection of formal academia, which started back in the sixties, was shared by quite a few delegations. It is another major symptom of the search for a new open paradigm.

7. Special attention was also given in Cartagena to reviewing the relations between the *marginal and central* in popular education. Many dissident educators have worked at the margins of institutions, experimenting with participation and with ludic expressions or games. To our surprise, these marginal spaces have sometimes expanded considerably, and the methods of work devised there have been adopted or coopted for use among millions of people (in Australia, South Africa and Chile) and even in formal school or university programs. We may recall here that for the indigenous people of Australia the recovery in the

eighties of their traditional instruments and music (inventively combined with rock), through the efforts of young teachers using P(A)R in the schools, also signified recovery of their dignity as a people.

8. This transition from the margins towards the center of educational institutions raises certain questions. Are the new participatory methods making a difference and producing better results in both teaching and research? How do we respond to the change in power relationships that this involves, for the purpose of transforming institutional practices? How to ensure that changes taken to the center from the margins are not subsequently lost at the margins?

   These questions were partly answered by Jaime Niño Díez (Chapter 3), a sociologist and Colombia's minister of education, in recounting the history of the *New School*. The challenge was originally rural, that is, marginal to the country's educational institutions, and involved raising the level of teaching in difficult material conditions, with a poorly trained teaching staff. After fifteen years' practice the results are encouraging, the idea has spread to other countries and received attention from UNESCO for its new *MOST programs* (Chapter 4). However, according to the minister, the present situations make it advisable for the New School to be given a fresh technical and methodological impetus, including research training, and P(A)R has been recommended and adopted in the ministry to serve as a guiding light in this campaign.

9. The challenges faced by *universities* are equally great but better known. The process of cooptation there has led to participatory research being taught today in thousands of lecture halls across the world (a very great number of universities were represented at Cartagena). But attempts at fieldwork by professors and students have been hindered by curriculum inflexibility, academic cycles (semesters or years), and the requirement of presenting an individual thesis to obtain a degree. As we have seen, PR fieldwork is of medium- or long-term duration and requires a minimum continuity, with perseverance and personal or group commitment, at least on the part of professors and students who keep up the pace of the work beyond a particular semester.

Institutions do not always present the necessary combination of this condition for building links between university and society by participatory means. Elitism and business carry a lot of weight. Even so, it is easy to see that determined efforts to build such links would lead to fundamental transformations in university structures and functions. This is something that many young students have been feeling and demanding for some time to make the universities more attuned to life beyond their sphere and to the realities that condition us all.

In general, the working groups agreed with the theses put forward by Stephen Kemmis, an Australian educator and Congress rapporteur, to the effect that "teachers could form critical action-research working groups in their schools that gradually involve students and other school members in a collaborative exercise of self-reflection. At systems level, this means that curriculum advisors, organizers and supervisors should give back the responsibility for educational policy to teachers and others in the field. Such is the nature of emancipatory action-research as an expression of the critical science of education".[3]

COMPANIES AND MICROBUSINESSES

As regards businessmen and micro-entrepreneurs, the aberrant persistence of a savage, exploitative neoliberal capitalism in the Third World has left them out of participatory campaigns, although a measure of ideological injection is beginning to reach them through the idea of "economic solidarity" and humane concepts of efficiency. In this connection, helpful presentations were made by Davydd Greenwood and William H. Whyte on the Mondragón Cooperatives in Spain,[4] and by systems theorists who extended the techniques and concepts of soft-systems theory to business administration.[5]

The experiences presented by the so-called "Scandinavian school", referred to earlier, showed that participatory techniques improved work performance and plant operation, bringing greater fairness for the workers and greater satisfaction to the manufacturers. Besides these experiences, case histories from Sweden, Australia, South Africa, Philippines and Venezuela were reviewed.

1. Indeed, it seems to be demonstrable that greater productivity and better results in companies are directly related to *worker participation*. In Swedish steelworks, on the basis of direct explorations and recommendations by the workers involved, the designs of control booths have been modified, with excellent results. In Australia, worker participation has received considerable university support from professors' involvement in *extracurricular activities* in the community, though still with institutional difficulties. Such difficulties have been formally studied in Venezuela by a group at the Centro-Occidental University concerned with management decision-making.

2. When Nelson Mandela became President of South Africa, *interracial groups* were organized to introduce support and tolerance activities in the factories, companies and entities where group members were employed. Major self-evaluation and participatory exercises were also organized and continue to be performed to this day in this reconstruction process. The Congress did not go deeply into racial problems or inter-racial tensions occurring in the rich countries, but it did clearly express its support for the claims of all groups subjected to exploitation or oppression for racial (or religious or gender) reasons.

3. In the Philippines, participatory forms of communication and action and special projects were used in implementing a large-scale program for the *transfer of technology* to microbusinesses run by small farmers. The program sought to increase farm income, improve workers' efficiency and vitalize the rural economy. Workers and farm owners took an active part in designing and carrying out these projects, with very positive results.

4. We agreed that, if capitalism continued to globalize its well-known exploitative system, as seemed inevitable that it would to the point of self-collapse, we would have to combat its insidious effects on companies and, beyond them, on the communities they operated in and on the local people. These aspects were explained by Rodolfo Stavenhagen of Mexico (Paper 9). It should not be forgotten that, in economic terms, the greater part of production and employment, and a good part of consumption and investment takes place, after all, at

regional, national and, especially, local levels; and that *globalization*, particularly of money markets, has many ramifications and is largely elitist.

To promote combat against large-scale exploitative globalization (discussed in detail below), attention was drawn to how important the informal sector or economy is to the business dynamics of the most defenseless part of the population, the part that does not fit in the dominant models. These informal sectors of microbusinesses and tradesmen, which include women, children and marginal groups, are beginning to discover forms of communication with one another and of socio-economic organization that may lead them to create their own systems of administration and management. This P(A)R response, if it is intensified, can help to remove sharp contradictions in today's world.

NOTES

1. An important contribution was made in this connection by the (Colombian) Caribbean Coast Regional Encounter, sponsored by Cartagena University, COREDUCAR, and the Workers' Circle of Fundación Social, and organized by Carmen Cabrales, Javier Hernández, Raúl Paniagua and Rosa D. de Paniagua. The Encounter's publication, *Una visión participativa de la Costa Caribe colombiana*, Cartagena: Universidad de Cartagena, June 1997, contains 25 interesting papers, and rapporteurs' reports by Victor Negrete, Liliana Pérez, Edgar Rey Sinning, Ana Pombo de Cordero, Julio Sierra and Kenia Victoria. Seven other university and regional encounters were held in Colombia (Bogotá, Medellín, Bucaramanga, Villavicencio, Yopal, Ibagué and Pamplona) in preparation for the Congress; their papers were submitted to the working groups. These events were coordinated by CINEP (Centro de Investigación y Educación Popular) represented by Marco Raúl Mejía and Marco Vargas, and CLEBA represented by Alfredo Ghiso.

2. The speakers in these groups were: Sue Thrasher, Helen M. Lewis, Mary Ann Hinsdale, Carol Añonuevo, Losandro Tedeschi, Jorge Jeria, Derek Mulenga, Paul Wangoola, Carmen N. Hernández, Veronica McKay, Allan Feldman, Ximena Zúñiga, James Blackburn, Vicki Creed, Yusuf Kassam, Ben Osuga, Deborah Johnson, John Thompson, Julián Gonsalves, Bunker Roy, Gabriel Kaplun, Flor Alba Romero, Luis E. Alvarado, Salomón Magendzo, Mike Sarakinsky, Colin Fletcher,

Cristina Frodden, Elijah Sekgobela, Gerard Rademeyer, Jürgen Hagmann, Edward Chuma, Mike Connolly, Ricardo Cetrulo and Sergio Haddad. Jorge Osorio of Chile set up the group with John Gaventa.

3. Carr and Kemmis, cit., 224.

4. The case of the Mondragón Cooperatives was upheld theoretically and professionally as a "humanistic enterprise" by Mark A. Lutz, an economist, and Kenneth Lux, a clinical psychologist, in their book *Humanistic Economics: The New Challenge*, New York: The Bootstrap Press, 1988. This book denounces neoclassical economics as a mathematical expression of scholasticism. The authors turn back to the original tradition of political economy, which appears to be more congruent with the theses and theories of participatory research as discussed in Cartagena, because it does not divorce economics from society.

5. P.B. Checkland and J. Scholes, *Soft Systems Methodology in Action*, Chichester: Wiley, 1990. The working group was coordinated by Ernesto Parra. The main speakers were: Anders Machs, Bertil Olsson, C.K. Christensen, J.J. Watters, C. Arcodia, Y. Ryan, P. Weeks, Kathleen Collins, Julieta R. Roa, Javier Escalera and Alicia Sanabria de Camino. This group was set up by Fernando Rojas.

17. IMPLICATIONS IN GEOPOLITICAL TIMESPACE

The large concept of geopolitical and transformational TimeSpace expounded in Cartagena was employed by some working groups in discussing strategic issues of international scope: globalization, developmentalism, democratization and local government, social and cultural movements, justice and conflict resolution, poverty and hunger, biodiversity and natural resources.

GLOBALIZATION

The group coordinated by Socorro Ramírez and Juan Tokatlián,[1] both political analysts, clearly identified the general characteristics of the globalization, transnationalization and homogenization processes cyclically inflicted (from the time of modern empires) on all societies, particularly indigenous communities, for control of the natural resources they possess. Global processes, driven today by technological change, are now causing subordination of societies through the overwhelming force of the capitalist market, especially of financial capital, a fluctuating mass hurtling unpredictably around the world.

Capitalist globalization, it is well known, has deleterious effects on identities, cultures, relations between countries, and democracy. Guided by a neoliberal ideology (regarded by many as equivalent to neoconservatism), it makes for uniformity in the management of national economies and in consumer values and patterns, and tends to devitalize autochthonous cultures. It is anti-participatory. It gives rise to integrations, exclusions and differentiations that limit the national and regional dynamics vital to human solidarity-not even the richest and most advanced nations escape from this. And what seems worse: at global level the resulting phenomenon would not be democratic but hegemonic and potentially imperative or autocratic. Not even the United Nations, in its haven of safety, has managed to avoid this tendency. Unipolarity can turn capitalist globalization into a suffocating mantle over small and medium-sized nations, depriving them of their autonomy, despite the would-be democratic theses upheld by its adherents.

Globalizing processes are made possible by a number of mechanisms, some of them disastrous, others more or less benign. The communicators' group coordinated by Martín-Barbero drew attention to information technologies and the mass media, asserting that their chief impact today is pluralization and dissemination of knowledge. They attributed this to displacement of the hierarchies that used to choose and decide what was to be known and by whom, and to dispersion —away from the center— of the social settings in which knowledge is built. A new global space is thus produced, in which: collective demands and new expressions of identity become visible; relations are forged between cultures which are no longer successive; and different narrative forms (oral, written, audiovisual, virtual) are employed together and interact with one another.

The challenge of globalization involves loss of certain social values considered vital to democratic participation, such as solidarity, collective trust, and a sense of personal and even national security. Three types of safeguards were proposed by the other working groups against such loss: cultural safeguards, to lay stress on things local, diversity and otherness; economic safeguards, based on alternative programs, such as those of the "barefoot economy;" and political safeguards, to emphasize radicalization of democracy wherever possible, reconsider the present role of an authentically democratic socialism, and foster the creation of a "global civil society".

1. With regard to local diversity/otherness (as treated by Tzvetan Todorov), the philosophers in Guillermo Hoyos's group expressed themselves in favor of a multiculturalism that forges bonds, which they described as the "issue of the moment". Multiculturalism is both the driving force and origin of resources for the participatory decentralized democracy that is being fostered in many countries. As a result there has been a revival in both the North and the South of spatial entities such as

region, ethnic group and community that serve as deep-seated antidotes or cultural checks to globalizing tendencies. The local aspect is very important, for it holds the roots of people's reality. In the former socialist world, in European countries with autonomous regions (Spain, France, Italy, Belgium, Germany), and in Latin America there are many cases of decentralization in which the process of territorial reorganization has served or is serving to democratize institutions and induce greater political participation by local communities.

Locally rooted cultural and political tendencies are making themselves felt, even in poor neighborhoods and communities in or near large cities. We saw this in Cartagena on field trips to Henequén (a neighborhood of collectors of recyclable waste materials), and to Arroyogrande (a fishing village endeavoring to protect its marshes) (see Video 3). In these two localities there are effective mechanisms for safeguarding communal life, manifestations of important social movements, and a fostering of local cultural expressions, which have allowed the inhabitants to regain a good measure of respectability and dignity. The same can be said of many other similar cases on all five continents, for the North also has its South. This phenomenon can be expected to articulate resistance against globalization. In this practical way participatory research can "deconstruct" uniformization and, according to many participants, work towards a common front of cultural action to bring together the interests and identities of the South's poor and the North's exploited, induce congruent policies of general and world-wide concern, and help to humanize rampant capitalism.

The transformation of capitalism was highlighted in Cartagena as a very dramatic, almost impossible, task. For it means giving capitalism not only "a human face" but also a change of heart. How is this to be done by quixotic individuals? Granted that, with the reversal of socialism, capital has become globally victorious, it is showing a monstrous Gorgon-eyed face hugely capable of producing good and evil with a single look. It is a fact that capitalism creates matchless wealth and unheard-of poverty at the same time and by the same act. Not as successive, mutually exclusive events, like night and day, but as fatally inseparable phenomena, like siamese twins. The efficiency of this monstrosity is inexplicable and seems to make it unrestrainable.[2]

But without the possibilities we see in regional cultures, local diversities and respect for gregarious otherness, we would be in even worse straits. That is why no other alternatives were found in Cartagena than to pursue the quixotic ideal of participation.

2. Economic response to these difficult issues is based on the kind of analysis and action Manfred Max-Neef has been expounding for many years, with reference to development indicators, agglutinating elements of civilization, and criticism of neoliberalism.[3] Not all growth (e.g. much-talked-of "development") is good. It may be inhuman and benefit only a few, as occurs now with capitalist globalization and as happened before with the so-called Green Revolution. According to Max-Neef, growth indicators, even in countries regarded as advanced, such as England, Denmark, Germany, Sweden, Austria and the United States, show that beyond a "threshold point" the curve for domestic production and the curve for satisfaction of basic needs diverge: inequalities multiply and poverty reappears even in situations thought to be buoyant. A certain tendency towards self-destruction then begins to emerge in global capitalism. It seems as though, like the mythological "uroboro", it were starting to devour itself from the tail, leaving behind amongst other things a social debt almost impossible to repay. No sustainable economic development is therefore likely to result from the present norms of globalization and free marketry. Viable alternatives will have to be found to ensure survival of communities; the World Bank's Working Group on Participation is presently engaged in seeking such alternatives. Max-Neef maintained in his address that the strengthening of local economies and cultures would provide considerable protection against this globalization, which was not sustainable indefinitely. There was no need to give it a new face or a change of heart; rather efforts should be made to induce its total decomposition or autophagy. Strong criticism was directed against the current theory and practice of "socio-economic develop-

ment" and against "macroeconomics;" this is further discussed below.

3. Political solutions were put forward, based on the belief that the response to capitalist globalization needed to be equally macro and at the same level as the challenge posed by it. But there was little clarity, much less consensus, on this issue, though it was felt that many leaders were clearly an integral part of the problem, and that they and their parties would have to be the target of action in any endeavor to bring about fundamental transformations.

Dominant Western nations are concerned with extending to the rest of the world the model of democratic representation based on the Westphalian concept of "state sovereignty". In many places this would lead to the establishment of more radical and more extensive democratic processes. In others, however, if respect is shown for the concept of local otherness-diversity (which recognizes the influence of cultural, political, ethnic, religious and other factors at the local level, as referred to above), there might arise forms of administration that are not necessarily democratic in the Western sense but are otherwise open, community-based, semidemocratic, or even authoritarian, and respond to the people's right of self-determination, asserted by invoking "popular sovereignty". This would not resolve the problem of a macro-response to globalization; in fact it would result in a dispersion of political forms of zonal or regional (not national, much less global) government that could not be easily articulated but would be more authentic and more autonomous. However, as a reaction or response against current globalization tendencies, they could come into play at any moment, as has already occurred in several places.

Another macro-solution proposed by some participants was a pluralistic socialism. Socialism was properly understood as a universal civilizing project embodying its primordial social values, not the personalistic and bureaucratic socialism known and suffered by millions of people in many countries, nor the false socialism of Kardelj's reported self-management in Yugoslavia. The aim would be, not direct seizure of state power by force of arms, as used to be mooted, but a social leap having practical consequences. This involves the creation of political movements of a new, democratically participatory kind, like the Workers' Party in Porto Alegre (Brazil), or the movements set up in Villa el Salvador (Peru) and Montevideo (Uruguay) to fight for social justice and defend the classes exploited by landowners, businessmen, and practitioners of savage capitalism. It signifies a swing of the historical pendulum towards the "left", as has occurred periodically and seems to be heralded by the latest elections in France, England, Mexico and Argentina.

Many of the injustices and imbalances discernible in the current tendencies could be remedied by a renovated, global social democracy which looked back with respect on Marx and other critical thinkers and martyrs of a socialism that deployed the values of life and joy (rather than tanks of war), a social democracy that respected organized civil society. It would be more than just an "open society" in which a "better" capitalism continued to hold sway. Rather the intention would be to civilize and humanize capitalism, as mentioned earlier, to change its egoistic, exploitative, usurious nature. Perhaps the efforts needed to eradicate poverty would give rise to a unifying global ideology capable of eliminating the present aberrations of capitalist globalization.

Lastly, another political alternative discussed in Cartagena was to foster global networks by using such resources as electronic media and the Internet to build up a "global civil society" with sufficient self-identity, moral force and civic power to rectify existing defects and counterbalance the power of the multinational corporations.[4] The Souths could unite their voices and efforts against the Norths to induce them to undertake a corrective review of the system predominating in their own midst.

In conclusion, it would be well to follow Manuel Castells's recent, timely advice on this matter: "We need a compass and an anchor —the compass: individual and collective education, information and knowledge; the anchor: our identity— to know who we are and where we have come from, so as not to lose our way to where we are going".[5]

DEVELOPMENTALISM, POVERTY AND NATURAL RESOURCES

The working group coordinated by Arturo Escobar and María Cristina Rojas[6] agreed that the usual concept and practice of "development" were in crisis, development being an idea associated with criticizable modernity. Its results are not convincing on the social or economic front: though production rates may have increased, distribution of the wealth generated has not improved. The debate has been going on for some years now in Europe and North America (see references above to Escobar, Sachs and Rahnema), because the problems and strains resulting from oft-attempted "development" outnumber its accumulated benefits. When the failures became apparent, new formulas were nimbly invented by attaching "participatory", "sustainable", "integral" or the like to "development", without making it any more convincing. For these qualifiers fail to mask the original sin of that first developmentalist proposition conceived in the North on Harry Truman's Point IV (1948) and imposed on the South as a model to be replicated.[7]

In Cartagena observations on this issue mainly confirmed Max-Neef's view that "sustainable development" is impossible to attain with the recent economic liberalizations and the dominant norms of global capitalism. And even evolutive attempts to combine the old state interventionism with freely competitive capitalism will not make it any more attainable. Privatization of state-owned enterprises does not make for greater participation, either. In fact, "development" creates an entropy which steadily demolishes the very resources (natural, social, cultural, human) that development feeds on. Reaching zero growth may satisfy the advanced countries' present hopes about population increase, but it would destroy the productive roots of the tropical and subtropical Third World. This would be an intolerable situation, particularly for countries that look to growth for the well-being of their people.

A serious threat looms over the globe from developmentalist ecological abuse, which, stimulated by savage capital, has so far proved impossible to control. Yesterday's defective Green Revolutions have turned into today's environmentalist campaigns fostered by international technocracies, often with no attempt to adapt them to pressing social, cultural and political needs.

Moreover, this ecoglobalism is presented as the "responsibility of all" on planet Earth. Yet the capitalists of the advanced countries are more to blame for environmental depredation than people in the poorer countries. As a matter of fact, many poor communities, including indigenous groups, have been seen to show greater respect for the environment than the rich or powerful.

Such arguments led Escobar's group to ask: From what perspective, from what cultural, social and cognitive fronts, can we supplant "development" as we have seen it practiced, with such doubtful results? Alternatives are presented in different parts of the world which may be interrelated on three fronts, as discussed earlier: social movements; cultural, social and ecological practices; and knowledge-producing processes.

On the one hand, since local worlds continue to exist —they still make themselves felt by expressing significant differences with dominant models and successfully resisting them—, the universe could be rethought from these micro-perspectives, by learning to see, hear and present those local worlds with a greater insight obtained from non-conventional forms of knowledge. On the other hand, to protect them it is best to set aside the customary dualisms (global/local, capitalist/non-capitalist) and by getting a better understanding of power and its multiple fissures, such as those created by various ethnic groups and communities, move in through such fissures with determination and commitment to make the necessary transformations.

This means breaking the complicity of social discourse with the present organization of power, without being taken in by the siren songs of neoliberalism, economic liberalization, and globalization. Survival of all worlds will depend on this and on the consequent changes in contemporary conceptions of production, consumption, democracy and ethics, particularly as regards natural resources and their use—where capitalism has been most rapacious and destructive. And such changes, in turn, will reduce the rate of destruction by global entropy.

These vital aspects were also discussed by the working groups on poverty and hunger (coordinated by Elssy Bonilla),[8] and on biodiversity, natural resources and habitat preservation (coordinated by Marc Lammerink and Timmi Tillmann).[9]

There is no doubt that these problems are connected with neoliberalism and the disastrous "development" policies criticized above. A dangerous time bomb is ticking away: it is the historical social debt owed to the poor classes, exploited and oppressed by dominant systems with their callously gained wealth. To be able to eradicate poverty, it is necessary to find out about and get to know the power elites from the inside. This was corroborated in Cartagena by important evidence of general disasters in Ghana, Colombia (Cartagena, Cauca, Ciénaga Grande de Santa Marta), New Zealand, Brazil, Nicaragua and the Himalayas, in which the iron hand of the oligarchy was discernible. Two very great dangers were stressed: 1) lack of water, already a factor in several armed conflicts in Europe and Africa, and likely to cause more savage confrontations elsewhere; and 2) deforestation, a cause of climatological changes, increased erosion, and air pollution, and a threat to what little is left of frontier forests in Asia, and to tropical jungles in Indonesia, Brazil and Colombia. A disturbing question asked in Cartagena was: Why are existing cutting-edge technologies not being used immediately and fully to solve such serious problems as those arising from present energy use, which causes so much ravage? It is for governments to answer.

Regarding the accumulated social debt, there is a "poverty-and-hunger trap" implicit in "development" policies; and the usual practices of top-down transfer of technology have proved a failure. It is particularly disturbing to see what is happening to genetic banks, which are seizing from indigenous communities by pharmaceutical companies under exclusive patents. Fortunately, however, there are also positive developments such as: effective Regional Research Committees; applied Participatory Planning; credit initiatives designed to offer "the poor of the world fairness and self-reliance as a liberating process", such as SOCED (Ecumenical Development Cooperative Society), created by the World Council of Churches; technical and educational programs for water and environmental protection (such as those organized from Holland); socio-economic techniques of waste recycling; and intelligent application of Participatory Rural Assessment. In all these experiences, as reported in Cartagena, there have been fruitful horizontal exchanges between external agents of change and leaders and entrepreneurs, so that suitable modifications of approach and behavior may reasonably be expected. This would include a return to policies for autonomous promotion of many local activities such as afforestation, farming and industry (other than ranching) in less advanced countries, and defense of such activities from foreign competition, which often arrives subsidized.

Once more we concluded that an alternative to the phenomena of "misdevelopment" referred to above would be based on and inspired by popular participation and political struggle. Such an alternative has already been proposed, studied and adopted by many institutions. The main methodology applied so far with some success in these cases has been participatory action research.

DEMOCRATIZATION, SOCIAL MOVEMENTS AND LOCAL GOVERNMENT

The individual working groups on democratization, coordinated by Franciso Leal Buitrago[10], on social movements, by Jaime Arocha,[11] on social integration, by Elías Sevilla Casas,[12] and on participation and local government, by Tomás R. Villasante[13], converged on at least two points: 1) that grass-roots or local democracy needs to be revived by means of civil-society movements, and imbued with positive or non-reactionary values and concepts such as active citizenship, hybrid culture, ethnic reconstruction, otherness, local identity and inter-group transmission of meaning; and 2) that neoliberalism holds a danger of fostering freedom-less democracies (elaboration of one of the theses expounded by Agnes Heller at the Congress).

To begin with, Anibal Quijano of Perú pointed out that, in the context of modernization, citizenship-building was entering a state of crisis. P(A)R, with its liberating effect on thought, word and feeling, could contribute to exerting a countervailing force in the balance of power, and developing novel theses on "governability". Popular and civic movements organized for this purpose are displacing the old discredited, patronage-wielding parties and moving towards diverse expressions of "popular power". According to President Cardoso, citizenship for its part involves more than voting: it calls for developing a kind of political wisdom that goes beyond self-interest.

Social movements (whether cultural, economic or political) are subject to discontinuous or spiralling cycles, which determine whether they will survive, become strengthened or disappear. Reference was made at the Congress to the historical backgrounds of movements that had run the cyclical course from initial protest to lasting political proposal. A case in point were the English Chartists (1838-1848), whose movement led to the creation of the Labour Party once they had become wealthy through utopian socialism and Rochdalean cooperativism. It was apparent from later cases and also contemporary ones that movements might need periodical renovations and changes of leaders if they wished to remain in existence. This is clearly seen in movements like those of Colombia, which have been sharply curbed through cooptation, corruption and assassination, combined with media control and silence.

The kind of leadership required is a mystery. Charisma alone is not enough because of the decisive importance of both the context in which the leaders operate and tactical opportunities. Much may depend also on the composition of the anti-elitist organizations that displace dominant groups. Nor is the usual leadership training either definitive or formative, for it tends to become merely a generally useful experiential attitude.

The Congress seemed to feel that no characteristic portrait could be drawn of movement leaders. Lists of desirable qualities are often made, but a combination of such qualities is just as likely to produce an easily manipulated puppet or a Frankenstein. There is however evident danger from people with authoritarian tendencies, a lack of humility, or no sense of self-criticism, or who neglect to become attuned to the communities. Nor did a collective or rotating leadership seem all that practical or advisable to the Congress.

Instead, the idea of promoting "servant-leaders" was mooted in Cartagena as one way of obviating bureaucratic temptations and building trust among followers. Without such trust no movement can carry out its action cycles or accomplish the transformations it has postulated. Leaders with formal education (like Gandhi, Nehru, Nyerere or Deputy Commander Marcos) are able to translate their education into a liberating experience to remain in touch with the bases, act on their commitments and find possible solutions.

It was said in Cartagena that civil society movements and action groups should study technical-scientific discourses and models of projects to improve the quality of life of social groups, such as those employed in the United States in the "War on Poverty" twenty years ago and later in "Empowerment Zones". Classical schemes of "adoption and application of technological innovations" should be set aside. For there are traditional, premodern or popular actors capable of mobilizing to create and obtain acceptable results from their own practices.

Sufficient evidence of this is provided currently by the successful example of the Movimento dos Sem Terra in Brazil (and formerly by peasant movements in Colombia (ANUC) or in Chiapas, Mexico). Equal success is being achieved in Zimbabwe by the Organization of Rural Associations for Progress (ORAP), comprising 600 units coordinated by Sithembiso Nyoni (presently a minister of State). The thousands of movements in India, from the Bhoomi Sena to those of Chipko, Bhopal and the Narmada Valley, are other endeavors of far-reaching significance in which participatory research has played a part.

Communication between outside "experts" and lay users also deserves attention from movements, according to Tomás Villasante of Spain (Paper 117), for it is necessary "to move on from traditional rituals for reproducing knowledge and standards of conduct, to counter-rites that are conducive to reflective, complex, practical constructions." It is important to "charge and potentiate synergies"[14] in all this process of reconstructing and protecting the local and one's own, so as to forge a new imagery there around the idea of participation through community fronts, civic fora, popular concertation panels, area councils and the like. Moreover, care should be taken not to recede with reactionary movements (such as certain religious, political, racial or gender groupings) that insist on using violence and were in the past known sources of oppression, exploitation, prejudice, fanaticism and killings.

Repudiation was expressed at the Congress of the idea of "peoples without history", with its inadmissible racist and ethnocentric connotations, as evidenced by the realities of African-Americans in the United States and various ethnic groups in Latin America. These peoples (from the inhabitants of Bahia to those of

Ciudad Bolívar in Bogotá and the communes in Bucaramanga studied by participatory research) possess a tremendous dynamism that cannot be explained by current theories of marginality or functionalism. Participatory methods have been employed in ethnic reconstruction, for example among the Oyomán of Venezuela. However, ethical failings have been perceived in some NGOs, either because their leaders preach participation but deny it in their own internal practice, or because, in aiming to replace the State in the provision of services, they become infected with the State's defects, according to reports on Senegal, Mozambique and other countries. Some colleagues, including Smitu Kothari of India, were in favor of renaming the NGOs "social action groups" or something similar that reflected their commitment to the popular classes and a greater striving to fulfill it.

VIOLENCE, CONFLICTS AND REPRESSION

The working group coordinated by Camilo Borrero[15] focussed on violence as a persistent, serious problem in both urban and rural settings. There was consensus on the fact that a cause of violence in all countries is to be found in unequal criteria for distributing the wealth generated by the productive classes; this has grown worse with the recent neoliberal policies of liberalization, which have polarized societies economically. Lack of fairness, justice and generosity in this respect amounts to treason against humanity and has to be remedied, otherwise it leads to intensified internal confrontations and national decomposition, as is sadly the case in Colombia today.

P(A)R's contribution to resolving conflicts of this kind was recognized at the Congress. Discussion also turned on a key question that has been little studied: How is it that some societies, such as those of Central America, become ripe earlier than others for a peaceful solution to their conflicts? We saw that P(A)R can reveal the imageries and representations underlying the logic of acts of violence, and can also provide keys to preventing them; no other methodology is known to do this.

The possibility of fostering peace projects even in extreme circumstances is a positive fact. Such was the conclusion reached not only by the working groups, but also by the plenary panel discussion coordinated by Gustavo De Roux (author of the much applauded "Exhortation for Peace" (Chapter 6)) and Marja Liisa Swantz. Six popular leaders sat on this panel: Manuel Serna (Cimitarra, Colombia), Eduardo Tinkam (Mosquitia, Nicaragua), Leonor Zalabata (Arhuacos, Colombia), C.S. Kilala and Mwajuma Masaiganah (Tanzania). (See Video 7)

The forces seeking the disintegration of society and culture are now more varied, more powerful and usually armed, according to the panelists. Repression is often irrational, excessive and heedless of local and regional realities. The panelists wondered what society would be like if, for example, the United Nations' resolutions on disarmament and prohibition of landmines were complied with, munitions factories were turned into plough foundries, and human rights and the rights of peoples and ethnic groups to self-determination were fully respected. The denouncement was made that it was the very forces of States that were responsible for sowing and spreading violence.

Administration of justice has been transformed in many countries, from simply enforcing rights, to linking them to equity and providing new mechanisms and safeguards for settling small community actions. This has led to greater attention being paid to the cultural aspect of civil society —to the way in which communities develop and apply such concepts as justice and injustice, equity, authority and power—, in order to induce positive social and political transformations.

Both the panel and the working groups were perturbed by repressive practices and their disturbing local consequences, as reported from Pakistan, Colombia, Guatemala and Bolivia. It is imperative to establish a dialogue between the actors in processes of conflict and policy-makers; it is equally imperative to expand negotiating capacity, handle information with care, and support and adhere to decisions for peaceful co-existence. Because it is obvious that the free or preferred use of repression and punishment against people protesting for just causes is not the way to meet their needs but to make them worse.

Notes

1. The speakers in the globalization group were: Elizabeth Whitmore, Maureen Wilson and Maritza López de Rodríguez, besides Ramírez and Tokatlian.
2. This paragraph draws on a speech made by Julius Nyerere, former president of Tanzania, on October 23, 1997 in Bellagio (Italy) at a conference on global community-reconstruction campaigns, organized by the Rockefeller Foundation. This interesting event was attended by several of us who had participated at the Cartagena Congress.
3. Manfred Max-Neef, Antonio Elizalde and others, *Desarrollo a escala humana, una opción para el futuro*, Uppsala: CEPAUR, Dag Hammarskjold Foundation, 1986. See also Max-Neef's presentation in Chapter 8, and his book *La economía descalza*, Stockholm: Nordan, 1986.
4. This thesis is also maintained by Hubert Campfens, whose book, *Community Development Around the World* (Toronto: University of Toronto Press, 1997, 465-466), briefly introduced at the Congress, was welcomed for his realistic criticism of the community development movement in several countries.
5. Manuel Castells, "La insidiosa globalización", *El País* (Madrid), July 29, 1997, 9. Immanuel Wallerstein's book *El futuro de la civilización capitalista*, Barcelona: Icaria, 1997, received very close to the time of the Congress, deals with issues relevant to discussions at Cartagena: the prospects of capitalism, the dilemma of accumulation, that of political legitimation, that of geoculture, and the crisis of the historical system. *Cf.* Peter F. Drucker, *Post-Capitalist Society*, New York: Harper, 1992, and his not-very-consistent emphasis on the cognoscent type of society, social citizenship, and the evolution of the nation-state towards a kind of mega-state.
6. The speakers on developmentalism were: María Keita, Debbie Fredo, Smitu Kothari, Soren Hvalkof, Libia Grueso, Carlos Rosero, Rigoberto Lanz, Maia Carter, Sara Torres, Alma Estable, Lisa Taylor, Marc Craps, Maruja Salas and Timmi Tillmann.
7. *Cf.* Arturo Escobar, *Encountering Development: The Making and Unmaking of the Third World*, Princeton: Princeton University Press, 1995. This is essential reading for understanding the nature and origins of developmentalist discourse, whose ideological-political components are laid bare, using Foucault's schemes. The limits of this discourse are clearly discernible in national case-studies, such as those presented by Campfens, cit., for Canada, Holland, Israel, Ghana, Bangladesh and Chile, as are the failures of development policy in these countries.

8. The speakers on poverty and hunger were: Richard Couto, Rosemary McGee, Uwe Kievelitz, Jaime Joseph, Solón Barraclough, Amaury Padilla, Armando de Ávila, Beatriz Salas, Carmen Cabrales and Javier Hernández.

9. The speakers on natural resources were: David Deshler, Kwesi Opoku-Debrah, Helen Ritchie, Fanny Becerra, Ismael Acosta, Günter Meinert, Robert Dilger, Juan Gaviria, Nancy Gradens-Schuck, Patrick Christie, Bertha Simmonds, Oswaldo Morales, Helle Ravnborg and Maruja Salas. Darío Fajardo, of Colombia, set up the group.

10. The speakers on democracy were: Aarón Zazueta, Ponna Wignaraja (in absentia), Rosario Saavedra, Stella Carrillo, Lourdes Regueiro Bello and Aníbal Quijano.

11. The speakers on movements were: Asafa Jalata, Lynda Schneekloth, Robert Shibley, Helen Safa, Jean Stubbs, Lourdes Martínez, Victor Negrete, Jaime Eduardo Jaramillo, Carlos Arango Cálad, Isabel Guerrero, Laura C. Cogollo, Vera Gianotten and Ton de Wit.

12. The speakers on integration were: Bob Finlay, Eileen Pigott-Irvine, Judith McMorland, Hilda Valenzuela, Javier Hernández, Carmen Cabrales, M. Saleem, A. Hussain, D. Abroze, Xavier Albó and Yolanda Wadsworth.

13. The speakers on local government were: Alí Arión, Ángel M. del Castillo, Carlos Rodrígues Brandão, Leonor Zalabata, Carmen López, Javier Encinas, Jaime Ruiz, Josefa Cabello, Susan Boser, Arlés Caruso, Beatriz E. López de Mesa, Marta Gutiérrez, Carlos Guerra, Pedro Ferradas, Miguel Martínez López and Óscar Grillo.

14. On the subject of synergies, reference was made to the important but little-known analysis of Colombian peasant experience by León Zamosc, "Campesinos y sociólogos: reflexiones sobre dos experiencias de investigación activa en Colombia", in Foro por Colombia, *La IAP en Colombia*, Bogotá: Foro, 1987, 24-25.

15. The speakers were: Alaf Hussein, M. Saleem, Ms. Dilferoza, Giulio Girardi, María Clara Jimeno and Víctor Hugo Torres. Francisco de Roux, of Colombia, set up this group.

18. COMBATING THE ETHOS OF UNCERTAINTY

With so much information in hand as we have seen, the Cartagena World Congress on Participatory Convergence regarded this turn-of-century period as the cruel reign of violence, vice, consumer squandering, hunger and poverty. In doing so, it confirmed what had been asserted at the start of the Congress by some of the key speakers: that our societies are suffering from a general malaise, from a disturbing ethos of uncertainty. The resounding failures reported and analyzed at the Congress are the efficient cause and circular effect of this harmful ethos. Not knowing where we are going and how we are doing makes us uneasy and anxious.

How is the vicious circle of uncertainty of our time to be broken? From the first day of the Congress some speakers suggested creating an alternative ethos that would include as one of its elements certain rebellious attitudes, of heresy, subversion and liberation, committed to bringing about greater justice through transformations. Agnes Heller spoke to us of setting our sights on not-too-distant horizons, and of the responsibility we bear as thinking, acting beings towards others, in dealing with present issues. Without rejecting utopias, Agnes Heller pointed out the inconsistencies and frustrating hazards of long-term planning and neoliberalism.[1] The postmodern here and now has a distinct bearing on our feeling of emptiness or incongruence, which is what we must overcome. Immanuel Wallerstein, for his part, invited us to seek "not just any convergence but a just one, an intelligent one, a substantively rational one".

These critical, rebellious ideas and the commitment they expressed were reaffirmed by other speakers and found stimulating by participatory researchers, particularly the very large number of young people present at the Congress. We all discovered that, despite heavy assault from globalization, local reserves of common sociability and solidarity continue to exist and show resistance in base communities, villages, hamlets and slums, as they do in Arroyogrande and Henequén near Cartagena, visited during the event. We heard accounts of this too from Nicaraguan, Tanzanian and Colombian communities leaders who, in one of the best moments of the Congress, taught us how to try to rebuild peace by non-violent means and succeed in this hazardous endeavor.

There were two other major contributions in a self-critical vein: one from the group organized by Budd Hall to review histories of worldwide participatory-research networks, the other a "coup d'état" by a number of women delegates who decided to supplant the coordinators in the final days.

As regards historical accounts of participatory-research, the participants[2] pointed out in them the value of continuing to apply the reflection-action cycle in processes of social change. Several of the popular movements they described from personal involvement have grown strong in the respective countries, providing evidence of the efficacy of PR practice. Budd Hall, Marja Liisa Swantz and Kemal Mustapha recounted histories from Tanzania, Rajesh Tandon from India, Ted Jackson from Canada, among many others.

At least three issues were thus observed to have been resolved: the role of knowledge in a popular struggle (*episteme plus techne*); useful practice that gives a moral orientation to the work; and a sense of personal commitment that distinguishes between the logic of action and the logic of research.

The women delegates were led by Mwaluma Masaighana (Tanzania), Elssy Bonilla (Colombia), María Salas (Peru), Marja L. Swantz, Patricia McGuire and other colleagues. Overcoming an initial sense of frustration, they expressed their views on the event and on world issues from the perspective of gender. Their teachings and examples (recorded in Congress documents and in this report) left a strong impression, reinforcing the conviction that gender collaboration was essential to gaining the existential securities we all need.

Finally, the ideas discussed at the Congress led to the decision that we needed to converge for more effective action, in both space and time. And needed also to prepare ourselves to meet the twenty-first century with better methodological tools, with greater conviction of the rightness of our ideals, and with greater resolution to do our duty by history by transforming our societies without delay.

During the last days of the Congress some of the more important goals in geopolitical TimeSpace were analyzed in the form of questions: Shall we be able to steer for a new north, as represented by a universal altruistic brand of ethnogenesis providing for greater happiness? Shall be able to stay the bloody hands of the ethnocides, the paramilitary, the makers and merchants of arms, and the multiple agents of death, poverty and hunger that act like apocalyptic agents in a world that could be more respectful of life and better balanced? Shall we be able to accept the challenge contained in Paulo Freire's last message, addressed to our Congress, of "reviving dreams and utopias and kindling hope" in our worlds and cultures and in our time?

These questions were naturally left to receive such specific answer as Congress participants may make at each point of time and each place in future, as proof of their commitment to peoples and themselves and to the new humanism. We parted happy in the great idea that the prevailing universal uncertainty could be successfully combatted.[3]

Such was the scientific and historical responsibility of our World Convergence Congress in the face of the seriousness of the issues analyzed. We tried once more at the Congress to converge to protect vital human roots, in both the South and the North, and irrigate them with the sweat of our brow and our wisdom, and also with the tolerance and generosity we wish to continue to extend over the whole world.

These highly altruistic ideals and other aims were reiterated at the Final Panel Discussion, as we shall see in the next section.

NOTES

1. Bourdieu's misgivings —based on Husserl— about "concern" and "plan" (interfered with by cynicism) were relevant here (*Razones prácticas*, 144-152).
2. The participants were: Ted Jackson, Peter Park, Miguel Ángel Osorio, Xavier Albó, Rajesh Tandon, Yussuf Kassam, Vera Gianotten, Ton de Wit, Marja Liisa Swantz, John Gaventa, Anne Martin, Robin McTaggart and Orlando Fals Borda (see Video 8 and Paper 13 by Budd Hall).

3. In this connection it was very stimulating to receive around that the
    concordant Manifesto of the World Forum on Alternatives held in May
    1997 at Dakar (Senegal)and headed by Samir Amín, Pablo González
    Casanova, François Houtart, and other personalities. The Forum, too,
    laid emphasis, among other things, on the fact that "the time has come
    for convergence: the convergence of struggles, of different kinds of
    knowledge, of resistance efforts, of hearts and minds", to find "viable
    alternatives to neoliberalism and unilateral globalization." The "swing
    of the pendulum", which has brought social democracy back to power
    in Holland, France and England (and may do so in Mexico, Argentina
    and other countries), has also raised new expectations of political
    change of broader range and scope, as reported in the previous chapter.

PART IV

THE FUTURE OF PARTICIPATORY CONVERGENCE

The Final Panel of the Cartagena Congress was led by Marja Liisa Swantz, of Finland. In the panel were present: Immanuel Wallerstein, Agnes Heller, Yvonna S. Lincoln and Denis Goulet. The session ended with a summary and farewell message by Orlando Fals Borda, Coordinator of the Congress.

19. THE POSSIBLE AND THE IMMEDIATE

Immanuel Wallerstein
and Agnes Heller

IMMANUEL WALLERSTEIN

The most useful thing that I can do is to reflect on the point, how this Conference is different from any large meeting of this kind that could have been held thirty years ago.

First, there are ways in which it is very much the same. One heard analyses after analyses of the contemporary world, and a sense of deep complaint about the degree of its problems and injustices like the inhumane economy, as one of our speakers characterized it. And though the analyses here were perhaps in detail different from what it would have been given thirty years ago, the tone of the analysis was the same. Not only in the negative appreciation of social reality as it is in the moment but in the sense of a deep resistance: that people felt part of that negative social reality and had a great determination to somehow change it. This is exactly the same today as I remember things thirty years ago.

But there are differences. Thirty years ago people were more sure that history was on their side. There was almost an arrogant assumption about the future. I don´t find that today. I find hope, perhaps, I find effort, but not certainty. Personally I think that is healthier but in any case it is certainly different.

Secondly, thirty years ago if people put forward the solutions, most of those solutions had to do with getting the States to do something. The tone of the solutions thirty years ago was: "Change the States!" Change the people in power in the States! Change the policy of the States!

I do not hear that today. I hear this other word: "local". Local is a vague word, it can mean many different things. But I think it is very significant that people are using the word local and not the word "State". There is an orientation that is different .

Thirdly, thirty years ago I would have heard about organizations and parties. Perhaps I would have heard from different people about different parties, but I would have heard about parties, world organizations, national organizations. In this Congress and in other congresses today I hear about "networks". Networks are different from parties, they work differently, between each other and with the world. That is different.

And the fourth thing that I find that is very different from thirty years ago, is that thirty years ago the emphasis would have been on the fact that everyone was really the same. If they are the same today, they would surely soon be the same tomorrow. But now I hear a celebration of heterogeneity and of difference. Not merely an acceptance of it but a celebration of it, as though that were a great virtue (and I think it is a great virtue).

So I think the world has indeed changed in thirty years. What has changed most is the way we —who are confronting the things that we think are inhumane— are still resisting them.

AGNES HELLER

I will enjoin what Professor Wallerstein has said, so that we can have here a real conversation. He said (and I agree with him) that a group of people like this coming together now, has not really lost much by passing the grand universal narratives and global visions. Because when it comes to action, caring and being interested in people who surround us (persons whom we normally know, whose issues and problems we are familiar with) is far more relevant than acting for a goal that we don't know how it will be realized, or believing that in order to act for a goal we can use all possible means. Because this is what went together with the grand vision: that we believed if we had the good goal inside, we could use all possible means to achieve this goal.

This means that we have lost sight of moral responsibility. This conference was also about moral responsibility. At least I heard mentioning ethics by many of you and in different contexts and occasions. But the central category of ethics is responsibility. Remember, then, that responsibility is two fold:

We can have retrospective responsibility, which means that if we have done something which is not right, we may say "excuse me, we take responsibility for this". And if someone asks whether you did this or that, the answer might be positive: "Yes, I did it". But there is another kind of responsibility which can be called prospective responsibility. This is the responsibility of the captain of a ship, or of the school teacher who is in charge of children. I do not think that retrospective responsibility is similar to the responsibility of the captain or the responsibility of the teacher, because the people who are under charge are not children, nor the crew or passengers. In prospective responsibility there is a mutual bond for taking care of each other, that we take charge of others, and others are in charge of us.

The loss of grand visions basically strengthens this conviction that we are mutually responsible for each other. The great French moral philosopher Levinas said that the Other, the stranger, is always facing us. That the Other, the stranger, raises claims on us that we should satisfy.

By stranger, Levinas did not mean the person whom we don't know (we can know the stranger). It means that he raises claims upon us from the outside. Certain claims are not easy to satisfy. Sometimes they are demands which we do not like to fulfill. But responsibility for the Other mutually includes to at least be aware of those claims. Responsibility as taking charge of each other is very important in what action is today.

Now, Levinas is only one philosopher among many. You can formulate this issue of responsibility also in different manners. You can recall with Emmanuel Kant that you should not instrumentalize another person. That your responsibility is expressed by not instrumentalizing, by not using the Other as mere means.

Participation, participative action and participative knowledge have to do with non-instrumentalizing. If you participate and collect any experience by participating, then you really cannot merely instrumentalize the Other. Of course you would say that this is still possible, because the question is, Where do we participate? In this meeting, it was said that participation is not yet taking full responsibility. The question is thus broadened to Participating in what?

Responsibility then implies not to instrumentalize the other person. From this follows that it is best to participate in movements which are not autocratically organized, in movements and groups where there are no gurus, where there are no self-appointed leaders, where there are no organization heads or secretaries. That is, it appears best to participate in a group that you can really take charge of and hold responsibilities for one another. This is a relationship of symmetric reciprocity, as everyone can contribute to the activity of the group.

This kind of activity is very important because it is political, without being political. For what is directly political takes place always under the limelight, that is, in the collective or in a central or public sphere. Thus, if someone acts directly politically, he/she can be sure that his/her name will be appearing in the newspapers, that she will be on the t.v., that everyone will know her. And if someone participates in an action which is indirectly political, he/she may not be in the limelight. This person cannot expect his/her name to be well known, that it will appear in the newspapers. Basically he/she accepts not to be seen. This is a most beautiful thing, when he/she takes responsibility for the Others without being resentful for not going public. This is a really authentic, ethic-motivated action, when things are not ends in themselves, when one does not demand celebration or acknowledgment.

Of course, acknowledgment, even if not demanded may be always there, as happened when Fals Borda spoke at the beginning. This kind of acknowledgment must be dearer and more precious for morally motivated persons than being constantly in the limelight. It has much to do with morality.

20. COMMODITY AND PARADIGM

Yvonna S. Lincoln *(Texas A&M University)*
and Denis Goulet *(University of Notre Dame)*

YVONNA S. LINCOLN

I see four possible arenas for action in the future for researchers, PAR practitioners and teachers. Clearly, my list is far from comprehensive. It is shaped by the experiences, biases, knowledge, aspirations, gender and culture that I brought to Cartagena.

First stage. We have many up-hill battles, but one of them, particularly for those of us who teach the next generation of field workers, is to resist the pressure to commodify, that is, to turn into nothing more than a commodity, the knowledge we have generated or mid-wifed into existence over our lives. With globalization, especially in the North, we are seeing a commodification of virtually everything important in our lives:

- The spiritual, such as with the televangelists.
- Our death, and the ritual process of letting go, as Jessica Milford described more than thirty years ago.
- Our leisure, the commodification of which has been tantalizingly explored by Chris Rojek.
- Our bodies, by the beauty and cosmetic industry treated by Susan Faludi and others.
- Our emotional lives, as explored by the sociologist Stjepan Mestrovic.

In an information age, knowledge is in danger of becoming just another readily marketed set of goods, services and processes. Our universities, which have as their primary mission the creation of new knowledge and the transmission of ancient and modern cultural knowledge, are sensitively poised both to co-opt our work, and at the same time, to punish us for engaging in non-traditional and participatory forms of inquiry and action.

Therefore, some of the important work we will do should be transformative and subversive within our own institutions. For some of us old gazers, academic life feels more secure. But for a younger generation, life in universities feels risky, threatening, and precarious. –We owe them a new academy, one which gives them the security and autonomy to be able to throw their full hearts into work of meaning and genuine worth.

Second stage. We need to find and create extended connections outside of ourselves. We have heard here many speakers on human, ecological and biodiversity violence. After hearing Max-Neef, we may not wish to make the World Bank our political bedfellow. But other organizations might make loyal helpmeets and boon companions. I am thinking, as an example, of a structure which might help us communicate with, for instance:

- Amnesty International, on human rights abuses of which we have first-hand knowledge.
- The World Wildlife Fund, on the maintenance and preservation of fragile biological and ecological habitats.
- The Seed Savers Exchange, on dissappearing biodiversity in food and agricultural crops, and the preservation of heirloom seeds.
- Greenpeace, on the prevention of degradation of air, water, and marine resources.
- Habitat for Humanity, on issues of simple, safe, decent housing for the poor.

The other night at dinner, I heard Pat Maguire talk about her favorite metaphor, the Grand Canyon. She pointed out that this geological miracle, more than a mile deep, more than a mile wide in places, was formed by a small amount of pressure over a very long period. In fact, to extend the metaphor, the Canyon was formed not only by water. It was also shaped by minute underground tectonic forces and by wind erosion.

If we should become an inexorable Colorado River, we might also find some assistance from our friends the tectonic plates and the winds.

Third stage. We have to think more systematically on the problem of mentoring. During this conference, we have honored

our pioneers. But there are still among us senior experienced colleagues who know much, and who hold wisdom born of hard work,
heartache, and celebration. We have at the same time young people
yearning for help, support, encouragement, and advice.

What we need now is an adoption programme. Many junior
colleagues came with, or were brought by, their mentors and
teachers. We need to think about how we effect this special
convergence across knowledge, wisdom, and the unique and
tender time of generations. We have little time for this purpose.

Fourth stage. We need to think more extensively and systematically about the authentic in PAR. From my perspective, there are
fundamental problems in the determination of authenticity in
participatory work. For example:

1. With our energy and zest for action, we have sometimes not
   attended to reflection nearly enough. Nor have we attended to
   the systematic production and elucidation of strong, defensible,
   widely debated criteria for high quality and authentic participatory work. We have been doing the right work but sometimes
   we are not certain that we are doing the work right.
2. Another facet of the authenticity problem in PAR is that this is
   not amenable to criteria as we normaly talk about them. That is
   because half or more of what we do is what a dear friend calls
   "heart work": work from, and in, the realm of the heart, the
   spi-rit, the soul. This is born of caring, empathy, altruism, hope,
   love, and a growing selflessness. Our only ways of judging this
   particular truth, this form of authenticity, reside in our own
   experience, wisdom, character, capacity for forgiveness, tolerance and love. Those have always been the bases of knowing
   the heart of another. But there are no ways to quantify this form
   of authenticity.

And so we have a dual problem. Our public rationales and
justifications for our work are not always clear to those who do
not work in this way, and our second judgments about authentic
work can only come from the heart and the spirit.

In the first instance, we must work out (and write about) our
methods and the criteria we use to ensure high-quality work.
However, it is only by enacting and honoring the spiritual and the
sacred that we will ever know the truths before us.

DENIS GOULET

Tides are changing in development and in the way to do social science. I will restrict to comment just on the second point, as a new pragmatic knowledge model might be in gestation. It is a new way of looking and considering the nature and forms of the technological, as well as those of social organization. It is a second tide which is changing not just the development model, but the scientific knowledge model as well.

I am under the impression that in this Congress —for its size, diversity, for the conceptual seriousness of the contributions and their enlightenment— this new science is reaching a critical mass. The analogy comes from atomic physics: when someone is able to produce an implosion, or may be an explosion, this may result in a new authenticity.

Our friend Paulo Freire used to say that there is no such thing as a neutral education, that every kind of education is designed to domesticate or to liberate. I have the impression that new approaches, focuses and outlines for research, learning and education displayed in this Congress, converge in suggesting, without demonstrating, that the social sciences are not value neutral; and also, as Freire said about education, that they may domesticate, enslave or emancipate the mind.

In my country there is an institution which grants "good house-keeping seals of approval". This seal of approval is given to a product to certificate on its safety, health and high quality to use at home. I think alternative social science has been conquering this seal of approval. To use an analogy suggested by my local visit at the "Inquisition Palace", heretical knowledge has been certified as less heretical now.

We are in the process to gain a new science, but this is not yet adequate. We are lacking wisdom to go along with our sciences. Wisdom is unity and simplicity for the explanation of totality. It is obtained by intersecting and confronting contradictions, complexities and negations, whereas simplicity, naiveté or unconsciousness may offer unique and simple explanations at the cost of avoiding contradictions and complexities.

This type of wisdom on the level of our sciences is necessary. I look at it rising between ancient wisdom and modern rationalities.

Such a dialogue does not have necessarily to be expressed only by linguistic or conceptual ways. It can be by artistic, symbolic or mysterious means.

I remember some years ago when I talked to a Tupi Guaraní chief at the Paraguayan East. He had seen his nation thrown out of the forest for the construction of a dam. He held regrets not because of the dispersion of his nation into the city, which made them lose their language and culture, but because the people could not celebrate their Sacred Dance.

I asked him: Why is the Sacred Dance so important? He explained but I did not understand him because I wanted to put it in terms of my own concepts, not on indigenous ideas according to his way of thinking. After many attempts he finally said: But, don't you understand that the Sacred Dance gives support to our cosmos!

Now, we have to discover another Sacred Dance to sustain our own fragmenting cosmos.

21. MAKING SENSE OF CONVERGENCE:
THE NORTH STAR OF ALTRUISM

Orlando Fals Borda

As you could probably feel at the Final Panel just held, the main themes of our Participatory Convergence Congress have criss-crossed during this week in many ways. They have given rise to infinite questions related to theory-making, process management, systems thinking, the educational challenge, and philosophical, socio-economic and political problems. There have been lots of stimulating ideas, but never claiming what Percy Bysshe Shelley called the "divine right of intellectuals", especially poets, to be "the unacknowledged legislators of the world".

We have not been so arrogant but have exercised a certain healthy pique produced by our desire to exorcize, through participation, the sin of imposing our own ideas and practices on unsuspecting common peoples. Rather we have tried to respect and learn from popular knowledge, and we have repeated this experience these days right here.

In my own view, this complementarity of academic and popular knowledge has been one main tangible result of our discussions this week on ethics and fieldwork; on systemic practice; on local government and political and cultural movements; on the globalization challenge; on industry and human economics; on action learning and creative teaching; on justice and peace; on the counterdiscourse of development; on possibilities for participant micro and macro work; on environmentalism; on hunger and poverty; and on the intricacies of creativity and communication.

We have received good lessons and warnings from President Fernando Henrique Cardoso of Brazil and political leaders, historians of movements and promoters of networks, from literary figures, engineers, sociologists, economists, entrepreneurs and, last but not least, from our late friend Paulo Freire. Most of them tended to set limits to rampant postmodernism and neoliberalism.

Yet I also feel that, beyond ideas and arts, the driving force of this event has been *action*, that is, our overall concern with the practical and with what to do in our respective environments. We want to proceed and do our work more thoroughly, although with the bearings of a theory enriched with concrete pertinence, and with the supports of a personal commitment reinforced by ethics. This has been rather clear to me also at the Final Panel. It would also clarify the relations between the intellectual and the politician, and between the academy and the real world.

As you know, in sociological tradition there have been many studies of social change and social dynamics, but not so many analyses of action mechanisms themselves, like the cause-and-effect linkages determined by recent chaos theory, as recalled by Wallerstein. W.I. Thomas in the 1930's had contributed in this specific direction with his concept of "definition of the situation step by step". His empirical stance was useful, but it turned out insufficient. Jaspers then complemented it with a vision of history based on a "hermeneutical situation", meaning the situation in which we find ourselves with regard to the tradition or heritage that we are trying to transform. Hence the contemporary, applied hermeneutics about which we have learned so much from Agnes Heller.

Now as we depart for home, I find helpful to suggest grounding our future work on Jasper's and Heller´s lead about applied hermeneutics, and on Wallerstein s grand vision of the SpaceTime theory as we heard it this week. In this way we could choose better on what we want to do, and improve our praxis within well-specified contexts.

Gadamer also helps us along this useful path by pointing at three relevant elements: 1)The "life experience" as such, which includes not one step (understanding) but three steps, with the addition of interpretation and application (remember that for him application was not blind technology or simple expertise but political reason); 2) "Practical acuteness or wisdom" which was how Gadamer interpreted Aristotle's ethical concept of *phronesis*; and 3)The "fusion of horizons" as a way to discover angles beyond the near to improve actual conditions, a method to focus better the fringes between disciplines. Certainly this looks to me like an appropriate formulation to overcome scientific, political, and technical shortsightedness as well as institutional staleness, especially if we want to talk about new scientific paradigms.

If we could make praxis, *phronesis* and *ethos* converge and place this combination on a fusion of horizons perspective, we might also gain two other benefits: 1) We could be more sure, persistent, and effective in our work as it becomes clear that the purpose of our knowledge as a fluid phenomenon is to guide and govern better our daily action; and 2) We could also move toward the construction of paradigms that would be practically, intellectually as well as morally satisfying. I would think Professors Goulet and Lincoln would agree on this point. Goulet accepts that our new paradigm may be achieving a critical mass. And Lincoln specifies criteria for this difficult task. All of which takes us somewhat beyond Thomas Kuhn.

Of course this task of paradigm building calls for a quest for creativity so that we can select relevant topics of inquiry and ground them as pertinent subjects of research and action, hopefully without fear of violence or threats from vested interests as has often happened. Here is where imagination as well as courage come into play in science-making: we need them urgently in some holistic measure to overcome our present frustration and partial paralysis in the face of such acute world problems. We need courage and imagination in order to become effective builders and defenders of ethnogenetic civilizations and cultures (as De Roux invited us to do in our opening session), to stop the self-destructive rituals of exploitative dominant systems. We have protested here and on the streets this week in a very eloquent manner. So we need to turn our eyes again to the North Star of altruism, and to concede to altruism all its subversive potential in today´s decomposed world.

In this rather grandiose manner, to make the instrumental converge with the axiological —to combine a clear head with a lion heart— appears like a worthwhile effort to redefine and reconnect our disciplines and arts, and to recapture the positive essence and meaning of our scientific and practical concerns.

We are now more assured than before by this week's speakers that there is an immanent validity of critical methodology in the sciences, both "hard" and "soft", that there is only one logic of scientific investigation. But we require more than a unifying method, we require also to entwine it with real experience, *Erfahrung*, or *vivencia*. The many schools of participatory research which met here to clarify how they differ and concur (with predominance of the immanent convergences just mentioned) appear to be the closest today to that ideal of science and service that we tried to articulate at this event. Even with obstacles and ups and downs, our participatory schools are demonstrating *in tandem* a valid field method and a satisfactory philosophy of life. This is quite an achievement. Thanks to you for this great proof of pertinence and effectiveness, which answers in part the two questions on scientific method and political project made to this Congress by President Cardoso.

Hence the importance of continuing to work with this intelligent, soul-filling flexibility as well as with seriousness of purpose, if we want to reconstruct our institutions, our lives, and our relationship with nature.

Of course, to give meaning to imperiled institutions and damaged lives, we will have to discard some things and to refashion others according to our renovated fusion of horizons. This process of revamping is nothing new in the history of humanity. It may be painful like Sisyphus' ordeal, but at present we would not feel under any insurmountable curse to do and to undo as happened to him in mythological times. Apparently we still can survive as humans and manage our own man-made disasters.

As new horizons rise in the near future within transformational TimeSpace, other hopes and possibilities appear. It is likely that our age will keep on giving us some additional space and some remade time for our convergent knowledge to acquire significance, and thus save us from anomie and greater stress and frustration.

Therefore I invite you finally to take advantage of this dynamic, historical leeway for hope. May we go home now, even more able and decided to keep on planting everywhere some of the good seeds of social reconstruction that were sown amongst us during this week.

APPENDICES

APPENDIX A. REGISTERED PAPERS

Appendix B. Videotapes
(NTSC FORMAT-VHS)

1. Memories of Convergence .
   General summary of the event / English, Spanish (90 min).

2. Opening Session.
   Opening statements, tribute to Freire and pioneers / Spanish
   (40 min).

3. Field Outings.
   Henequén, Arroyogrande. English, Spanish (45 min).

4. Music in the Congress.
   Programs at the Convent (45 min).

5. Women at the Congress.
   In plenary plus the posters. English, Spanish (30 min).

6. Literature, History and Society.
   Panel with Galeano, Molano, Parra, Sánchez, Giraldo. Spanish
   (45 min).

7. Popular Thought and Action.
   Panel with popular leaders from Nicaragua, Tanzania and
   Colombia / Spanish (45 min).

8. History of Participatory Movements.
   World and regional PAR networks. English (60 min).

9. Max-Neef and the Rhinoceros.
   His complete lecture. Spanish (60 min).

10. Wallerstein and SpaceTime.
    His complete lecture. English. (60 min).

11. AGNES HELLER AND HISTORIC HORIZONS
   Her complete lecture. English. (60 min).

12. GALEANO Y LOS PERSEGUIDORES DEL PUNTO.
   His complete lecture. Spanish (90 min).

13. FUTURE ACTION.
   Final Panel with Wallerstein, Heller, Lincoln and Goulet
   and closing statement by Fals Borda. English, Spanish (60 min).

14. SCHOOLS AND METHODS.
   Panel with scholars. English. (90 min).

15. THE INTELECTUAL AND THE GOVERNMENT MAN.
   Videotape sent by Fernando H. Cardoso,
   President of Brazil. Spanish (20 min).

ADDITIONALS SHOWN AT THE CONGRESS

A1. ADVENTURES OF A RADICAL HILLBILLY.
A2. THE BEST MADE PLANS.
A3. PENSAMIENTOS DE MUJER
A4. AMERINDIOS, CAMPESINOS Y NEGROS.
A5. INVESTIGAR LA REALIDAD PARA TRANSFORMARLA.
A6. CAMPESINO A CAMPESINO.

These videotapes from IDS (Sussex) and University of Calgary
should be ordered from there directly.

Producers: Édgar Álvarez, Yasmid Beltrán and Eduardo Roberto P.

APPENDIX C.
RECORDINGS OF MUSIC AND NARRATIVES
(Played at the Congress)

Colombian Caribbean.
Writer David Sánchez Juliao introduces us to the basic culture of the Caribbean region taking oral tradition as his point of departure with PAR. He tells us in a lively manner about the struggles and penuries of these peoples through the case of a boxing "champ", Flecha. (1972). (In Spanish).

Colombian Caribbean (II).
Accordeon player Máximo Jiménez, a founder of protest "vallenato" music from Montería, is composer at bestsellers like "The Indian from Sinu" and "Struggling Donkey". He utilizes different styles and rhythms extolling the struggles of coastal peasant communities as they become articulated through PAR (1972).

Cuban Caribbean.
Well-known singers Silvio Rodríguez, Pablo Milanés and Juan Márquez sing about the vicissitudes of revolution and daily life in Cuba. They present poignant messages to further the quest for human liberty.

Proletarian Mexico.
Judith Reyes, a pioneer of protest singing, dwells on Mexican history and daily life in her country, especially among peasants, workers, and students of her time (the 60's).

The Amazon.
Indians like Múrui-Muinane find musical expression for their reality and cosmic visions. This recording shows the Sukii dance, a ritual for the renewal of life. The records were made between 1979 and 1980.

Ancient Afrocuban Songs.
These are rituals from Eastern Cuba, showing a mixture of religions in dance and song. Processional singing, the old Columbia rumba, the Wemba chants and the rites of the Secret Abakúa Society are outstanding.

Peoples in Chile.
A Cantata on Santa María de Iquique by the famous Quilapayún musicians (1970's) tells about the bloody strike by saltpeter mineworkers in northern Chile at the beginning of the century.

Australian Music: Yothu Yindi.
This is an extraordinary group of aborigines musicians from the Northern Territories of Australia, a winner of national awards. The recordings present ceremonial and religious renditions of the spiritual unity between man and nature by combining traditional and modern instruments and rhythms.

Eric Bogle.
His music tries to open up hopes by marking a synthesis of friendship and conflict, with the purpose of converting life and the audience in a permanent concert for love.

John Williamson.
This recording presents his efforts to redefine contemporary music through lyric poems rendered in song and guitar.

Struggle Songs in Colombia.
These songs for and from popular struggles among Black communities in the Cauca Valley celebrate social movements during the 80s to recuperate land taken from descendants of former slaves. Produced by Grassroots Organizations Network, Cali.

Candelario Obeso.
Obeso is a precursor of Black poetry in the Americas. Born in Mompox, Colombia, he died in 1870. His well known poems, like "The Absent Boatman" and "The Bushman", are here sung in Spanish by Antonio del Vilar and Adolfo Barros. They reflect the harsh realities of life in Magdalena River communities in mid-19th century.

este libro se terminó de imprimir en junio de 1998
en los talleres de tercer mundo editores.
cra. 19 no. 14-45, tels.: 2772175 - 2774302 - 2471903.
fax 2010209 apartado aéreo 4817
santafé de bogotá, colombia